THE LAST CHRISTIAN

THE LAST CHRISTIAN

ADOLF HOLL

Translated by Peter Heinegg
DOUBLEDAY & COMPANY, INC., GARDEN CITY, N.Y.
1980

This book was originally published in German under the title *Der Letzte Christ* (© 1979 by Deutsche Verlags-Anstalt, Stuttgart).

Library of Congress Cataloging in Publication Data

Holl, Adolf.
    The last Christian.

    Translation of Der letzte Christ.
    Bibliography.
    Includes index.
    1. Francesco d'Assisi, Saint, 1182–1226.
2. Christian saints—Italy Assisi—Biography.
3. Assisi—Biography. I. Title.
BX4700.F6H5213   282'.092'4 [B]

ISBN: 0-385-15499-2
Library of Congress Catalog Card Number: 79-7868
Translation Copyright © 1980 by Doubleday & Company, Inc.

CONTENTS

CONTENTS

CONTENTS

THE LAST CHRISTIAN

I

"I, YOUR LITTLE BROTHER FRANCIS"

About eight hundred years ago people in a number of European cities began to feel a peculiar and unheard-of desire: They wanted to know what time it was. Of course, there had always been church bells. They summoned the faithful to worship, proclaimed the arrival of death, warned of fire and approaching enemies. Their chimes divided the day into morning, afternoon, and evening. Nobody had a watch.

Then in the year 1188 the citizens of Tournai, in Belgium, got permission from the King to set up a clock in a suitable spot, to strike the hours, "for their pleasure and for the city's business."[1] The first mechanical clock was installed in 1309 in Milan,[2] and it wasn't long before every sizable town had one. Thus people began to live in a new era. They called it "modern times."

Nowadays, after eight centuries of modern times, and a generation of living with the atomic bomb, we find our enthusiasm for modernity somewhat dampened. We wonder what went wrong ever since people started asking what time it was.

Around the period when men first felt the urge to divide their days into shorter intervals, for the sake of business engagements and deadlines, a son was born in Assisi to a cloth dealer, Pietro Bernardone. *The Last Christian* is about that son—Francis of Assisi. It argues that in the person of Francis the premodern world, so to speak, gathered itself together before coming to an end. For one last time, before the forces of progress thundered off on their triumphant path, one man looked into the motivating thrust behind the whole thing and decisively rejected it: Francis of Assisi, the last Christian. No one after him worked as strenuously against the forces of modernity as he did, with his body, with his very life. Francis had no new theory to offer, but an old practice—the practice of Jesus Christ.

This is the crucial difference between Francis and later prominent figures of European Church history. All of them, belonging as they did to the modern period and indebted as they were to it, had theories that they disseminated in manuscript and, later, in print. We can see this most clearly in the case of Martin Luther. But Francis mistrusted books and refused to have any of them. All the written material he left behind can be read in ten minutes.

After Francis no one ever took Jesus with such stubborn literalness—or to such stunning effect. Francis wanted to own absolutely nothing except a pair of drawers, a hooded robe, and a rope around his belly. Just as with Jesus, few people could imitate this sort of life. Nevertheless, in a way that can be compared only with Jesus, Francis has remained a haunting figure, and not just for Catholics. Somehow Francis awakens in us a kind of pain that draws us to him, a feeling of nostalgia. We shall see why.

Contrary to widely accepted opinion, the entrepreneurial avant-garde that transformed the face of the earth did not make its first appearance sometime after the Thirty Years' War: It was already alive and kicking eight hundred years ago, in the shape, for instance, of Pietro Bernardone from Assisi. Francis' father was one of the people who witnessed the birth of modern times—and Francis broke with his father.

This was no trivial "generation gap," but a decision on principle, an exemplary desertion at the start of the battle. We know now that Francis' father belonged to the winning side. Francis, by contrast, must be counted among the world-historical losers. His group of comrades remained a minority, and the name he gave it was well chosen: Friars Minor.

Yet Francis has not fallen into oblivion. In his obscure and undramatic way, he spoke to the numberless common people who, over the course of centuries, lit candles beneath his painted or sculpted image. Heretics, freethinkers, and enthusiasts all felt his influence. And even in the various Franciscan brotherhoods (still in existence today), sanctioned and controlled by the Church as they were, his disconcerting, independent spirit kept on bursting forth. The key to Francis' continuing power is the longing for the reconciliation of humanity with itself and with nature. This is a thoroughly Christian desire, but, despite the presence of a billion or so Christians, it failed to prevent Auschwitz and Hiroshima. Should we at long last give it a decent burial?

The problem of the value of Christian longing takes us back to the intersection of modern and premodern times, to Assisi. There we find, of course, no "essence of Christianity,"[3] or any such theoretical constructs.

We meet instead a strange individual: an obedient rebel, an earnest clown, an unworldly activist, an ascetical master of the arts of life, a restless wise man, a convivial penitent, a humble authoritarian. Behind these contradictions in Francis' character one discovers an inexorable resolution, a refusal to play games or give ground. Francis studied something you never learn in the Boy Scouts or the Social Democrats, in public schools or Christian homes: the science of social climbing—downward.

On the rare occasions when he spoke of himself, he used the tender, power-weary diminutive, *"Io picciolino vostra fra francesco"* (I, your little brother Francis).[4] The kind of company he felt drawn to was . . . lepers. When he slept one night in a cardinal's house, Francis got a severe anxiety attack. He wanted an imperial edict against the capture and slaughter of songbirds. But even this wish went unfulfilled.

AN URGENT CASE

This is the story they tell: It happened at the time when Francis had just begun to abandon his former way of life, and so had to suffer all kinds of mockery from his relatives and friends. Bernard of Quintavalle, one of the richest and most distinguished citizens of Assisi, was pleased by Francis' patience in the face of such harassment, and he determined to test Francis' character. Bernard invited Francis to dinner, and afterward they both went to bed. Francis immediately pretended to sleep, and Lord Bernard likewise began to snore loudly. When Francis felt safe, he got up to pray. He raised his hands and eyes to heaven and tearfully repeated, without pausing, till daybreak:

> *Iddio mio.*
> My God.

A lamp was burning in the bedroom.
Bernard became Francis' first companion.[5]

Francis, as everyone knows, is revered by the Catholic Church as a saint. Though many people today have little understanding of sainthood, it is the oldest descriptive category ever applied to Francis. Its origin predates the Catholic Church, the Roman Empire, and indeed recorded history. It is in a certain sense international: In the most diverse languages it expresses related feelings of piety and devotion. It is central to what we nowadays call religion.

In this book, however, Francis will not be presented as a saint. For the majority of people in modern industrial society the term carries only vague and faded associations. It has become anachronistic, and no longer evokes any common practices. At the same time it would be false to bypass

3

Francis' religious nature out of tact, as it were, and to treat him simply as a sort of humanitarian. The singular excitement that drove the man out of bed and made him pray to God all night long belongs to Francis as much as his tunic: Without it he becomes a face in the crowd.

And so we ask: What kept Francis from sleep? The most concise and telling definition of the God of the Crusaders, the mystics, and the poor—i.e., of Francis' medieval God—is one I found in Sartre: "A murmur from above: You were not born in vain. They're waiting for you."[6] The people of that era had a mandate that justified their existence. They weren't living in vain, even if they landed in hell. They still had an all-embracing context for things. They had not yet paid for the process of civilization, as we have, with the loss of cosmic meaning. Romantic spirits long for the return of this kind of security—without, however, caring to dispense with paid vacations, automobiles, and dental care. There was none of that in the Middle Ages. There was also no SPCA, no Red Cross, and no guaranteed pensions. In lieu of those there were public executions, epidemics, and famines. And the certainty of God.

The indeterminate yearning for this certainty, the longing for simple faith and the consolations of prayer, all such impulses seem like a search for a lost era. Nonetheless, we cannot simply consign our society's remaining searchers for God to the scrap heap. And so we find ourselves in a curious state of suspense. We know that our childhood faith is irretrievably gone, but we still won't give up on God once and for all. The situation isn't very satisfying, and one wonders why we don't break out of it.

In *Waiting for Godot* Samuel Beckett calls our attention to the fact that our need for "him" is too flabby and sluggish, that we don't wait enough for him, and that we lack, as Sartre puts it, the literally crazy stubbornness that alone could qualify us as an urgent case. Godot tells himself that there's no hurry, "I'll come by when I've taken care of my affairs."[7] Or else our cries are so weak that he simply hasn't heard them.

True, Beckett's unsurpassable description of this situation is relentlessly pessimistic, but there's more to the picture than that. He claims that waiting is pointless, but nobody deserts. And in the end we hear a distinctly messianic word:

VLADIMIR: We'll hang ourselves tomorrow. (*Pause.*) Unless Godot comes.
ESTRAGON: And if he comes?
VLADIMIR: We'll be saved.[8]

Francis had that crazy stubbornness that we lack. He arouses our interest, but not because he prayed to his medieval God. Many people did the same in those days, out of habit as it were, and many still do today—

President Carter, for example. Francis prayed in secret—that is, he did something rather unusual for that period. The force that kept him from sleep doesn't belong to the usual religious routine. Bernard, his eavesdropping witness, was so impressed by the scene that he made a radical change in his life on the strength of it.

It would be easy enough to say that Francis was just an especially religious person, but that wouldn't explain a thing. On the other hand, we can readily understand Francis' nocturnal behavior if we view it as a struggle with a familiar problem: the loneliness of bourgeois existence. In his origins and mentality, Francis was a bourgeois. He was one of us. He had that quality that makes us what we are and at the same time causes us such grief: the consciousness of individual identity. He felt alone and he sought "the Other"—God. Were those tears of happiness that he shed amid his sighs? Did he find himself, while Bernard spied on him, in the state of "union," of blissful fusion of the Self and Not-Self? No, he was still groping in the dark.

But he was obstinate. The hours went by, and Francis would not yield. He wanted to free himself from the oppressive power that held him back. But what was it? Francis was contending with his bourgeois ego. This son of a rich trader already sensed the adversary who inhabited his flesh. Off in the distance Godot began to pay attention.

Francis' battle lasted for twenty years, up until his death. During that time he experienced sudden illuminations and overpowering certitude. But he found peace only at the end, in the form of a final, shattering denial of his body: the stigmata of Christ impressed in his skin. We shall observe Francis in this venture, as Bernard watched him in that bedroom. We shall not, to be sure, give away all our property to the poor, as Bernard did, and head out into the world without a penny. The police would arrest us for vagrancy. What anyone with conviction could do then has now become an anachronism.

And that is why we have such a hard time with God. Our problems on this score are the results of the past eight hundred years of European history, which took a direction that Francis resisted. The fact that in spite of this we still can't quite forget about God, speaks for the indestructibility of the instincts Francis continually followed.

A NEW LIGHT

The forty-four years of Francis' life, from 1182 to 1226, were uneventful. In comparison with the Popes and Emperors of his time, including such outstanding figures as Innocent III and Frederick II, Francis' career was almost hidden, provincial, with hardly a headline in it. From a journalistic point of view, his life can be summed up in a few sentences.

We learn that at age twenty Francis took part in a battle between Assisi and the neighboring city of Perugia, and was taken prisoner. Following his release, he was sick for some time, and after recuperating he remained rather pensive, sought out solitude, and even undertook a pilgrimage to Rome. Then a crucifix spoke to him, and he decided to restore a ruined church in the neighborhood of Assisi. For this purpose he sold a bolt of cloth from his father's store, was called on the carpet for it, and had to give back the money. In a sort of trial before the bishop of Assisi, Francis dissociated himself from his father, but stayed on in the vicinity of his hometown, lived on charity, and worked at the renovation of abandoned chapels. At twenty-six he knew what he wanted. He began to speak openly about the need for repentance and peace, and led an ascetical life. Before long he had several companions. In the year 1209 he succeeded in getting an audience with the Pope, who approved his intentions and gave him permission to preach. During the next ten years he wandered around, went as far as Dalmatia and Spain, and finally journeyed to Palestine. He was recalled from the Holy Land by an emergency at home: His companions now numbered in the thousands, conflicts had broken out among them, there were hostile factions. Francis named a deputy, and therewith gave up the leadership of his Order. Weakened by various illnesses, he spent a good deal of time in his final years in out-of-the-way places. He gave his consent to a written "Rule," to guide the lives of his "Friars Minor." During his stay on a lonely mountain the wounds of the crucified Christ broke open on his hands and feet. He died near Assisi, almost blind, totally exhausted, and widely revered as a saint.

Only three years after his death the first biography of Francis appeared, commissioned by the Pope. Its author, Thomas of Celano, was a Franciscan. Francis' presence, he wrote, shone on the men and women of his time like "a new light from heaven"[9] that scattered all darkness and despair. That sounds like a flowery exaggeration, in the customary style of that day. But there is truth nevertheless in the unusual contrast between Francis' comparatively uneventful life and the tremendous impact he had on the world. Barely a century after his death he was hailed by Dante as the "sun" that had risen in Assisi.[10] At the same time Francis had triggered a violent ideological crisis in the Church. The argument raged over Francis' *Testament*, over his ideal poverty, and its effect on a corrupt society. In 1318, three years before the death of Dante, the first radical Franciscans were burned at the stake in Marseilles.[11]

Francis was not the first mendicant. Long before him many Christian men and women, orthodox and heterodox, had modeled their lives around the strict voluntary poverty of Christ and his Apostles.[12] These "good people," as they were sometimes called, led lives of exemplary unselfishness. They never touched money; they preached in the town squares and marketplaces, studied the Bible, and criticized the greedy, dissolute monks and clerics. They were concentrated in the regions of Europe with the liveliest social and economic activity in the twelfth century: Belgium and Holland, southern France, northern and central Italy. The Church authorities watched their doings with decided mistrust, and on occasion extreme radicals among the mendicant preachers were quickly done away with. Around this time, independently of Francis, several mendicant Orders were founded with the approval of the Church: Dominicans, Augustinians, Carmelites.

Still, for Dante (and for others, too) Francis stands alone as the true spouse of Lady Poverty.[13] For eleven hundred years since the death of Christ she had lived as a widow, without any suitor. Now at last someone had courted her, and she was no longer forlorn. Thus far Dante, extolling Francis in barely veiled language as the second Christ. Francis did not become a new Christ because of his original discovery of a new manner of life, but because of the character traits he combined in a way that only happens once in a thousand years.

This is the story they tell: When the Friars Minor met at Assisi for Pentecost, Lord Cardinal Ugolino, who later became Pope, was among them. Several learned, cultured brothers asked the cardinal to talk Francis into following their advice and allowing the establishment of a Rule on the model of St. Augustine, St. Benedict, and St. Bernard, so as to organize the brothers' lives in a methodical fashion. When he heard this admonition from the cardinal, Francis took him by the arm, led him before the assembled crowd of brothers, and spoke to them: "My brothers! My brothers! God has shown me the way of simplicity. I cannot bear to have a Rule forced on me, neither St. Augustine's, nor St. Benedict's, nor St. Bernard's. The Lord wanted me to be his simpleton—there lies all our learning. God will destroy you through your education and erudition, whether you like it or not." The cardinal froze and said not a word, and all the brothers were greatly afraid.[14]

The man whose hand Francis seized so boldly would, as Pope Gregory IX, do two things. He would quickly canonize Francis (1228), and codify the Inquisition's procedures against heretics (1233). This two-pronged bureaucratic operation strikes one as surprisingly modern. The people were granted a blessed wonder-worker for their quiet veneration. But only the proper Church officials could interpret his teaching. Anyone who thought otherwise would have to face some unpleasant consequences. Thus the authorities managed to neutralize the "dangerous" elements in Francis' personality.

We shall not make the mistake of seeing Francis through the eyes of clerical functionaries, nor of using their terminology. We shall consider Francis neither as a saint nor as a heretic, Gregory IX notwithstanding. We shall look upon Francis as a fool (his own word), as the sort of man who takes the powerful of this world by the arm, as a child might, to tell them the truth—with a force that stuns them to silence. Which is only fair: Day in, day out they deafen us with their talk.

II

DANGEROUS STORIES

In the great cloister at Assisi the executors of Francis' "estate" have preserved a crumpled piece of parchment, sealed in glass and framed with pretty decorations, like a miniature baroque altar, with heads of *putti* all around it.[1] This is a note on which Francis wrote a forceful blessing, with the additional words, "May the Lord bless you, Brother Leo."

The archives of the Cathedral of Spoleto contain a short letter, likewise written by Francis himself, that begins, "Brother Leo, Greetings and peace from your brother Francis."[2] The letter has a number of grammatical errors.

The note in Assisi and the letter in Spoleto are the only documents left in Francis' own hand, and both are addressed to Brother Leo. Leo was not Francis' actual brother, but his most trusted companion. He was also, as a priest, Francis' confessor. He could write with fluency and a good hand, and he composed letters for Francis, as his secretary. We don't know exactly when Leo first met Francis, but we are certain that Leo was continually at his side for Francis' last three years. He was present when Francis was working over the instructions for the life of the Friars Minor, and he wrote them down. He changed the bandages on Francis' hands and feet after he received the stigmata in ecstasy on Mount La Verno. When Francis died, Leo was permitted to keep Francis' prayer book. Leo outlived his friend by thirty-four years, and not everything that went on among the Franciscans during that period met with his approval. When he died in 1270, he was buried near Francis in the splendid new basilica of the Friars Minor in Assisi. By that time his many stories about Francis, which were written down and passed around, had already been officially withdrawn from circulation by the Order. Six hundred years later someone discovered a yellowed folio volume of these stories.[3] Since then a series of further copies have been found in old libraries (most notably in Perugia, Uppsala, and Rome).[4] Why were they suppressed for so long?

Just two years after Francis' death the Pope had personally commissioned Friar Thomas of Celano to write Francis' biography. Six months later the book was ready and presented to the papal chancellery. Anyone who takes the trouble to go to Paris can examine Codex No. 3817 in the Bibliothèque Nationale. In it will be found this notice, in the handwriting of a papal clerk: The blessed lord, Pope Gregory IX,[5] received this *legend* at Perugia on February 25, in the second year of his glorious pontificate, confirmed it, and ordered that it be kept. Thanks be to Almighty God and to Our Savior for all his gifts now and forever. Amen. The year was 1229. The Pope resided in Perugia from 1228 till 1230. *Legend* literally means what one can read out loud. Nowadays we would call it reading material.

The Friars Minor read Celano's book with deep interest, and apparently made many copies of it. But the demand for more stories about Francis was great, and so in 1244 Celano was commissioned, this time by his superiors in the Order, to write a second life. The Friars Minor were called on to gather all the unrecorded oral traditions about Francis, to write them down, and put them at Celano's disposition. Brother Leo obeyed this summons. Along with two other companions of Francis', Rufino and Angelo, he put together a collection of more than a hundred episodes from Francis' life. Celano drew freely upon this, copying much of it verbatim. By 1247 he had gotten it all down; the book was inspected by his superiors and approved. The Friars Minor now had some more reading material—but not for long.

After less than twenty years, in 1266, the General Chapter of the Franciscans in Paris proscribed both of Celano's autobiographies, as well as the stories of Brother Leo.[6] In the meantime Giovanni da Fidanza, Professor and Doctor of Philosophy, called Bonaventure, had produced a smooth official biography. Bonaventure led the Franciscans from 1257 till 1274, and ultimately became a cardinal of the Roman Church. When his life of Francis was complete, the heads of the Order decided to do away with the previous biographies. They commanded that all existing copies of these books be destroyed.

Fortunately, not all the Franciscans were stupid enough to obey. Several copies of Celano's books survived, although his first biography didn't appear in print until 1768, and the second not till 1880. Again, one wonders what was so dangerous about these stories that they were forbidden for five hundred years.

Listen to Bonaventure's rather pathetic cry: "I would wish to be ground to dust, if I could bring the Order back to the purity of St. Francis and his companions, and to their original goals."⁷ But he adds: "May their spirit animate the new establishments that changing circumstances have made necessary." The "new establishments," of course, were the houses of study that the Franciscans had set up in all the university cities of Europe. In reality there was no going back to Francis: In Bologna, Paris, and Oxford the Friars Minor were too busy with their doctorates. One of them, Roger Bacon (who died in 1294), pursued the study of mathematics and the natural sciences along with theology. In his writings he sketched out a future society in which wondrous machines made life easier for people: permanently burning lamps, motor-driven wagons and ships, flying machines, and underwater vessels. Bonaventure ruled over thirty thousand Franciscans in fifteen hundred friaries, spread throughout Europe.⁸ He was, as we say today, a good manager. He was canonized. Francis would have cursed him.

Here is one of the suppressed stories: When Francis was walking from Verona on his way to Bologna, he was informed of a recently completed "brothers' house" in Bologna. When he heard that, he demanded at once that all the brothers, including invalids, leave the house as quickly as possible—which they did. And the brothers humbly accepted the harsh penances that Francis imposed on them as punishment. Only one man, the superior of the province of Bologna, named Pietro Stacia, who was a learned man, could not agree to giving up the new house. Francis cursed him.

Before he joined the Order, Brother Pietro had enjoyed great fame, and even among his fellow superiors he was highly respected for his knowledge and erudition. For this reason some of the brothers approached Francis and appealed to him to take Pietro back into his favor and bless him. This was at the time when Francis was close to death. He replied: "I can't bless a man whom God has cursed, and so the curse remains."⁹

Bologna was a university city. Before entering the Franciscans, Pietro Stacia had taught there as professor of jurisprudence. His confrontation with Francis took place in the early summer of 1220, shortly after Francis' return from the Holy Land. The "brothers' house" was a house of studies, built for the intellectual training of new recruits to the Order and for the promotion of advanced academic work.

After the death of Francis such houses of study were erected in all the intellectual centers, and the Franciscans were soon reckoned among the most learned men in Europe, along with their competitors the Dominicans. One can well imagine that by Bonaventure's time the leading Franciscan bureaucrats had no interest in trumpeting to the world the old story about that incident in Bologna. "Changing circumstances" were stronger than Francis' express desire—and have remained so. That is why Brother Leo's old stories and both Celano biographies were banned.

This book will not renew Francis' curse upon Pietro Stacia. Why should we play arbitrator in the disputes of the past? Francis took a remarkably strong stance in the face of certain developments in modern culture. This will make enough of an impression on the reader without any lecturing on our part.

A BOUQUET OF FLOWERS

Brother Leo's stories and both Celano biographies are our most important sources in dealing with Francis.[10] Beyond this we have, from Francis himself, his *Testament,* a few prayers (including the famous "Canticle of the Sun"), letters, and finally, two versions of the Rules for the Friars Minor. Then there is the so-called *Legend of the Three Companions,* dating from 1246, an anonymous collection of stories from Perugia.

The biography by Bonaventure, for centuries the only officially authorized text, is historically worthless. It adds little new material to the older sources and suppresses practically everything that makes Francis interesting. There remains the *Fioretti* (*Little Flowers*), which is today the most popular collection of anecdotes about Francis. It was not written down till comparatively late, around a hundred years after Francis' death. The stories in *The Little Flowers* were first told by Franciscan hermits who had settled in the country around Ancona—sufficiently removed from the now busy world of Assisi, but close enough to the home of their adored Francis to keep his memory alive.

These brothers wanted to follow Francis' original plan in silence and seclusion, and they were left in peace. In this kind of atmosphere Francis' image underwent an early transformation—in *The Little Flowers* history turned to poetry, to *belles lettres.* The book also records the disappointment of these hermits over the evolution of the Friars Minor. And, of course, this charming collection has many accounts of miracles. Here and there we discover old and authentic pieces of tradition, and we have to weigh each case to decide whether we're dealing with fancy or historical facts.

All in all, we are better acquainted with Francis of Assisi than with any other medieval man. His behavior strikes us as utterly spontaneous, his sayings are unmistakably his. One can imagine meeting him anywhere, even today.

In the Introduction to their collection of stories, Leo, Rufino, and Angelo write that they had no intention of composing an autobiography.[11]

They compare themselves to people wandering through a meadow full of flowers and who pick a beautiful bouquet. By flowers they mean the "conspicuous examples of Francis' way of life" (*conversationis insignia*) that they consider worth passing on to others. And as a matter of fact, they succeed in depicting precisely those details of Francis' everyday life that make him seem vividly present. For example: It was Francis' wish to take the teachings of the Lord Jesus literally and to practice them with scrupulous exactitude. For this reason he ordered brother cook not to soak the next day's vegetables in hot water on the night before, as was the custom. In so doing he wanted to comply with the instruction given in the Sermon on the Mount, "Take no thought for the morrow." So the cook never put the dried peas or beans in the water until the morning, after matins.[12]

One simply can't invent something like that. Perhaps it's clearer now why I like to call Francis the last Christian.

Here is another of Brother Leo's stories: One time the Lord Jesus Christ spoke to Brother Leo: "I weep for the brothers." Leo asked: "Why then, dear Lord?" Jesus answered: "Because they don't understand how I take care of them every day, without their having to sow and reap. Because they are lazy, they gossip, they quarrel with each other, and when they suffer injustice, they refuse to forgive."[13]

This dark, forceful picture of a helpless God complaining about his incorrigible children makes an obvious point. Once again, as in the story of the vegetables, we find the Jesus who preaches the Sermon on the Mount put forward as the absolute authority for proper conduct, contrary to the way people actually live.

The Leo stories reveal a conflict that we should like to get to the bottom of. We can readily understand how Francis with his "literally crazy stubbornness" had no chance, in the long run, against the Bonaventures, with their sharp eye for the ways of the world. One need not sigh about Francis' tragic failure, as contemporary biographies have gotten used to doing. Nowadays everyone takes thought for the morrow, except perhaps the Bushmen, and we would just as soon not head back in that direction. Still, we have to explain why Francis strove so obstinately to create a condition where one need not worry about the future, and where destructive energies would be superfluous.

Francis' unswerving passion for this ideal bore within itself the seeds of the conflict that would lead, forty years later under Bonaventure, to the banning of Brother Leo's stories. The suppression of the authentic accounts of Francis' life lays bare their potential explosiveness—we should not be deceived by Leo's pleasant style nor by the amiable image of a cluster of flowers. In point of fact the Leo stories became the favorite reading of the Franciscan opposition to Bonaventure and his party line.

FRANCIS THE MAN

The following quotation is taken from German writer Rudolf G. Binding's Introduction to his 1911 translation of *The Little Flowers*: "There, where the wind blows pure from the broad, gleaming ridge of the Apennines, and unites with the breezes of the Tiber plain, heavy with the sweetness of flowers and herbs and warm with the breath of the ripening wheat; there, where the sun is a laughing god; where the bees hum and the larks twitter the whole summer long, and it makes you a little drowsy, a dreamer in broad daylight; there where the landscape is one whole cry of joy to a Creator who seems to brood over it: There is where the little flowers of St. Francis grew."[14] The text combines a minimum of factual content with a maximum of "atmosphere," created by the piling on of calculated touches. (The summer isn't just long, it has to be "delightful" as well; the sun is not merely a god, but a laughing god to boot.)

We have here, from the pen of a master in this genre, a fully ripened sample of literary *kitsch*.[15] In the twentieth century this sort of thing has reworked Francis into someone whose chief occupation is talking to birds. This sentimentalized Francis is all wrapped up with the air of Italy, with picturesque poverty and dreamy little churches amid olive groves, with the soft light of Umbria and the dark forms of cypresses in the glow of sunset.

And such petty-bourgeois sentimentalization did not come about by accident. Before he was made over into a nature enthusiast and animal lover the Christian social movement between 1848 and 1914 had discovered in Francis a powerful patron. Thus in 1857 a study published in Italy investigated Francis' bearing upon the class struggle and the condition of the workers.[16] (It went through fourteen editions before the outbreak of World War I, and was translated into French and German.) Dozens of such books were printed around that time,[17] and read by Catholics and Protestants to whom the "social question" meant something more than a chance to practice charity. Their authors talked about "Christian democracy" (*democrazia cristiana*) and social reform—fighting words then—and appealed to Francis whenever they did. They didn't quite follow the Marxist line of Karl Kautsky (d. 1938), who made an exhaustive survey of early communistic movements in the Middle Ages,[18] but they did take a fresh look at the political content of Francis' preaching. Before the First World War the good Franciscan fathers had their hands full trying to steer the laypeople in their "Third Order" away from socialism, and to keep their attention focused on the kindhearted, peaceable Francis. They got help from a Danish Protestant writer named Johannes Jörgensen. In 1907 he published a biography that went through many editions and translations and that signaled the transition to the sentimental Francis of our time. Jörgensen later converted to Catholicism, which so overjoyed the Franciscans that they renamed a street in Assisi after him.

From the Introduction to the *Life of St. Francis of Assisi* by Paul Sabatier (1894): "[Francis] was of the people and the people recognized themselves in him. He had their poetry and their aspirations, he espoused their claims, and the very name of his institute had at first a political signification: In Assisi, as in most other Italian towns, there were *majores* and *minores*, the *popolo grasso* and the *popolo minuto*; he resolutely placed himself among the latter. The political side of his apostolate needs to be clearly apprehended, if we would understand its amazing success and the wholly unique character of the Franciscan movement in its beginning."[19]

Sabatier was the first to discover the old manuscript with the stories of Brother Leo. Sabatier had studied Calvinist theology and history in Paris, and was led by his teacher, the renowned Ernest Renan (whose novelistic *Vie de Jésus* was such an epochal book), to do research on the life of Francis. Sabatier's biography went into fifty editions. It is fluently written, it displays a solid knowledge of the medieval world, and it does a thorough job with the sources then available on Francis' life.

Sabatier set modern study of Francis in motion. He was the first to recognize and work out Francis' political significance, which led to a great hue and cry from Franciscan academics writing in learned journals. Since his time many books have appeared about Francis of Assisi, readable ones and scholarly ones loaded down with footnotes.[20] But Sabatier's is still unsurpassed.

People have often asked me—with reference to my earlier books—what my purpose is in writing. So let me offer on this occasion a word of explanation. As a historical study this book aims not to compile abstract information, but to aid in the understanding of contemporary social conditions, to show that our problems are not at all fortuitous. As a biography it aims to reveal what Francis the man was actually like. Beyond this I would like to meet with Christianity, now so exhausted, at that point in its long career where it fell among robbers, and where it has lain prostrate ever since. Perhaps it can be gotten back on its feet again.

III

A GOOD BOURGEOIS

Francis' century (1180–1280) was a period of economic growth, with business expanding and the population of Europe rapidly increasing. During this time an entire social class entered irreversibly upon a road that we, as members of the bourgeoisie, are still treading today. Francis refused to take this road, and that is the subject of this book.

Which means that we're stuck with the banal business of the relations between the individual and society, with the issue of Francis' "position within the historical context," and similar jargon-filled topics.

But we shall attack the question from a different angle. We shall ask what was going on in Francis' head before he proceeded, at the age of twenty-six, to give his life a new direction.

The question, then, is: What made him what he was, a good bourgeois?

As everyone knows, we call the time when Francis lived "the Middle Ages"—that is, the period between A.D. 500 and 1500. The Middle Ages conjure up thoughts of Gothic cathedrals and proud fortresses, of noble knights and the unbroken unity of Christendom. In reality, of course, there were no Sir Galahads running about in the Middle Ages. The knights were murderous ruffians who got into brawls at the slightest provocation, spat on the table during dinner, and seldom came into contact with soap and water.[1] The many books about the Crusades adequately demonstrate just how barbarous these people really were.

And Christendom? The lovely Gothic cathedrals mislead us into thinking of medieval society in Europe as deeply Christian. There's some truth to that, at least as far as religious conviction goes—it was strong. And people had more enthusiasm about going to church than they do now: There was a place of worship for every one thousand city-dwellers, whereas in our major cities the figure is ten thousand.

But if we take a closer look at medieval piety, we may well ask what was so specially Christian about the everyday behavior of Christians in those days. The love of one's neighbor, as Jesus preached it, had next to no impact on medieval society. Some of our stouthearted and simple-minded history professors may rattle on about the "medieval cosmos,"[2] but in so doing they slur over the coarseness and brutality that everyone took for granted then, from the savage childrearing practices[3] to the traditional wife-beating, the traffic in Christian slaves, and the extermination of entire districts in the name of the Lord. Instead of repeating the usual clichés about the Middle Ages, it makes better sense to take a more realistic point of view and judge the period for what it actually was: the cradle of modern capitalism.

Between the last ancient empire (Rome) and the first modern one (Charles V) there is a period of roughly one thousand years. From the standpoint of imperialism the European Middle Ages were a penny-ante epoch, when various country squires fought for the best acreage. Compared with Islam's international empire, which stretched from Spain to the Indies, Charlemagne was a rather trivial figure, and his kingdom merely a rustic province. One can well imagine how they smiled in the courts of the then civilized world, in Baghdad and Byzantium, at the news of his coronation as Roman Emperor in the year 800.

In the course of time the laughter died on the lips of those Arabs and Greeks.

In the forests of the backward corner of the globe later called Europe, forces were gathering that a thousand years after Charlemagne took control of the world.[4] They achieved this through the use of that philosophers' stone which brought forth an unprecedented, overflowing store of riches: industrial capital. The necessary groundwork for this development was laid in Francis' century. We have already mentioned the discovery of the mechanical clock, the model for all robots and automatic machines.[5] "The entire theory of the production of uniform movement was generated by the clock," wrote Karl Marx in a letter to Friedrich Engels in 1863. But clocks were not only a necessary condition for the organization of the modern factory, they also represented the critical breakthrough to what would be the characteristic feature of modern science and technology: precision.

Along with clocks came the desire to have a standardized calendar—an indispensable aid in doing business abroad.[6] The demand to begin the "civic" year on January 1 was first made in Francis' century, an altogether revolutionary proposal that ran contrary to the customary order, based on the holy seasons of the liturgical year.

Clocks and calendars, these hopeful children of Francis' age, would never have seen the light of day without the arts of counting and reckoning.[7] In 1212 appeared the *Liber Abaci*, by a certain Leonardo Pisano—the first popular presentation of arithmetic. It took many generations of untiring teachers before abstract mathematical quantities could determine the patterns of everyday life for the general population. Over the ages entire forests have been sliced into sturdy rods to beat numerical skills into the heads of children. An astonishingly successful operation, as we know. Our glance runs over the price tags of goods in the store windows, and we never give it a second thought—which is a mistake. Thoughtlessness is a poor preparation for dealing with Francis of Assisi.

We have something in common with Francis that we seldom pay attention to, because it seems the most obvious thing in the world: a bourgeois ego. We shall have to occupy ourselves with what might be called the archaeology of this ego. The Greek word from which archaeologists get their name conveys the notion of "beginnings" or "origins." I should like to discuss three origins of Francis' bourgeois makeup (and ours), in the order of their appearance. The first takes us back to ancient Greece, to around 650 B.C. The second lies in the Christian monasteries at the dawn of the medieval period. We shall look for the third in the cities of the high Middle Ages. At the end of these reflections we shall know, at least in general, what was going on in Francis' head when he rode with the militia from Assisi into battle with Perugia.

MONEY AND MIND

In a study published in 1977, Professor Rudolf Wolfgang Müller, of the University of Hanover, whom I have to thank for practically everything in this section, proposed a striking and well-documented thesis. He suggests that the birth of the bourgeois ego coincides with the beginning of coined money.[8] Both make their appearance together, in Greece, in the second half of the seventh century B.C. The transition from the bar to the coin form of money took place between 600 and 620 in the kingdom of Lydia (in the western part of modern-day Turkey). The metal used was electrum, an alloy of gold and silver. The transition from the non-ego to self-consciousness took place in the poems of a certain Archilochus, the first Greek lyric poet. He came from Paros, one of the Cyclades. He lived from around 685 to 640 B.C., and earned his living as a mercenary soldier. Professor Müller writes: "The thing that strikes one right away about Archilochus is that he speaks of himself, indeed that he thinks of himself as an individual."[9] Archilochus himself has this to say: "I understand the art that the Muses bestow." With this sentence, a self-conscious artist steps out on the stage of history for the first time.

And before this? Was there no ego, in the usual sense, before the time of Archilochus? No. To back up this stunning assertion, Professor Müller analyzes the content of both the famous epics that form part of our cultural heritage, *The Iliad* and *The Odyssey*. They were written down in the eighth century B.C. Barely a hundred years separate the Homeric epics from the poems of Archilochus, but the difference between them is essential. The heroes in Homer have no word for "decide," no future as we understand it, no term for "spirit," or rather "soul" in the sense of a personal self-consciousness. There are expressions like "my heart," in which we can make out a dim feeling of the ego's powers, but it never presses forward to reflect upon itself, to true self-consciousness. The ego of the Homeric warriors is rather the product of various forces, especially the tribal conventions of the ruling class. One seeks in vain throughout the Homeric epics the division, which we take for granted, between subject and object, and hence between an inner world ruled by the ego and a separate outer universe. Nowadays we know that this mode of thought, entirely foreign as it is to us, was once the general rule, and not only among the Greeks of Homer's day. In many languages (in Vietnamese, for example) to this day there exists no word for "I" in our sense.

The connection between self-consciousness and coined money is not accidental. Of course, Archilochus himself never held a coin in his hand, since he died around twenty years before the appearance of the first coin. But he was a mercenary, and as such he was paid with little bars of precious metal. These were the immediate predecessors of actual money. Archilochus belonged to that class of free but destitute Greeks, who appear in the seventh century B.C., mercenaries, craftsmen, handymen, traders and usurers, sailors and pirates, and who constitute the earliest bourgeoisie we know of. They don't make their living from the soil, since they own no land. They have to look elsewhere. In the ups and downs of an uncertain and constantly imperiled existence they need a stable ego to fall back upon. Archilochus writes,

"Soul, soul,/ Torn by perplexity,/ On your feet now!/ Throw forward your chest/ To the enemy;/ Keep close in the attack;/ Move back not an inch./ But never crow in victory,/ Nor mope hang-dog in loss./ Overdo neither sorrow nor joy:/ A measured motion governs man."[10]

Archilochus has only two things he can rely on: himself and the precious metals in his soldier's bag. He and people like him are the vanguard of a new mentality. They give shape to a kind of intelligence that has at its command a set of interrelated capabilities: self-consciousness, rational (purposeful, logical) thinking, abstract calculation, goal-oriented sense of time, and objective distance from things—as opposed to the old magic. In the foreground of this way of thinking stands the personal (!) acquisition of wealth in the form of money. Money and mind are the two faces of the Janus-headed god whom we worship to this day, though we've never given him a name. That isn't necessary, however, because, to put it plainly, we're identical with him.

Scholars will surely cast light on further connections between money and mind. For instance, consider the fact that the earliest Greek philosophy, Ionian cosmology, coincides geographically and temporally with the appearance of coinage. (Thales of Miletus, the first of this school, lived between 624 and 545 B.C. in exactly the same region where the first coins were put into circulation.) Around 550 B.C., Athens issued silver coins that shortly afterward became the first internationally accepted currency. Over the course of three hundred years of unparalleled development Athens also saw the minting of those bourgeois modes of consciousness that have continued to serve as the basis of modern society, practically unaltered, right up till the present.

It is no accident that the bourgeois revolutionaries of the eighteenth century appealed so resolutely to Greek and Roman philosophers and orators. They thought of the "dark" medieval period, with its feudalism and bigotry, as an interruption of the light of rationality that had first shone on ancient Greece. Three hundred years before this, Renaissance humanists had thought likewise. Today we have a clearer view of things. The medieval "interruption" of the bourgeois era, which began in antiquity, was only superficially a relapse into barbaric and prelogical patterns of life. Beneath all the boorish stagnation, the bourgeois ego was gathering new strength to play its part in the coming industrial age.

We are now in a position to appreciate the depth of the protest that led Francis, with his acquisitive bourgeois ego, to become a despiser of money. Francis was fighting a process that led, by the logic of history, from Archilochus to Rockefeller. To this day many people, especially the poor, view this logic as a rather dubious affair.

PRAYING AND WORKING

Along with ancient Greece, Christianity too is generally considered responsible for the forging of European culture. That sounds very nice, but it's all rather intangible. We can get a much more concrete notion of the part played by Christianity in the creation of the bourgeois ego if we think of the industrious monks. Over the many centuries since the fall of the Roman Empire, of all the institutions that have patiently toiled to inculcate discipline in people, the medieval monastery was the first, and its impact has been enduring.

Here is a little story from modern Italy: A manager of the Alfa-Romeo plant in Milan once told me there had been considerable difficulties at first with the workers of the Alfa-Sud factory in the southern part of the country. They couldn't understand why they were supposed to give up their siesta: They were in the habit of taking a little nap after lunch, which is altogether sensible in hot places. But this old custom was incompatible with modern assembly lines, which run all day long. So the workers had to learn about the "production of uniform movement"—and they had to give up their siesta. The results achieved in a relatively short time with the Alfa-Sud workers took many centuries to accomplish on the much larger scale of the European nations. In this disciplining process, which made medieval shepherds over into modern industrial workers, and dairy maids into office girls, much more was at stake than just a siesta. People had to have drummed into them the steady practice of certain virtues, without which trains don't run and letters don't get delivered. These include coming to work on time and the readiness to perform a specific operation at a specific time without complaining, slowing down, or pausing, except very briefly. In advanced industrial countries we exhibit these virtues around 240 days a year. In the Middle Ages people worked only 180 days a year.[11] In other words, at that time roughly every other day in the year was a holiday.

Nowadays everyone knows that medieval monasteries made a substantial contribution to European culture. Fewer people realize that these same monasteries, with their purposeful rationality, discipline, abnegation, enterprise, and inventiveness, developed the basic principles of the modern capitalistic economy. There were monasteries in the Far East at the time of Abraham, long before Christianity. But, needless to say, modern capitalism arose not in India, but in Europe.

Numerous scholars have racked their brains searching for the root cause of this development. One of these men was Max Weber, the sociologist, economist, and historian, who died in 1920. His research into the origins of the contemporary world economy was peculiarly extensive, thorough, and persistent, and his conclusions are still discussed today. In his best-known work, *The Protestant Ethic and the Spirit of Capitalism,* conceived during a trip to America, Weber traced the strange "elective affinity" between Puritanism and capitalism, between religion and business.[12]

Weber paid special attention to the period between John Calvin (d.

1564) and Benjamin Franklin (d. 1790). John Wesley, the founder of the Methodists (d. 1791), described in his day what happened over those 250 years in Geneva, Birmingham, and Philadelphia in the following terms: "Religion must necessarily produce both industry and frugality, and these cannot but produce riches. But as riches increase, so will pride, anger, and love of the world in all its branches. . . . So, although the form of religion remains, the spirit is swiftly vanishing away."[13] Weber cites Wesley as a fair summation of his own ideas, and he adds, "The Puritan wanted to work in a calling; we are forced to do so. For when asceticism was carried out of monastic cells into everyday life, and began to dominate worldly morality, it did its part in building the tremendous cosmos of the modern economic order. This order is now bound to the technical and economic conditions of machine production which to-day determine the lives of all the individuals who are born into this mechanism . . . and will so determine them until the last ton of fossilized coal is burnt."[14]

Weber's mention of the monk's cell shows how keensighted he was. He also notes the difference between European and oriental monasticism, drawing attention to the "rational character" of monastic life in the West, from the Benedictines to the Cluniacs to the Cistercians. In these observations lies Weber's answer to the question of why modern capitalism emerged in Europe rather than anywhere else. From the beginning of the Middle Ages, around the sixth century A.D., monks and nuns lived by a motto that represented a significant departure from all previous monastic programs. It was *Ora et labora!* (Work and pray!)

Before this, monks confined themselves to prayer and meditation as their ideal activity. Such manual labor as they performed to support themselves had nothing to do with any program; it was simply a necessity of life. After Benedict of Nursia (d. 547) daily work became a pious duty, placed on the same footing with prayer.[15] Eight times in twenty-four hours the bell for prayer rang out in the abbey church of medieval monasteries. The monks spent roughly five hours a day singing the Office and five hours toiling in the fields and workshops. Their daily lives were disciplined and regimented according to a detailed system. This is what Weber has called the "rational character" of Western monasticism. We can already recognize this systematized way of life in the "Rule" written by Benedict himself. Of the seventy-three articles in this medieval code more than half deal with discipline and administrative matters. One can feel the modern factory in the offing (and recall the ancient slave plantations) when one reads that every ten monks formed a working team under the supervision of a "dean."

More amazing still is the fact that from about the year 1000 medieval monasteries were the most important experimental stations for the machinery of the time. There were water mills in existence in China, Denmark, and northern Anatolia from the first century B.C.[16] They then appeared in massive numbers in Europe during the early Middle Ages. By the ninth century a resourceful monk in Picardy had greatly improved the old clattering mill. This man was obviously tired of crushing the mash by hand in his monastery's beer brewery. So he fastened cams to the axle of the waterwheel, and the cams activated a row of vertically operating beaters. This invention spread rapidly, and from the twelfth century on it was used for fulling wool, hammering iron, and sawing wood.

We can sense the medieval monks' enthusiasm for mechanization in an old text that describes how machines functioned in a twelfth-century Cistercian monastery: "The river enters the abbey as much as the wall acting as a check allows. It gushes first into the corn-mill where it is very actively employed in grinding the grain under the weight of the wheels and in shaking the fine sieve which separates the flour from the bran. Thence it flows into the next building, and fills the boiler in which it is heated to prepare beer for the monks' drinking . . . it is now drawn into the fulling-machines . . . its duty is now to serve [the brothers] in making their clothing. . . . [The river] does not . . . refuse any task asked of it. . . . Now the river enters the tannery where it devotes much care and labour to preparing the necessary material for the monks' footwear; then it divides into many small branches and, in its busy course, passes through the various departments, seeking everywhere for those who require its services for any purpose whatever, whether for cooking, rotating, crushing, watering, washing or grinding, always offering its help and never refusing. At last, to earn full thanks and to leave nothing undone, it carries away the refuse and leaves all clean."[17]

This agreeable song of praise to the mechanized abbey gains in significance when one reflects that most of the monasteries of the period enjoyed a system of machines like the one portrayed here. Today one can admire such a factory, a large building with four "departments," at the abbey of Fontenay in Burgundy. It dates from the twelfth century.

We can likewise observe the combination of working units in an efficient mechanized ensemble in the old architectural plans, still preserved, of the monastery of St. Gall, in Switzerland. The "rational character" of the monastic organization of labor, once one absorbs the details, strikes one as astoundingly modern.[18] It is hard to resist the temptation to go one step farther and call it "rationalization."

The motives of the pious brothers when they installed all those wheels and crankshafts were, in the beginning, noble enough. They wanted to spare themselves monotonous tasks in order to be free for jobs that took some thought, such as copying and illuminating books, for example. It's one of history's ironies that the "old Orders," as they are still called, with their progressive spirit, introduced a process whose final results they would scarcely find gratifying. Today, fifteen hundred years after Benedict, our life has been split into work and free time, and in the latter there is precious little praying—at least by the members of the modern technological elite, the scientists and managers. It may happen by chance that a computer programmer wanders into an old monastery while on his vacation, and is taken through the church and cloister by an obliging monk. At this meeting of the medieval and the modern each man, presumably, will have little to say to the other. They would be greatly surprised should anyone inform them that they are both children of the same spirit.

Francis got to know the monastic mentality at firsthand. There was a stately Benedictine abbey on Mount Subasio, a few kilometers from Assisi. The monks there owned a lot of land in the district and, as a concession to the times, they had also built a house in Assisi—a branch office, as it were.[19] Francis never gave a thought to becoming a monk. On the contrary, as mentioned before, he stubbornly resisted the idea of choosing one of the old monastic Rules as a model for his own companions. Evidently Francis had sensed in the monasteries the fatal connection between religion and wealth, and he wanted nothing to do with this sort of piety.

"CITY AIR SETS YOU FREE"

There is a hackneyed notion that stands in the way of understanding our collective past: the "deeply pious peasant." A hundred years ago this concept, now a nostalgic legacy from our grandparents, flourished in penny dreadfuls and cheap oleographs. Since then we associate this kind of religiosity with those figures wearing Breton or Tyrolean costumes, standing out in the fields saying the Angelus with bared heads or walking to Christmas carol services through the snowdrifts. Some people like to claim that the religious faith of country folk is still untainted, and vacationing urbanites mix with the supposedly devout villagers at church on Sunday.

People seldom ask, however, whether holding onto old costumes is equivalent to piety. One or two facts may serve as a corrective to these romantic imaginings: Judaism as we know it found its permanent shape in the city of Jerusalem. It spread throughout cities and regarded fellow believers who belonged to the peasantry as second-class Jews, if not basically godless. Similarly, in early Christianity the word "peasant" (*paganus*) meant the same thing as pagan. Medieval theologians too, among them Thomas Aquinas, treat the peasants with open contempt as inferior Christians. From the very beginning Christianity was first propagated in the cities of the Mediterranean basin, and later on the impulses for change in Christian life, whether orthodox or heretical, all ran from the city to the country, and not the other way around. This is the context where Francis belongs, shaped as he was by urban life. The will to shake off the yoke of the nobility and clergy came naturally to him—by birthright, as it were.

When the cities of Europe were still small and in their first flush of prosperity, around 150 years before Francis, they were controlled by the Church. With its abbots, bishops, and cathedral chapters, the Church held not only the souls, but also two thirds of the land in Europe. Religious authorities then were known collectively as "the dead hand" (*manus mortus*). Whatever came their way, by sale or bequest, was put under mortmain—that is, withdrawn from further exchange. Church property could not be alienated. The Papal States, for instance, belonged to St. Peter and St. Paul; and dead men, as we know, don't return things.

In the cities too, the dead hand ruled, alongside the barons, and nothing went on without it. As handicrafts and commerce gradually grew stronger and the towns began to stir, after the long stagnation preceding and following Charlemagne, the townsfolk set about defending themselves from the dead hand—at first with the weakling's weapon of cunning. So, for example, in eleventh-century Florence[20] people spoke quite ingenuously of how useful it was for the men to have discussions in front of church after Mass. Out of these conversations "assemblies" (*conventus*), and from there it was an obvious step to elect some trustworthy citizens as spokesmen for the assembly, in case they should have to consult the very reverend lord in the bishop's palace. A hundred years later Florence was ruled by elected "consuls," and the higher clergy were out in the cold.

This same pattern can be seen in some sixty Italian cities. On each occasion the burghers formed a conspiracy against the local bishop, and the coups were not always bloodless.[21] From the eleventh century onward successful revolts against the clergy were also staged in other European cities, and the control of town life passed from the dead hand to a living one. "City air sets you free"—six hundred years before the French Revolution this medieval saying signals the first triumphs of a new class, whose homeland was the city.

The bourgeoisie, consisting of merchants, bankers, and artisans, is the class Francis belonged to. In this context some writers have spoken of a new human type, dubbing it *Homo economicus*.[22] One might just as well call it *Homo hereticus*. For stride by stride with the formation of the urban middle class, from the year 1000 heresy too began to make its presence felt, as an expression of the awakening self-consciousness among the bourgeoisie.

Around A.D. 1000, an old chronicle tells us, in the region of Châlons-sur-Marne a man named Leuthard grew tired while working in the fields one day and decided to take a little rest. He fell asleep and dreamed that a huge swarm of bees had in some mysterious way gotten inside his body, only to escape from his mouth with a roar. With their stings, the man felt, the bees had given him an unheard-of inspiration. He ran home to his wife, and in a state of wild excitement declared their marriage at an end. He then hurried at once into the nearest church, ripped the crucifix out of its fastening, and trod it underfoot. As the peasants came running in, he preached that God had revealed wondrous things to him. There was no need to pay tithes to the clergy. Not everything in the Bible was holy and beneficial; it also contained all kinds of nonsense.

People listened to this sort of talk with pleasure, and increasingly large crowds gathered around Leuthard to hear his disclosures, until finally the bishop, a certain Gebuin, called him in for questioning. The bishop, so the chronicle reports, succeeded with his clever words in driving the man into a corner and convincing the people that his message was confused. In this way the danger was averted, and in the end Leuthard was abandoned by the people, fell into despair, threw himself into a well, and drowned.[23]

One could easily make a novel out of this strange story: *The Man Who Trampled the Cross*. Where did Leuthard get his knowledge of the Bible? In those days it was available only in Latin, and besides that, books were very expensive. (For a book one might give an entire dairy farm in payment, with buildings, cattle, and pasture.) Then, what of the dream with the bees, those learned, eloquent creatures? From time immemorial their buzzing and swarming, as well as their circumspection, their busy and frugal housekeeping, have appealed to people as symbols of inspired, single-minded intelligence. They descend upon Leuthard in an open field, in the noontime stillness of a hot summer's day. Suddenly he knows what he has to do: The things in his head, acquired from others or thought out for himself, the usual jumble, fall together in a recognizable pattern. In a burst of ecstatic clarity he leaves his wife and his hut, and does something dreadful: He stomps on the crucified God.

That is the core of the story. It contains, in a puzzling, obscure fashion, the essential combination of horror and attraction, as in the thinking of forbidden thoughts, which is the substance of heresy. Forty years after Leuthard's death, between 1043 and 1048, a certain Roger, bishop from the same region where Leuthard preached, wrote his episcopal colleague in Lüttich an anxious letter. He spoke of people who rejected marriage as absurd, abstained from meat, and refused to kill even the smallest living thing. And, to top off their blasphemous arrogance, they practiced the laying on of hands to administer the power of the Holy Spirit, which by hallowed custom only bishops may do. They also divided themselves up into masters and disciples (*perfecti et auditores*), and with their great eloquence poisoned the hearts of the faithful, so that very soon even simple souls began to feel superior to the most learned Catholic teaching.[24]

Here we have those men and women, still anonymous, who in Francis' day would form an extensive counter-Church in southern France and northern Italy—the Cathars, whence the German word for heretic, *Ketzer*, a name expressive of the most horrible sacrilegiousness.[25] The sword of the Holy Inquisition was forged for use against these people. And a holy war was waged against them in the South of France between 1209 and 1229, which saw entire towns wiped out in the name of God.

What made this new teaching so dangerous? We now know that it was brought in from the Balkans by itinerant traders. They believed in a different God from the one worshiped by Roman and Byzantine Christians, a twofold God, as it were, one good, the other evil. The world for these heretics was a battleground, an arena where one struggled for purity, with the help of a strictly vegetarian diet and sexual abstinence, even for married couples. The inner circle of this strange movement followed such maxims to the letter, but the sympathizers who made up the bulk of the membership were not obligated to so rigorous a life.

In every case it was city dwellers who joined the Cathars:[26] weavers, shoemakers, tanners, furriers, pickpockets, saddlers, ropemakers, millers, innkeepers, cartwrights, tradesmen, money changers—members of the bourgeoisie, in other words, who sat in their workshops and stores, enjoying a modest prosperity. The new faith freed them from their guilty Catholic conscience, troubled by interest and profit—for, since this last was a work of the evil God anyway, and thus belonged to the eternal order of things, believers might well be justified in finding a secret meaning in the joys of wealth and acquisitiveness. Only, at the point of death, these worthy people would call in one of their strict coreligionists and get themselves permanently enrolled in the ranks of the "pure" through the cheering ceremony of the laying on of hands. Then they could die in peace.

What led the bourgeoisie to heed the ascetical Catharist preachers was the ability of these men to provide them with a broad new outlook that, unlike their old traditional faith, suited the actual conditions of their lives. First of all, the Cathars questioned the need for any sort of clergy. They promoted a way of life that allowed the "laity" to find their way to God without the intervening mediation of their clerical masters. Luther, as we know, made the same case 350 years later, and in so doing greatly strengthened bourgeois self-consciousness. Evidently, the Cathars could be physically destroyed, but their ideas lived on.

Thus in Francis' time city air scattered the seeds of heresy (i.e., of independent thought) along with those of freedom. Medieval burghers did not merely personify concern with debit and credit, they also practiced what philosopher Ernst Bloch (d. 1977) called "going upright." They wanted to live without making any feudal genuflections, which had a pronounced effect on their religious posture as well.

For all his lifelong politeness to the clergy, Francis never wanted to be a priest. He meant his fellowship to be made up of laypeople, and to be legitimated by a Christlike way of life, not by Holy Orders and the study of theology. This desire was effectively frustrated, as we shall see later on. The fact remains that Francis sought blessedness in the lay state, and that on all the critical questions concerning his chosen way of life he always appealed directly to God and the Bible, never to any churchly rules or traditions. This essentially heretical attitude takes us to the heart of Francis' bourgeois mode of thought. Even after the decisive step that changed his life, Francis' bourgeois makeup continued to play an active role in everything he did.

For the rest, we observe nothing particularly original about this young man of twenty who leaps into the saddle to fight alongside his fellow citizens against their rivals from Perugia. Insofar as he has been shaped by the three "origins" that we have discussed, these forces from the depths of the ancient and medieval past, he stands before us as an anonymous and interchangeable figure, the son of a rich cloth dealer in a provincial town, cut out for a future in the family business. We shall have to watch him closely to recognize the problem that finally drove him to revolt against himself.

IV

A DISGRACE TO THE FAMILY

ONLY once in his life, at the age of twenty-five, did Francis engage in open, public rebellion. This act of revolt was directed against his father, and it was irrevocable. His gesture of throwing money and clothing at his father's feet transformed Francis for good. Before this they had quarreled over a considerable amount of money that Francis had stolen from his father.

This is the story they tell: When his father realized that he could get no satisfaction from the town authorities, he turned to the bishop of Assisi to lodge a complaint before him against his son. The bishop then informed Francis that he had to appear before his tribunal. Francis came at the appointed time, and the bishop said to him: "Your father is extremely angry with you. If you wish to act like a religious person, then give him back all the money you have, immediately! Once he has the money, his rage will be appeased." Then Francis said: "My lord, I shall not only return the money that belongs to him, but the clothes as well." Quickly he went into a chamber in the bishop's house, removed all his clothing, came back naked, and flung clothes and money at his father's feet. He said as he did so: "Hear this, all of you, and understand it well. Up until now I have called Pietro Bernardone my father. Now I am returning the money that he was so alarmed about, along with all the clothing that I have from him. From now on I will say: 'Our Father who art in heaven,' and no longer: 'Father Pietro Bernardone.'" His father in a rage seized the money and clothes, while the bishop threw his cloak around Francis. Thus Francis was free from everything, and ready for the service of righteousness.[1]

Naturally, this key scene had a prior history, and we shall have to deal with it. Information about Francis' childhood and youth is admittedly meager, but there is enough for us to recognize a broad pattern with a dominant theme. It's important that Francis had an opportunity to be reconciled with his father at the bishop's court. But Francis wanted to make a break: He denied his birth, his position in society, and his upbringing with a single blunt gesture. One has the impression that he wanted to start all over again, naked like a newborn child.

DOWNWARD SPIRAL

The first twenty years in the life of Francis of Assisi passed in cheerful obscurity. He went to school, learned reading, writing, and a little Latin. Later he worked in his father's shop, and visited the taverns with youths his own age. Since he had pockets full of money and was generous with it, he was chosen "king" of many feasts. As befitted the son of a rich businessman, his clothing followed the latest fashions. We may assume that Francis was not popular simply because of his money. He seems to have been a charming and high-spirited young man who knew how to sing French songs and liven up a party.

Francis' head was full of the usual tales of King Arthur and Roland, of courtly love and derring-do—and, more to the point, of animosity toward the people of Perugia.

The year 1198 had brought the town of Assisi a considerable increase in civic freedom.[2] The year before, in September, Henry III, a Hohenstaufen, King of Sicily and crowned German Emperor at the age of thirty-two, had died. His son and heir, the future Frederick II, was three years old, and this created a power vacuum in Italy and Germany. In the first week of the new year the Pope had also died, and the cardinals quickly elected a successor, the youngest pope in a long time, Lothar of Segni. He was thirty-seven years old, had studied in Paris and Bologna, and took the name of Innocent III. He set out from Rome in the spring to visit the papal territories, aiming to displace the Germans who had firmly ensconced themselves there. The young Pope also wanted to win back to the See of Peter the duchy of Spoleto, which included Assisi and had been under German domination for the past twenty years.

The journey was one long triumphal procession. Many Italian cities by this time had had enough of the Hohenstaufen. French troubadours passed through Lombardy, with satirical songs mocking the foreign counts and barons, and in Assisi too, young people quickly learned to sing the malicious little ditties in Provençal. In April the Pope was in Narni, thirty kilometers south of Assisi, negotiating with Lord Konrad von Lutzen over the duchy of Spoleto. Konrad had to yield and promise to withdraw. It was further stipulated that he hand over his three largest fortresses, one of which overlooked Assisi, to the Pope. The townspeople of Assisi reacted joyfully to the news. They didn't even wait to hear what the Pope had in mind for the fortress, but decided on their own authority to tear it down. One can imagine how the whole town worked all week long with crowbars and cramps, amid merry shouts and cups of wine. Francis, who was sixteen years old at the time, experienced the first high point in his life.

Then came the Pope in person. He granted the town a plenitude of sovereign powers it had never known before, including free elections. By the end of the year Assisi had its "consuls," it ran its own administration, and it merely had to pay tribute to the Pope. In the town the guilds set the tone, and among them the merchants' guild was the richest and the most powerful. Pietro Bernardone belonged to it, and he doubtless played an eager part in city politics.

The aristocratic enemies of this rising bourgeois class lived in strongholds out in the country, where they watched the signs of the times with growing uneasiness. Many of them had built themselves town houses to exert their influence as directly as possible, on the spot. A crucial sore point between the old nobility and the new bourgeoisie was the right to levy tolls.[3] Someone has calculated that a merchant traveling with his wares from the Po Valley to the border of the duchy of Spoleto would have to pay tolls no fewer than sixteen different times. But even after he crossed the border the nobles kept on stopping him to demand further payment, and that rubbed the tradesmen of Assisi very much the wrong way.

After the Germans pulled out, the tradesmen became bolder than before. Assisi had a civic militia, which was stronger than the handful of serfs who fought for the gentry. At this juncture the noble lord of Sassorosso (a fortress in the neighborhood of Assisi), who customarily charged a toll of every passerby, made a clever move[4]: He swore loyalty to the consuls of Perugia and applied for citizenship there. He did this on January 17, 1200, and a week later the entire clan of the Sassorosso was behind the walls of Perugia.

The Assisi militia marched out at once and leveled the abandoned fortress. Thereupon Perugia sent an ultimatum to Assisi, demanding restoration of the fortress and compensation for its lords. The ultimatum was indignantly rejected, and both cities found themselves in a state of war. Needless to say, the citizens of Perugia had not taken the lords of Sassorosso under their wing out of pure magnanimity. They themselves were involved in a conflict with the nobles in their vicinity, for exactly the same reasons as in Assisi and elsewhere. But the alliance with a noble family from outside the region was another matter: This way they could gain influence against a rival city. Obviously the businessmen governing Assisi and Perugia followed the logic of economic competition. The nobles held the balance of power, and as a matter of fact some aristocrats from Perugia fought on the side of Assisi.

For two years each side was content to engage in little skirmishes and, whenever opportunity offered, to burn the ripening harvest in the enemy fields. Each side formed alliances, Perugia with Foligno, Assisi with Spello and Nocera. Most of the noblemen around Assisi fled to Perugia. Their houses in the town were plundered and put to the torch.

This sort of activity was the business of the *popolo minuto*—that is, the common people, the "minor folk," to whom the name of Friars Minor alludes. These were not the respected tradesmen and master artisans, but the journeymen who had drifted into town from the countryside, handymen and idlers of every sort, corpse washers and grave diggers, ragpickers and dog catchers, washerwomen and working girls. Groups of poverty-stricken small tradesmen also belonged to this underclass, people who lived with their backs against the wall, on two thousand calories a day, in places with open sewers. They made up the majority of the population, in Assisi and elsewhere.

It goes without saying that these men and women seized the chance provided by the nobles who had fled town, and raided their houses, taking pots and pans, chests and bundles of fabric, sausages and hams. In Assisi all sorts of feasts were held around the bonfires of burning houses. Francis, as we see, had no reason to suffer from boredom in the years between 1198 and 1202.

One morning in the autumn of 1202 all the bells in Assisi began to ring. The town militia, as many as two thousand men, gathered before the cathedral. When everything was ready, they went off to battle against Perugia. The foot soldiers of the *popolo minuto* headed the parade, divided into groups according to the different parts of town, each part bearing its appropriate banner. Then came the middle class, arranged according to guilds, likewise marching on foot. A troop of archers followed them, and finally, riding high on horseback, the sons of the rich, and a handful of nobles who remained loyal to the town.

Francis, of course, was with the cavalry. At the end of the procession came a wagon drawn by white oxen, with an altar, priests praying before it, and miraculous relics. They all marched down the short path into the valley, then fifteen kilometers farther to the Tiber, the frontier between Assisi and Perugia. In the early afternoon the enemy came into sight.

Tradition does not record why the battle turned into a debacle, but the men from Assisi were soon racing across the plain, with the enemy in pursuit.[5] The scene provides a sort of "frozen frame" picture of European economic history at the beginning of the "century of wool."[6] When a man runs and his pursuer is on horseback, the running man experiences a vivid instance of class conflict, as he hears the pounding of hooves behind him. Perhaps at the last moment he turns around, sees the rider swinging his sword, and raises his arms to ward off the blow.

Today Perugia has five times as many inhabitants as Assisi.

On the evening after the battle Francis sat, dirty and exhausted, along with his fellows in the dungeon beneath the fortress of the "Capitano del Popolo" of Perugia. Perhaps his hands and clothing were still blood-stained. But in the Middle Ages people preferred to imprison knights rather than kill them, with an eye to ransom money. So Francis remained under arrest for a year, during which time he became seriously ill. (We don't know what he was suffering from.) It is not very likely, as we shall soon see, that Francis engaged in any deep meditation while he was in prison.

In the winter of 1203 his father finally managed to ransom him. Francis came home and was nursed back to health. By the next summer he was feeling so good that he decided to ride to Apulia, along with a young friend from the nobility, to join the army of Walter of Brienne. He planned to fight for the papal cause, in hopes of winning honor, fame, and perhaps even a title of nobility. The year in prison, even with his sickness and recuperation, had not changed Francis at all. His bourgeois ego was quite intact, it had to be up and doing, whatever the cost. His father gave him money and a splendid outfit. He did this deliberately, not because he had a soft spot for a spoiled child. As a *nouveau riche* he needed prestige, especially in a town so full of misfortune.

Francis took off, complete with retinue, dressed like an aristocrat, the elegant companion of noble lords. A few days later, to the town's surprise and his father's chagrin, he came back home. The reason? Francis had had a dream.

This is the story they tell: Shortly before his departure Francis had given away all his ornate and expensive equipment to an impoverished nobleman. The night after that, Francis had a dream. He was called by name and led about a spacious palace, full of costly weapons, magnificent shields, and all sorts of gleaming armor. As he wondered whom this splendor belonged to, it was intimated to him that it was all for him and his fellow nobles. Francis took the dream as a favorable omen for his adventure. But when he got to Spoleto, on his way through to Apulia, he fell into a deep reverie. He still intended to go through with his plans, but when he lay down and started to doze, all of a sudden it seemed as if someone were asking him where he thought he was going. Francis told him. Then he was asked: "Who can give you a better gift, the master or the servant?" "The master," Francis replied. "Then why are you leaving the master for the sake of a servant, a rich man for the sake of a poor man?" Francis was bewildered by these puzzling words, and he wanted to know what he should do. Once again the voice addressed him: "Turn around!"[7]

The story, which exists in three variant forms, should be taken with a grain of salt. The original texts are full of conventional tropes from pious conversion tales, with all sorts of allusions to the Bible. In keeping with this tendentious stylization, Francis is compared to St. Paul on the road to Damascus: He hears heavenly voices and has the inevitable instantaneous change of heart, brought on by an overwhelming force from above.

The core of the story is nonetheless remarkable, a master-slave dialectic we can follow easily enough. One might interpret Francis' gift to the poor nobleman as *nouveau riche* behavior—his father probably bought him a new outfit. And the ensuing dream of the castle (which in another variant comes complete with a beautiful princess) derives from contemporary images of social advancement, and is not especially noteworthy in itself.

But then the story takes a surprising turn. The masters abruptly change into servants, conventional wealth turns into poverty. A new master, another kind of wealth speak to Francis. We cannot yet identify them, but they create a decisive reversal in his values, as he dives to the bottom of his soul in broad daylight. Francis lapses into a state that is neither waking nor sleeping—this sort of thing does happen. Nowadays mysterious voices fall under the jurisdiction of the psychiatrist. But at that time people had different ideas on the subject, as may be seen in a writer as recent as Schiller: They thought that dreams come from God.[8] Francis obeyed his voice and for the first time in his life did something unusual. He snapped his fingers at the knights in Apulia, and went back home.

Shortly thereafter Francis had another fit of abstraction. The brotherhood of a *brigata*, a convivial club, chose him as host for a banquet. Francis did all the honors and paid for a lavish meal. Later that night the young gentlemen marched through the streets singing, with Francis at their head, bearing the staff of master of ceremonies in his hand. Then we are told: All at once Francis dropped behind the others. He stopped singing, and was lost in thought, for God had suddenly touched him, and so great a sweetness filled his heart that he could neither move nor speak. He felt only that sweetness, and could perceive nothing else. So enraptured was he, as he himself said later, that he could not have moved from the spot, even if they had cut him to pieces. When at last his companions noticed that he had fallen behind, they turned around and saw him transformed into a different person. "You must have a lady (*donna*) on your mind. Are you thinking of bringing her home?" "Yes, I really am! And the bride that I'd like to bring home is nobler, richer, and more beautiful than anyone you've ever seen." His friends laughed. Yet Francis had not said this on his own account, but through divine inspiration.[9]

Thomas of Celano and the *Legend of the Three Companions* hasten to explain Francis' strange remarks by insisting that the incomparable bride he spoke of must naturally be understood to mean true religion, to which he was about to consecrate himself. We shall be more cautious on this point. We shouldn't forget that Francis' reply to the obvious question about the reason for his absent-mindedness comes out like the first words of anyone who's been abruptly awakened—that is, partly uncensored. He seizes on "the lady" mentioned by his companions, and he wants to answer in jest, to smooth the awkwardness of the situation. But he only succeeds in part. The level of his consciousness that isn't fully awakened yet affects his speech, and what it's trying to say is: "You've got the wrong idea, my friends. I'm after something unusual, which defies all the common categories, and is better than any of them. I'm about to make a choice." Francis says, while he's still not quite all there, "nobler, richer, and more beautiful." The rising progression seems to be an attempt to express his denial of the familiar world of experience. Something is undoubtedly wrong with Francis, but he doesn't know yet what it is.

In the story of Francis' abnormal psychic state after the merry banquet, we find a hint that shouldn't be neglected: "So great a sweetness filled his heart that he could neither move nor speak." And, "He felt only that sweetness, and could perceive nothing else." To our ears that sounds rather sentimental. But, in my opinion, this prejudice blocks an important access to our understanding of Francis. The *topos* of sweetness appears so often and in so many different passages of the Francis stories that we have to pay attention to it.

We should start with the fact that Francis experienced real and quite powerful sensations, and that he called these feelings "sweet." Unfortunately, we are not now in a position to ask him for fuller explanations. But we can do something different. We can try to understand how Francis' contemporaries used the word "sweetness" (in Latin, *dulcedo*; in Italian, *dolcezza*; in French, *douceur*). It goes without saying that they applied the term to a spoonful of honey and a piece of cake. But what about the metaphorical meanings?

I found one surprising clue in the life of Savonarola.[10] After being imprisoned and even after undergoing torture (customary at the time), Savonarola expressly thanks the authorities for their indulgence in making him submit to the least painful form of interrogation. He chooses the word *dolcezza* to describe the lenient treatment he received, and in this context "sweetness" would surely be a mistranslation. The term was commonly used in Florence in the figurative sense of a specific kind of urbanity, as opposed to unrestrained cruelty and coarse manners. The Florentines were proud of their supple amiability.

But clearly we can't draw conclusions about thirteenth-century Assisi from fifteenth-century Florence. This is meant solely to illustrate how careful one must be in interpreting certain key words. Still, the detour through Florence was not just a digression. Florentine *dolcezza* was historically related to "courtesy," which was modeled after the great courts, primarily those in southern France.[11] This is where the troubadour movement arose, which in Francis' day was still widespread, not only in France, but in Italy too. Francis' description of his profound feelings of happiness as "sweetness" has the ring of the troubadour mode, and may very well bear some connection with it.

Here we have a young man who, much to his amazement, began experiencing intense and extraordinary emotional states, comparable to those of a poet. Francis was, in fact, a poet—a point to which we should now draw some attention. His "Canticle of the Sun" was one of the first vernacular poems written in Italy. We shall not make the mistake of replacing the cliché of Francis' "saintliness" with a label marked "genius." For the time being it will suffice to think of Francis as a man of unusually strong feelings. What made him stop dead in his tracks that evening was more than the faintly tipsy sense of well-being after a copious dinner. It was a feeling that the French to this day call *doux*. The corresponding noun *douceur* means sweetness, mildness (as in Florence), smoothness, loveliness. One can understand why this word is employed so often in the songs of the troubadours, because it synchronizes three sense perceptions— sight (lovely), taste (sweet), and touch (smooth). That night in Assisi Francis was filled with tenderness toward the world. Now we have the right translation.

In Thomas of Celano's second biography there is an important passage, immediately following the story of the outburst of tenderness. It consists of two brief chapters of remarkable psychological acumen. We immediately note the most significant sentence for our purposes: "It was that triumphant sweetness, which from the beginning flooded over him in such profusion that it never left him as long as he lived, but led him and drew him on."[12] Putting it more explicitly, Francis had a (for him) inexplicable experience that was both extraordinary and highly positive—of deep tenderness and benevolence without an explicit object. After he came to himself—that is, to ordinary consciousness—he had only one wish: More of the same, please! But how was he to get it?

The burst of tenderness had come over him spontaneously and involuntarily, Francis couldn't simply conjure it up at will. Nevertheless he tried to. Celano tells us: "He sought out lonely places, far from the public eye."[13] Celano gives the following account of what was going on in Francis' mind: "While he visited hidden places, which seemed as if made for prayer, the devil strove to divert him from his purpose through a stroke of malice. He caused a woman to appear before Francis, a horrible hunchback who lived in his hometown and the sight of whom made everyone shudder. He threatened to make Francis like this woman, if he would not come to his senses and leave off what he had begun. But he was strengthened by God and rejoiced over the saving answer granted to his prayer: 'Francis, exchange the vain and fleshly things you have loved for spiritual. Take bitter for sweet. If you wish to know me, despise yourself. In return you will delight in what I tell you, even if the old ways are overturned.' "[14]

In contrast to Thomas of Celano, we don't believe that Francis had an open line to the Chief. Nor do we believe in the devil and his whispered promptings. Still Celano's account remains noteworthy. First of all, the old woman. Her unexpected appearance in Francis' thoughts makes sense, if we recall for a moment his daydreaming outside of Foligno, more specifically the stress on the possible change from "rich" to "poor." If the rich, he must have thought, are actually poor, then the poor devils of this world are actually rich. This conclusion, at first, gave Francis a violent start. The old beggar woman, known all over town, occurred to him as the embodiment of human degradation. Francis must have said to himself: "If that mysterious voice I heard outside of Foligno is right, then my salvation lies with the lowest of the low—for example that hunchbacked beggar woman. Then I would have to become like her." Not an especially pleasant thought for a rich young man. So Francis let the opportunity pass this time, and turned to more agreeable things, such as his second ecstasy and its wave of sweetness. How could he summon it back again?

Francis was in a blind alley. His efforts to work things out in unfrequented spots, we may safely assume, were fruitless: Going off by himself simply did not do any good. Then he got the idea of linking ecstasy No. 1 with ecstasy No. 2. Perhaps there was a tie-in between turning to the beggar woman and the longed-for wave of sweetness. Take bitter for sweet, even if the old ways are overturned. Francis decided to put this crazy notion to the test. He went on a pilgrimage to Rome.

Celano tells us: "Francis soon made his appearance as someone especially fond of poor people. He had already made such a blessed beginning that one could tell what he would be like when made perfect. He often removed his clothes and traded them with poor men for theirs, for, although he did not yet really resemble them, still in his heart he strove to. Once, when he came on pilgrimage to Rome, out of his love for poverty he took off his fine clothes and sat down gaily in some beggar's rags in the vestibule of St. Peter's—right in the middle of all the poor people who were there in swarms. He also ate with them, and just as greedily as they did, in order to be like them in everything."[15]

I am fairly certain that the experiment in Rome worked immediately, on the very first try, even though I have no documentary evidence. I feel that the first time he traded clothes, as the text describes, he experienced that overwhelming tenderness he was searching for. In this regard Celano makes an illuminating remark. Francis, he says, would have gladly repeated his appearances among the poor "if shyness in the presence of his acquaintances had not prevented him."

Francis had taken an important step forward. He knew now what he had to do to get to that state of profound happiness which had so marvelously swept him away. He simply had to do whatever went against the grain. He still hesitated to make a complete fool of himself in people's eyes. But that was a running fight by a beaten army. In reality he was already headed "downward" at full speed, down to the "least of my brethren," as Jesus called them. This movement followed a spiral course, which kept bringing Francis face to face with poor wretches, and it shocked him every time he met someone poorer than himself.

This is the story they tell: It happened once during a preaching tour that Francis met a man who was completely down and out. Francis said to his companion, "This man's poverty puts us to shame, it seems to rebuke us." The other man asked how this was so. Francis replied, "I chose poverty in the sight of everyone, as the pledge of my true well-being. And so whenever I meet anyone poorer than myself, I feel ashamed."[16]

The critical sentence here is so revealing that we may quote it in its literal form. "I have chosen holy poverty for my mistress, for the sake of my joys and riches, spiritual and physical." (*Cum sanctam paupertatem elegerim pro mea domina et pro meis deliciis et diviciis spiritualibus et corporalibus.*) We know the joys Francis speaks of. Once he realized how he could share in them, nothing in the world would make him give them up. Again and again Francis would discover that he had not yet reached the absolute bottom, that he had compromised, that he wasn't radical enough. So he kept on moving downward, literally, until his death. On his deathbed he would bid his companions, once his agony began, to lay him naked on the earth.

It is clear that all of Francis' later conflicts, especially the one with his father, were preprogrammed, so to speak, in that very first contemplative fit outside of Foligno, with its pattern of exchange: riches for poverty, dominion for servitude, bitterness for sweetness, carnality for spirituality. Francis denied the carnal, i.e., the family ties—in his quest for tenderness. This meant that the "old ways" would be turned topsy-turvy, but that was no concern of his. The psychic energies released during this "confinement" were strikingly powerful. One wonders where Francis got them from.

THE THRESHOLD OF NAUSEA

From childhood on Francis had a psychological problem. Had he been a well-balanced individual, he would have spent his life selling wool. This time let him speak for himself. The beginning of the *Testament* of Francis of Assisi, written in 1226, the year he died: "The Lord granted me, Brother Francis, to begin to do penance in this way, that when I was in sin, it seemed to me very horrible to see lepers, and the Lord himself led me among them and I helped them. And when I left them that which had before seemed to me horrible was transformed into sweetness of body and soul. After that I remained only a little time before I left the world."[17]

We have here, psychologically speaking, a very substantial phobia. Francis' fear and nervousness in the presence of lepers was so strong that he felt impelled to avert his eyes whenever a leper crossed his path. Celano reports: "So greatly loathsome was the sight of lepers to him at one time, he used to say that, in the days of his vanity, he would look at their houses only from a distance of two miles and he would hold his nostrils with his hand."[18] Assisi's leprosarium was located down in the valley, just two miles from town. All Francis had to do was catch sight of it, and he would be forced to hold his nose.

In the Middle Ages leprosy was a widespread disease. There were thousands of leprosaria in Europe then, since people understood the danger of infection and isolated the victims. They were not permitted to enter public buildings or speak with children, they had to wear gloves and ring a little bell whenever they traveled outside the leprosarium.

This is the story they tell: During a ride in the country around Assisi Francis met a leper. Though he was filled with terrible disgust, Francis got hold of himself, dismounted from his horse, gave the man a coin, and kissed his hand. The man returned the kiss of peace. Shortly thereafter Francis took a sum of money and went to the leprosarium. All the lepers rushed toward him. Francis handed each of them a coin and kissed his hand. When he left there, what had once been bitter was truly transformed into sweetness.[19]

At this point contemporary psychopathology raises its ugly head, but we shall spare ourselves any such digressions, for two reasons. First of all, eight hundred years have passed since Francis' childhood. The application of modern categories to earlier periods has proved to be a dubious procedure. To give a sound diagnosis of Francis' compulsive fear of lepers, one would have to know a great deal about both medieval childrearing practices and Francis' relations with his parents. We need detailed information, and we don't have it.

The second reason for exercising restraint here lies in the fact that modern studies of outstanding personalities simply haven't succeeded in mediating between the banality of psychological commonplaces and the uniqueness of a particular individual, with a specific impact on his environment. To take an especially painful example: The attempt to "deduce" Adolf Hitler and his effect on the masses from psychological laws has failed, despite some notable efforts.[20]

Perhaps by shuttling back and forth between the sociological (or political-economic) and the psychological spheres a biographer can portray his subject as an "individual universal," as Sartre has done for Flaubert. But Flaubert wrote prolifically, from childhood on, and Sartre had a considerable body of material for his exhaustive analysis. He required several thousand pages to get through with Flaubert, and Sartre was really writing as much about his own neuroses as about Flaubert.

Let us assume that Francis spent the spring of 1205 in Rome, with the beggars of St. Peter's. (Experts on Francis quarrel about the exact chronology of this decisive year in his life.[21]) That would give him almost two years before the revolt against his father. Celano tells us that Francis repeatedly went out for walks with his best friend to remote places, especially to a grotto in the neighborhood of Assisi. Francis claimed to have found a precious treasure. He would vanish into the grotto, leaving his friend (unnamed) to wait outside. Thus screened from sight he would pray for a long time in seclusion, enduring great torments of soul, and emerging from the cave each time "exhausted from the strain." During his hours of prayer "contradictory thoughts" arose, and "their importunity disturbed him greatly."[22]

These are clear indications of a spiritual crisis. Evidently, changing clothes with the beggars provided only passing relief, so he tried stronger measures, and drew near to the center of his secret anxiety, the compulsive disgust he felt for lepers. After his grand appearance in the leprosarium he immediately sensed a powerful rush of sweetness (*dolcezza*, in the Italian version of the *Testament*). He felt overwhelmed by his reward, and knew he was on the right track. Like the beggars, the lepers would preoccupy

Francis all his days; they were his invisible companions. He oriented himself toward them, felt the reproach of their life, longed to be like them.

This is the story they tell: One day, when Francis returned from a walk, he met Brother Jacob, a simple, modest man, in the company of a leper with festering wounds. Although Francis had always encouraged the brothers to take care of lepers, he chided Jacob for bringing him into the brothers' quarters. Scarcely had he spoken when he began vehemently reproaching himself for putting the leper to shame. Francis confessed his mistake and resolved to eat out of the same dish as the sick man, which he did. The leper had bleeding wounds on his fingers, and every time he put them into the dish, blood flowed onto the food. When the brothers saw that, they were aghast, but for fear of Francis they didn't dare to say anything. The man who wrote that saw the incident with his own eyes and can bear witness to it.[23]

When Francis wrote his *Testament*, looking back on his life, he thought only one event from his youth worth mentioning—that visit to the leprosarium, with the happiness that ensued. Crossing over the threshold of nausea was for Francis the beginning of a new life. The logical thing in those days would have been to join the pious brethren of the Order of St. Lazarus, who devoted themselves to the care of lepers.[24] Had he done so, Francis would have been lost in the anonymity of a regulated life, freed from his neurotic fears by the daily practice of a sort of behavioral therapy. But such a simple disappearance from the scene was not Francis' way of doing things. He needed spectators, and he got them.

THE VOICE OF THE CRUCIFIED

This is the story they tell: One day, as Francis passed by the church of San Damiano, he felt the urge to go in and pray. When he stood before the image of the Crucified, he heard a gentle, kindly voice from the cross, "Francis, don't you see how my house is in ruins? Go and restore it!" Trembling with excitement, Francis answered, "Gladly will I do so, dear Lord!" He left the church and went to the priest who dwelt nearby, and gave him money to keep a lamp burning before the picture. Then, full of joy over Christ's command, Francis took a bolt of colorful cloth from his father's store, saddled a horse, rode to the market in Foligno, sold the fabric and the horse as well, and returned at once to San Damiano. He kissed the priest's hand and tried to give him money for the renovation of the church. But the priest wouldn't take the money, because he suspected a nasty practical joke, and also out of fear of Francis' parents. Francis threw

41

the purse full of coins on the windowsill and earnestly begged the priest to be allowed to stay with him. This was granted.[25]

The little church of San Damiano, a kilometer down from Assisi, is still standing today. The talking cross, painted on linen, can likewise be seen, in the church of Santa Chiara in Assisi. Since then it has never spoken again.

Finally Francis was being put to use, he had a mission. The voice of the Crucified set his life astir. As though it were the most normal thing in the world, Francis stole from his father. In addition he moved into new quarters in San Damiano: the process of detaching himself from his parents was taking concrete shape. As we shall see, Francis' father reacted with sharp irritation to this development, and it was only a few weeks before father and son made the final break.

The order of events may have run something like this: In the late summer of 1204 Francis had his two ecstatic experiences. In the spring of 1205 he went on pilgrimage to Rome and traded clothes with the beggars. If we allow a year for the further development of his spiritual crisis, the crossing of the threshold of nausea may have occurred in 1206. Then the Crucified spoke with him in late autumn of the same year. In February 1207 Francis publicly broke with his father, at the age of twenty-five. Regardless of the amount of time that may have elapsed between Francis' fraternization with the lepers and his experience with the cross, the psychological gap that yawns between these two incidents is enormous.

Psychiatrists will be glad to inform us about the various kinds of hallucinations, particularly the delusion of hearing voices. They meet this sort of thing all the time in their clinical practice, in connection with every imaginable psychic "disturbance." We may take it for granted that nowadays Francis would be in danger of winding up in a mental hospital, where he would be sent to be "sedated." Fortunately, in the Middle Ages pressure to conform and be inconspicuous was just beginning to be felt. People did not yet have the institutions later invented for applying it—prisons, barracks, lunatic asylums. (Even schools were quite underdeveloped.) And so we needn't put Francis on the couch.

Of course, we won't get much help, either, from the notion that the voice at San Damiano was a call from the Savior in person, coming from the other world. This book deals not with heaven, but with the earth. It deals with the exemplary need for tenderness in a young man who turned to beggars and lepers—an abyss of indigence.

All of them, the insulted and injured of this world, spoke to Francis with a single voice—the voice of the man of sorrows in San Damiano.

Francis, as we say today, identified so closely with him that nail wounds opened in his body.

Seen from this angle, Francis' concern with the Crucified seems to grow out of his relations with beggars and lepers. One could consider it as a sort of condensation of his experiences over the previous two years. We could imagine how Francis' love for Christ might have led to a career of charitable works—to the founding of a nursing Order, for example. In this case the voice at San Damiano would have commanded Francis to care for the sick and the poor. But in fact Francis was told only to renovate an old chapel. Why?

Historians have recently conjectured, on plausible grounds, that Francis' father was a secret heretic, a Cathar.[26] There is no documentary evidence for this assumption; it remains purely hypothetical. But even so it could be quite useful to us, as we attempt to reconstruct Francis' state of soul.

As a cloth dealer Pietro Bernardone traveled a good deal, particularly in France. There, in Champagne, six great fairs were held, which went on throughout the year in different places. Each of them lasted six weeks, and they were the principal emporiums for the most important commodity of that time, woolen cloth. The wool came from England, was processed in Flanders (Ghent, Ypres), and marketed at the great trade fairs of Champagne. Merchants from Germany, Sweden, Norway, Denmark, England, Portugal, Spain, France, and, above all, Italy (Genoa, Venice, Pisa, Milan, Florence, and Siena) bought the cloth and forwarded it to their customers all over Europe, even as far away as North Africa and the Levant.

Just how attached Francis' father was to French manners is clear from his behavior after the birth of his son. As was customary then, the mother had had the child baptized as soon as possible, giving him the name Giovanni. Bernardone was away on a trip at the time, and when he came back, he did something unusual: He gave his offspring a new name, Francesco, which means "Frenchman." We may assume that he imparted to his little Frenchman, along with songs and stories, a predilection for things French, both in style and substance. Perhaps Francis' father also inoculated him, in carefully measured doses, with the teaching of the Cathars.

The Cathars flourished precisely in the places where Pietro Bernardone stayed so often, and their ideas found an especially receptive audience among the merchants. In addition, there were organized Catharist communities in Umbria, Francis' native province—at Viterbo and Orvieto in particular. In Assisi itself a known Cathar named Gerardi di Gilberto was appointed governor of the city (though only for a few months). This was in 1204, when Francis had just come home from imprisonment in Perugia.

It has been suggested that the dilapidation of so many churches in Francis' day was due to the spread of Catharist teaching. This much is certain: The new heresy could tolerate neither crosses nor churches, that it heartily despised priests and sacraments as tools of the evil God, and to that extent at least was quite Voltairean, some six hundred years before the Enlightenment. Which is why it was so cruelly persecuted.

We cannot help noticing how gently the bishop of Assisi dealt with Francis during the final break with his father. After all, Francis had manifestly violated the Fourth Commandment: Thou shalt honor thy father and thy mother. In his little speech the bishop deliberately ignores this fact. Was it by accident, or did the bishop know that Francis' father sympathized with the heretics, and did the bishop therefore see no need to deal very strictly with the disobedient son? Once again, we don't know.

Regardless, however, of Bernardone's heretical inclinations, we may consider one thing highly probable: Francis' father was no friend of the Church. He and the men like him, the new patricians, were locked in an epochal struggle with the ever-present political and economic power of the Church. And this struggle was unquestionably accompanied by ideological conflicts. Anticlerical, laicizing attitudes, of the kind still met with today, especially in Italy, have a long history.

Mocking words about worshiping bits of bone of some long-dead monks, passing jabs at greedy, scheming canons—these are the sorts of things Francis would have heard over the dining-room table while his mother nervously crossed herself. Had Francis stolen that bale of fabric to pay off gambling debts, his father's rage would have quickly passed. But the idea that Francis wanted to spend money to restore a decrepit little church touched his father to the quick. Thus the command from the cross reveals a remarkable psychological delicacy.

BRANDED A FOOL

In the weeks following Francis' removal to San Damiano, Assisi had plenty to talk about. Father Bernardone drummed up friends and neighbors and hurried with them down to San Damiano, to bring Francis back to his senses. But he by chance had found a good hideout in the house near the church, some sort of walled space that may have had a hidden entrance from the outside, half underground. They couldn't find him for an entire month.

The priest from San Damiano evidently took the part of his new protégé. Francis didn't have to worry about food, and could think out his next step in peace, even though his surroundings weren't the most comfortable. He must have known that his actions were legally punishable with exile from the town and the entire region. The facts in the case—filial disobedience and misuse of his father's property—were clear. How would Bernardone react to them?

For the first time in his life Francis knew the feelings of a man who has broken the law. There is no evidence that Francis put himself in this unpleasant situation on purpose. He had heard the voice of Christ—that was how he perceived it, till his death—and had spontaneously done what seemed to him the most natural thing: He went and got some money to obey a divine command. Now he was a thief in everyone's eyes.

To his surprise Francis found that in spite of all this he had never felt so elated. Celano tells us: "Although in a dark hiding place, unspeakable joy, such as he had never tasted before, poured over him."[27] Once again Francis learns the lesson he first happened on when he changed clothes with the beggar, and when he crossed the threshold of nausea: Whenever he acted contrary to sound common sense, he had been happy. It was the same all over again. What was the maxim he had followed for two years now? Take the bitter for sweet! One fine day Francis left his hideout and walked up to Assisi.

At once the children of the town were at his back, with their sure instinct for the helpless outsider, playing the merry policemen of prevailing mores, shouting, *"Pazzo! Pazzo!"*[28] We have already met this word, in the story of Francis' confrontation with Cardinal Ugolino. There we rendered the passage, which is not easily translatable, as "The Lord wanted me to be his simpleton." In the original text Francis says, *"Et dixit Dominus mihi quod volebat quod ego essem unus novellus pazzus in mundo."* (The Lord told me that he wanted me to be a new fool in the world.) Fifteen years later Francis could still hear the children's cry as they informed him of his new social position: fool. The divine message from the mouth of children was reinforced by a shower of stones and garbage. Francis, whose appearance had not exactly improved during his stay in the hideout, maintained his dignity and went on, toward the center of town, the *mercato,* which was also the site of his parents' house.

When he got there, the scene was in an uproar. Shrill women's voices, laughter from the men, and loud adolescent horseplay filled his ears. Bernardone came out with measured steps to see what the noise was all about. "When he heard the name of his son," Celano informs us, "he hurried forward. As the wolf pounces on the lamb, with a fierce expression he seized his son and dragged him home"[29] amid "shame and disgrace," Celano adds, with his feel for theatrical effects.

We know only the bare outline of what followed this scene, in the bosom of the family. There was house arrest, furious reproaches, a box or two on the ear. We are not informed whether Francis tried to explain his motives to his father, or whether he even had a chance to. In any case, and this is the crucial point, the gap between father and son proved to be unbridgeable.

Undoubtedly, Francis felt innocent. He had the unshakeable conviction that God had told him what to do. And he had irrefutable proof that he was behaving correctly: Those repeated states of tender happiness were more important to him than anything else. Only now, in this painful confrontation with his father, did Francis grasp how deep and insoluble their conflict really was.

Francis recognized that in the past two years he had moved away, step by step, from everything his father lived for. Francis tried to find an expression for the insuperable obstacle that had come between them. Left by himself, he thought over his father's furious speeches and stumbled over a word that kept recurring in them like a leitmotif: money.

Up until then Francis had thought of money as a servant, ever ready to do his bidding, so obliging and unobtrusive that he paid no special attention to it. He had taken money so much for granted that a short while before, when Christ had bid him restore the church at San Damiano, the first thing he had thought of was money, good old money, to carry out the order quickly and conveniently. He had likewise come to an understanding with the lepers by offering them coins.

But now he began to appreciate the fact that rebellion against his father was the only possible choice if he wished to lead a happy life, and Francis saw money from a different point of view. It became the enemy he would fight inexorably for the rest of his days. He would positively hate money as the incarnation of the cold insensibility that he now felt surrounding him in his parents' house. Later on he would categorically forbid his companions even to touch money, much less spend it. And although he would urge his brotherhood to go begging as a Christlike way of life, Francis never allowed the Friars Minor to accept a coin as alms.

This is the literally crazy stubbornness that made Francis an urgent case for the God who had grown bored and hard of hearing and that accounts for the effect Francis has on people.

Anyhow, Bernardone had no time to go on arguing forever with Francis; he had his business to worry about, and so he left town for an important appointment. Now for the first and last time Francis' mother, Lady Pica, enters the picture as a character in her own right. "His mother remained by herself with her son. She disagreed with her husband's actions anyway, and she spoke lovingly to Francis. When she realized that she could not deter him from his resolution, her motherly heart had compassion on him. She undid his fetters and set him free."[30] Francis disappeared in the direction of San Damiano.

After his father's return, Lady Pica got a violent scolding. Then Bernardone ran "raving and roaring" (Celano) down to San Damiano. But this time Francis did not hide; he faced his father and refused to return home. Bernardone sensed that he was running into a granite wall, so he went to the Palazzo Communale to lodge a formal complaint against his son. Since Bernardone was acting within his rights, the magistrate sent a messenger down to San Damiano, who stood before Francis and cried out: "Francis, son of Pietro Bernardone, you are hereby informed that you have been arraigned before the consuls, and must appear in their presence."[31]

But Francis proved equal to the situation. Since he was in ecclesiastical territory and working in the service of the local priest, he pleaded immunity from the secular authorities. He too was within his rights. Apparently the priest at San Damiano knew a thing or two about canon law, or, more likely, Guido, the bishop of Assisi, had by now joined the game on Francis' side.

We know how the affair ended. Bernardone preferred charges before the bishop, and Francis came at the appointed time. The bishop sat, wearing a violet cope, miter on head, and crozier in hand, on a chair set up before the entrance to his church, Santa Maria Maggiore. Everybody in Assisi was there, of course. There were trumpet blasts, an address by the bishop. Then the explosion, with a short speech by the stark-naked Francis. Red with anger and shame, Bernardone gathered the money and articles of clothing together and vanished in the direction of his house. He appears in the Francis stories only one more time—implacable as ever.

This is the story they tell: Whenever Bernardone met Francis in Assisi, Bernardone would curse him. Then Francis found an old beggar named Alberto. Francis asked the man to accompany him, and promised him a share in the alms. Then, every time Bernardone uttered a curse over his son, old Alberto, following instructions, would make the sign of the cross over Francis, and in this way give him a fatherly blessing. At that time almost everyone looked on Francis as a madman.[32]

We learn only incidentally that Francis had a younger brother, Angelo. Once when Francis was going about begging in Assisi and trembling from the cold, his brother mockingly advised him to sell his sweat. We may assume that this Angelo later took over his father's business.

V

MAKING REPAIRS

For a whole year, from February 1207 till February 1208, Francis spent most of his time doing masonry. He renovated three dilapidated chapels in the neighborhood of Assisi: first the previously mentioned church of San Damiano, with the talking picture of the cross; then the chapel of San Pietro della Spina (no longer standing); finally the little church of Santa Maria degli Angeli, down in the valley, called in the vernacular "Portiuncula" (little plot).

In later times a pompous cathedral was erected over the Portiuncula chapel. In the midst of the giant baroque nave stand the primitive ruins of the little church, looking like a foreign body and a glaring anachronism. Francis would barely recognize the "little plot" if he returned to visit Assisi today. His followers' passion for architecture would greatly astonish—and distress—him. For his part Francis never erected a new building anywhere. He even resisted having fixed residences, and remained a vagabond all his life.

Once he left his parents' house for good, however, the "poor and abandoned" churches, as he calls them in his *Testament,* held a powerful attraction for him. In one of them the crucified Christ had spoken to him and bid him restore the ruined building. This order, as we have seen, led to Francis' quarrel with his father. After the break Francis stood all by himself, a true fool in people's eyes, and completely penniless to boot. But he had a friend who needed him—the Lord Jesus Christ in person.

The old sources tell us nothing about the formation of this Jesus complex, so central to Francis' character. They are content to refer to the miraculous voice of Christ at San Damiano as a heavenly intervention that changed Francis' life. But we demand more than this sort of information.

48

We would like to know why Francis was so enthusiastic about repairing churches—that is, we question the nature of Francis' religious sensibility.

IN ALL THE CHURCHES IN ALL THE WORLD

If one reads the old narratives of Francis' development, up till the break with his father, from an atheistic standpoint—that is, without any religious presuppositions—one makes a surprising discovery. There is not the slightest reference to any particularly pious achievements on Francis' part.[1] Let us recapitulate: Francis has, out of the blue, as it were, two exceptional psychic experiences. Subsequently he discovers the crucial law of the metamorphosis of bitterness into sweetness. One can understand his feeling that Jesus, the supreme model of all suffering and humiliated people, had actually spoken to him. Furthermore, it is important that Francis saw Christ not as ruler and conqueror, as was customary then, but as a God fallen into destitution and abandonment, whose roof threatened to collapse. Jesus became for Francis the physical incarnation of human degradation. When he welcomed such degradation, he was obeying a rule he could no longer doubt: Take bitter for sweet!

All this is an intuitive reading, which makes no appeal to the supernatural. It is striking how at this point in his development Francis did *not* choose a life of charitable works, but worked instead at repairing churches. Francis discovered "religion" in the year after the scandal with his family.

But first we must listen to a tale of robbers from Celano. Immediately after the explosive scene in the presence of the bishop, and dressed in whatever clothes he could borrow, Francis left Assisi and headed North, to Gubbio (thirty kilometers away), where he had a friend. Singing French songs as he went along, Francis came to a forest, where a band of robbers fell upon him. Celano tells us: "When they asked him in a ferocious tone who he was, the man of God replied confidently in a loud voice: 'I am the herald of the great King. What is that to you?' But they struck him and cast him into a ditch filled with deep snow, saying: 'Lie there, foolish herald of God!' But he rolled himself about and shook off the snow; and when they had gone away, he jumped out of the ditch."[2]

The story sounds authentic, with the exception of Francis' overbearing language. The evening after this incident, a not infrequent one in those times, Francis found shelter in a monastery, where he worked in the kitchen. After a few days he seems to have been thrown out of there, then finally reached his goal, the town of Gubbio, where his friend, Count Spadalunga, welcomed him and gave him something to wear. In Gubbio Francis spent some time doing exactly what every amateur psychologist would expect of him: He went to the leprosarium and took care of the lepers.

Had Francis been the sort of Christian we still meet today—the selfless, considerate type—he would have ended his days in the Gubbio asylum, nursing the sick, in the peaceful uniformity of an anonymous existence. But in reality Francis never thought of making such a choice. Much as he would struggle against it all his life, he needed to be in the public eye. He was, we begin to suspect, an actor. The role which he would grow into until he had identified himself with it was a hard one—the part of Jesus Christ—but no one ever played it with more bravura than Francis of Assisi.

Once the weather improved, Francis walked back to Assisi, to the crucified Christ of San Damiano. The time spent thinking things over in Gubbio had made him realize something that wasn't as obvious as it sounds: He could tackle the job of renovating churches with his own two hands.

In the Middle Ages no member of the upper class would have ever dreamed of seeing any value in manual labor. The ruling opinion—i.e., the opinion of the rulers—classified men as prayers, fighters, and workers, which corresponded exactly to the self-consciousness of clerics and nobles.[3] Folding one's hands or fighting wars brought social prestige, but not the sweaty business of the remaining 95 per cent of the population. Francis was the son of a *nouveau riche* who, as a wool merchant, stood on the threshold of nobility, and Francis was raised in this disdainful philosophy of the Christian West. As a man destined to be a master, Francis had been trained to look upon the peasants working the soil as part of nature, like animals.

Perhaps on his walk back home Francis looked thoughtfully at his hands: They had an aristocratic softness. The priest of San Damiano was no doubt amazed when Francis showed up again at his house.

This is the story they tell: Returning to San Damiano with holy joy, Francis made himself a hermit's outfit. Then he began to beg in the streets of Assisi for stones for the chapel, calling out: "Whoever gives one stone will get a single reward! Whoever gives two gets a double!" Many people laughed at him and thought he had gone crazy. But others were moved to tears, because they saw the sincerity of his purpose. He, the pampered son, now dragged along building stones on his own shoulders. He cried out to passersby, "Come and help build the church at San Damiano!" Francis also begged for oil for the church lamps, patiently bearing the ridicule that was heaped upon him.[4]

No doubt about it: Francis set about leading a religious life, complete with a hermit's outfit (monk's robe, leather belt, sandals, walking stick) and conventionally pious behavior. We find the motivation for this in Francis' *Testament*. We have already cited the beginning of this remarkable document, with its terse formula, *Ed uscii dal secolo* (And I left the world).

He meant the separation from his family. In medieval linguistic usage, anyone who lived with his family, bound up in the omnipresent ties of kinship that regulated all social relations, counted as a "worldly" person. Whoever disowned these bonds, as a monk or hermit, in a nun's habit or priestly costume, belonged to the host of the "religious." In contrast to its usual modern sense, in the Middle Ages this word designated not just the pious practice of believers, as opposed to unbelief or indifference, which might be found at any level of society. In Francis' day one recognized a religious person rather by external appearance—by the clerical tonsure, the hermit's staff, the various habits of the Orders, male and female. All these people were to some extent marked, negatively by their breaking free from the web of kinship, positively by their availability for "religion." They formed, therefore, a class by themselves.

Francis had already made public his decision to enter religious life during his memorable appearance before the bishop of Assisi, in a theatrical and, to the taste of his contemporaries, altogether scurrilous fashion. After his return from Gubbio Francis behaved from the first like a religious, wearing a hermit's garb, and serving God by repairing churches. He also tells us why he did this.

In his *Testament*, immediately after the statement that he left the world, we find this passage: "And the Lord gave me such faith in churches that I used to pray simply, like this, and say: 'We adore you, Lord Jesus Christ, here and in all your churches in all the world, and we bless you because with your holy cross you redeemed the world.'"[5]

The "Lord" in this text is not God the Father (in heaven), but God the Son (in all the churches). The shift of emphasis here is characteristic for Francis. He needed a corporeal God, not a distant, invisible one. The wave of tenderness that first seized and transfigured him that night in Assisi yearned for an absolute—that is, a divine—love object. All the beggars and lepers were to be gathered together in this Other: Francis wanted to clasp them in a single embrace.

That is why he heard the voice of Christ on the cross in San Damiano. Furthermore, Francis never carried the bourgeois repression of sensuous existence so far that he could be satisfied with purely spiritual experience. The key word, which betrays his secret longing for a physically blissful life, can also be found in Francis' *Testament*. It is *sensibilmente* (with the senses). And it is the reason why Francis dragged stones to San Damiano.

The *Testament* says: "I do this because in this world I see nothing of the son of God most high in a tangible sense, except his most holy body and blood, which priests receive and priests alone administer to others. This most holy mystery I wish to honor and venerate above all others and to house in precious pyxes."[6]

Francis' grief over the sad condition of San Damiano was part of his instinctive tenderness for the corporeal Jesus who comes among men under the species of bread and wine, in all the churches in all the world.

WE COULD USE A BROOM HERE

Almost twenty years separate Francis' work as a restorer of churches and the drafting of his last will. During that time he made the acquaintance of Popes, cardinals, and theologians. He became the head of a brotherhood that rapidly multiplied and was soon playing a crucial role in Church politics all over Europe. Francis' experience with the realities of life in the Church was by no means entirely gratifying, as his meeting with Cardinal Ugolino makes clear. At the end of his life Francis had to recognize that the Church in her prudence had poured a great deal of water into his wine. For the last time, as he dictated his *Testament,* Francis tried—what a moving effort!—to fix his original plan in writing, to save it from the Church's compromises. Still, he never lets fall a word of criticism against her.

On the contrary, immediately after the passage on his faith in the Christ who dwells in all the churches in all the world, Francis solemnly affirms his loyalty to the priests: "Afterward the Lord gave and gives me such faith in priests, who live according to the model of the holy Roman Church, on account of their orders, that even if they should persecute me I wish to run back to them. And if I had as much wisdom as Solomon, and found poor and humble secular priests in the parishes in which they lived, I would not wish to preach against their will. I wish to fear, love, and honor them and all others as my masters; and I do not wish to consider sin in them, because I discern in them the son of God and to me they are masters."[7]

Twice in rapid succession Francis characterizes the priests as his masters. We have already seen the reason for this imperturbable meekness, not to say subservience: because priests alone have power over the body and blood of Christ. So Francis resolutely sheds his benevolence on everything that bears a direct, sensuous relation to his Jesus complex—the body and blood of Christ, the priests as servants of this sacrament, the churches as its repository.

As we can see from the perspective of the *Testament* he dictated twenty years later, the repair work Francis did as a young man on decrepit chapels should in no way be construed as the pastime of a wavering character. He displayed amazing consistency in following the inner logic that led from the bewilderment of his first contact with the crucified Christ up to his reception of the stigmata.

In the process he reached an important decision: Never would Francis make the (heretical) distinction between the "true" Jesus of the New Testament and the Church's corrupted version. Jesus always comes to Francis through the mediation of the Church. Consequently, any direct rebellion against the Church is, for Francis, out of the question. At the same time, by the very manner of his life he stood as a living rebuke to all clerical power—right under the nose of the churchly authorities and with their approval.

This peculiar and unsettling state of affairs caused Francis acute suffering, especially in his last years, but he never found a solution for it. Toward the end, when he was already near death, he had himself carried from the bishop's palace in Assisi, where he had been cared for, down to the "little plot," to die. There is something conclusive about this wordless refusal to end his life in a prelate's house; it contains an unspoken truth. In this way Francis said good-by to the institutional Church forever.

Of course, from the very beginning Francis has been treated as a Church reformer. Even the first command of the Crucified, we are told, didn't really have to do with restoring the chapel of San Damiano, but the renewal of Catholic Church in the broad, general sense.[8] Only in his simplicity Francis failed, at first, to understand this. Not until later did he become fully aware of the magnitude of the command.

This sort of pious partisanship runs all through the nice little story about the Pope's dream, as reported by Celano. The Holy Father saw in his sleep the principal church (at that time) of Christendom, the Lateran basilica in Rome, on the verge of collapse. But suddenly a plain-looking man appeared who propped it up with his back, and so kept it from falling down. When, shortly after this, St. Francis came before him to request permission to preach, the Pope recognized in him the man who saved the church and cried out, "Truly, this is that man who will shore up the Church of Christ with his teaching and his deeds!"[9]

This kind of stylization is understandable, given the fact that in those days the idea of Church reform was widespread in Europe, and had been for some time. By the year 1000, when heretical movements began cropping up, there was, to take one example, a priest in Germany named Heimrad who was living in voluntary poverty. The monks, who were personally poor but collectively rich, gave Heimrad a terrible thrashing. Then the bishop of Paderborn, who disliked the priest's ragged appearance, had him whipped in public. Like Francis, Heimrad refused to make any provision for the morrow. He begged his way to Jerusalem, and died at last a widely venerated hermit.[10] Heimrad's life bespeaks the desire to follow the original Lord Jesus. This will was still inchoate and inexplicit, but it nonetheless ran headlong into the clerical-monastic Establishment.

In another corner of Europe, in Arras (France), a group of artisans created a formula in 1025 that became the motto of many innovators down through the centuries: We must live like Christ and his Apostles.[11] The "Friends" of Arras found that their maxim about the "apostolic life" tied in rather well with contempt for the Church's hierarchy—for which they were subjected to a brutal interrogation.

These early signs of dissatisfaction with the status quo came out of the social and economic upheavals of the eleventh century, which affected both the cities and the countryside. Impoverished peasants listened eagerly to the ascetic preachers who soon began appearing everywhere, attacking usurers and the money economy, simony and clerical luxury. It has been proved that many of these ascetics came from the lower nobility, which saw itself as particularly vulnerable to the growing economic problems.[12]

Dissatisfaction could also be found among the upper nobility, more precisely among the younger sons of this group. Owing to the law of primogeniture, most of these people were destined for the clerical state. They made their living from a great variety of ecclesiastical benefices; and these were always managed with an eye to the material interests of the family, to whom they owed their bishopric or abbey. In the second half of the eleventh century some of these young nobles among the clergy began to talk about reform and the "freedom of the Church," invoking the days of the distant past, when the Church had been above reproach.

Behind these aspirations, which reached their climax in the struggle over investiture, stood the determination of a churchly power elite to free itself from traditional feudal ties. Gregory VII (1073–85), famous for his quarrel with Henry IV, and one of the leading figures of this reform movement, reorganized the papal finances when he was only a Roman archdeacon, applying the most advanced techniques of the contemporary money economy. He also backed a Milanese coalition of the lesser nobility, merchants, and guild artisans against the greater nobility and rich clergymen. This "Pataria," as it was called (after the old-clothes market in Milan), made use of the city's proletariat to intimidate the high lord *capitani* and prelates.[13] The ideology of the movement appealed to the perfection of the primitive Church and insisted on the poverty of Jesus and his Apostles as the only proper way of life for the clergy.

For five hundred years, from Gregory VII to Martin Luther, Popes and heretics, hermits and theologians, poor wretches and noble lords, nuns and guild masters all spoke of "reforming" the Church (and thereby reforming society as well). Behind these words lay the most diverse interests—and meanwhile the really poor devils had, along with a fine slogan, their bare two thousand calories a day, consisting of millet gruel or bean soup.

Even Innocent III (1198–1216), to whose city Francis made a pilgrimage in the spring of 1209, was considered a reforming Pope.[14] In addition, he was the most powerful figure ever to sit on the chair of St. Peter. Never again could a Holy Father move and shake the world as he did. As a young cardinal, he wrote a tract on the misery of mankind (*De miseria humanae conditionis*), which dealt, to be sure, more with the sins of men than with the thin bean soup of the peasants. When Innocent died, he left the Papal States twice as large as he found them.

There are several versions of Francis' audience with Innocent, including the one already mentioned concerning the Pope's miraculous dream. The most credible account of the first meeting between Francis and the Pontiff has them coming across one another in the Lateran palace in Rome, the official papal residence in those days, in a lobby where the Pope was walking back and forth.[15] In the Middle Ages access to the mighty was relatively easy and unceremonious, and so we can imagine how Francis might have presented his petition to the Pope without much ado. He asked for the Church's approval of his brotherhood—still quite tiny at the time—and for permission to preach. The Pope listened and scrutinized the petitioner at his leisure. Francis' clothes were torn and dusty, his hair long and unkempt. Bushy black eyebrows and a long beard gave the strange brother a rather wild appearance, and it is not inconceivable that the Pope's nose detected a distinctly rank odor.

When Francis had said his piece, the Pope replied: "You will surely find a few swine, brother, to take you into their pen. You may preach to them, and perhaps they will adopt your Rule. In any case you resemble a pig rather than a human being." Despite this something less than successful interview, Francis managed to get his preaching license. We can reconstruct the chain of events as follows.[16] Guido, the bishop of Assisi, was in Rome on business at the time. He got Francis together with Cardinal Giovanni Colonna, who first tried the usual routine of urging him to enter one of the already established Orders. But Francis had no intention of going into a monastery. He and his companions wanted to live like Christ, without a settled residence, and from hand to mouth.

The cardinal knew that the Church had never yet given such a fellowship her blessing. On the contrary, vagabond monks had long since proved to be a real plague, a thievish, unruly rabble, averse to any kind of steady work, and addicted to every possible vice. Then too, characters like Francis gathered into bands with crazy ideas in their heads. In the papal Curia complaints were piling up from bishops all over Europe about the troubles stirred up by lay preachers: They turned the heads of the faithful and created all sorts of unrest in those already restless times.

Besides this, there were the heretics, those awful Cathars, as Cardinal Colonna knew very well. He himself had been in southern France as a papal ambassador. His successor, Peter of Castelnau, had been murdered the year before by the heretics, and now a war was going on—the first crusade within the Christian West. Despite all that, Colonna interceded on Francis' behalf.

What decided the issue was Francis' utterly childlike demeanor toward priests. He represented a combination of two elements that the papal diplomat had never met before: unconditional loyalty to the Roman Church and the most radical will to follow the Gospel to the letter. Cardinal Colonna went to the Pope. We may assume that he took care to make Francis bathe and cut his hair.

The discussions took place behind closed doors, but we do know of one remarkable argument that Colonna used to answer the obvious objections to Francis' mad scheme. "This man asks," the cardinal said, "permission to lead a life in accordance with the Gospel. If we reject his petition, and say it is all too difficult, a risky and untested enterprise, then we are taking offence at the Holy Gospel. For if anyone says that following the Gospel runs counter to the experience and the sound sense of men, then he blasphemes Christ the Lord, the author of the Gospel."[17]

This is a rare moment of truth, transcending tactics, calculation, and churchly politics. Suddenly from behind Francis' ridiculous figure there emerges the godly man, the eternal reproach to "realism." Francis was brought in, along with his companions. "Go with the Lord, brother," said the Pope, "and as He sees fit to prompt you, so preach repentance to all men. Then, as soon as the Almighty has multiplied you in numbers and in grace, return joyfully to me, and I shall grant you greater favor and a larger mission more freely than I can do now."

Francis and his companions knelt down before the papal chair, and one by one laid their hands in the Pope's, and promised him and his successors reverence and obedience. Then the *amplexus* (liturgical embrace) was given, and Francis found himself in the service of the Father of Christendom. Later he was tonsured, as an emblem of his official (thanks to Cardinal Colonna) religious status.[18]

Colonna died in 1215, and Pope Innocent followed him a year later, in Perugia, on July 11, at the age of fifty-five. A French cleric, Jacques de Vitry, who arrived in Perugia on the afternoon of that day, recorded his impressions in a letter. He writes: "I found one comfort in these regions [i.e., in Perugia]. Many there were, men and women, rich and worldly, who have left all for Christ, fled the world, and were now called Friars Minor and Minor Sisters. They are held in great respect by Pope and cardinals."[19] In the seven years since Francis' trip to Rome the brotherhood had in fact grown, to the number of some three hundred persons.[20] Cardinal Colonna and Pope Innocent had made a clever decision that day in Rome when they gave their *placet* to the ragged eccentric from Assisi.

The papal license to preach in no way turned Francis into a busybody or world saver, with the fate of the Christian West weighing on his shoulders. He never worried his head over the powers that be, as intellectuals in every age are so fond of doing. Instead he got himself a broom, to sweep the churches in the neighborhood of Assisi.

This is the story they tell: At the time, when the group of Francis' companions was still small and he was preaching repentance in the villages around Assisi, Francis carried around a broom, to sweep the churches, for it greatly grieved him when he entered so many churches that had not been cleaned for so long. And so, in such cases, he liked to get the priests in charge of them in a secluded place, where the laypeople couldn't hear. Francis would preach to them about saving their souls, and especially urge them to care for the cleanliness of their churches and altars.[21]

Francis' procedure looks quite unmasculine. In contrast to the high-and-mighty planners and reformers, he reached for a housewife's utensil. Not even Jesus Christ would have thought of such a thing.

VI

"THAT'S WHAT I WANT"

By THE beginning of the year 1208, after concluding his work as a repairer of churches, Francis had become a man of decision, someone who knew his own mind. At the age of twenty-six he could no longer be confused with anyone else.

Not long ago, while Francis' tomb in the basilica of San Francesco in Assisi was undergoing restoration, scientists took a look at his bones. He was, studies of his skeleton revealed, a small man with a slight frame. He also suffered from malnutrition—obviously a consequence of his frugal way of life.[1] Francis' first biographer, Thomas of Celano, portrays his hero as ". . . a man with a gay countenance and a kindly expression. His body was small rather than large, his head round, his face rather elongated, his brow smooth and low, his eyes black and clear, his hair black, his eyebrows straight, his nose regular, thin, and straight; his ears were small but prominent, his temples flat, his teeth closely spaced, even, and white, his lips thin and soft. He had a black beard, not specially thick, a slender neck, straight shoulders, short arms, slender hands, long fingers with long nails, thin legs, very small feet, delicate skin. He was very skinny."[2]

Celano also tells us of the impression the Pope had of Francis, on the occasion of the miraculous dream: "an insignificant, homely looking man."[3] And Celano passes on a comment by Francis about himself, after a dream in which he had seen a little black hen surrounded by many chicks: "I am the hen, small in build and black from birth."[4]

Francis knew that he was neither handsome nor impressive. When the bishop of Terni, on the occasion of a sermon Francis gave, and in front of all the people, called him a pitiful sight, Francis thanked him effusively for this apt remark, not without a certain coquetry.[5] One of Francis' contemporaries, Thomas of Spalato, observed him preach in Bologna. Thomas wrote, "His robe was dirty, his appearance wretched, his features unpleasant."[6]

There are no authentic portraits of Francis, despite the many pictures painted of him after his death.[7] Nevertheless, on the basis of the descriptions of his person we can imagine what he looked like. We have before us a small, lively, unkempt man; a slender, nervous type with a good deal of charm—and protruding ears. He wears a sacklike garment of coarse, dirty-gray material, full of patches, gathered around the waist with an ordinary rope. He goes barefoot winter and summer, lives on whatever food his begging brings in, spends the night in barns and caves, and is often on the road. His constitution is not at all robust, stories of sickness run through his life like a theme song. The energy that keeps him going is certainly not in his muscles.

We have to say that, contrary to the standard modern cant about positive thinking, his willpower came from a negation of everything that makes bourgeois men and women—us—function efficiently. He pigheadedly rejected the moneymaking, the planning and saving, the social classes and prestige, the hierarchical pecking orders, the hunger for power and influence, the instrumental use of sex. That is why Francis lacked that archetypal bourgeois mixture of envy, impotent hatred, and furtive admiration of successful people that makes up our resentment. Moreover, in sharp contrast to the bourgeois ego, Francis had no fear of death, the uninvited guest in our solitude. He reached what we all dream of—a kind of immortality. This book is further evidence of Francis of Assisi's remarkable power to survive.

One thing we find completely missing in Francis, in terms familiar to us, anyway, is an emotional and intellectual involvement in politics. One might object to this that Francis' unshakeable loyalty to the Pope constituted a political choice, in the context of the almost daily coalitional shifts in Italy. Parties vacillated between the German Emperors and the Roman Popes, inclining now to one power, now to the other, depending on which way the political winds were blowing. In Assisi, for example, just in the years between 1198 and 1210, the city fathers did a political about-face at least five times: They were anti-imperial and propapal in 1198, antipapal in 1204, pro-imperial in 1205, propapal in 1207, pro-imperial in 1210.[8]

Francis was by no means so detached from the world that he couldn't see through these political games: In the final analysis they were staged by the class he had been born into and whose rules he knew by heart—the higher circles of the so-called *maiores*. The *minores*, the common people, to whom the name of his society alludes (Friars Minor [*fratres minores*]), were, in the normal order of things, Francis' social enemies.

We have already seen how Francis betrayed his own class by breaking with his father and choosing an anomalous way of life. But—and this is the crucial political question—did he thereafter throw in his lot with the underprivileged? Did he actively take sides against their masters, and fight against oppression and exploitation?

The answer is no. The people's friendship, Machiavelli tells us, is easily gained. All they ask is not to be oppressed. Did Francis comprehend this desire? Did he try to satisfy it, as a political activist, or even as a rebel? No. Nevertheless, the people, as Sabatier says, saw him as one of their own. They accepted him and loved him—a remarkable fact, which we shall have to deal with.

We look for the red flag of heresy and political rebellion in Francis' life, but we won't find it. In his *Testament*, glancing back over the early years with his first companions, Francis writes: *"Ed eravamo idioti e soggetti a tutti."* (We were ignorant and submissive to everyone.)[9] At the same time it is true that soon after Francis' death his brotherhood created a notable ferment of resistance against the ruling class, with open heresy and active agitation against the established order. One wonders whether such resistance cannot be traced back to Francis, whether the flames of revolt were not smoldering in his submissiveness.

In addition we mustn't let ourselves forget that we are in the Middle Ages, not the eighteenth or nineteenth century. Compared with the bourgeois revolutions and the labor movement, all earlier collective struggles for liberation are "prepolitical" (Eric J. Hobshawm[10])—i.e., they lack a rational political theory. They are provincial, isolated, poorly organized. It follows that we cannot simply apply modern political watchwords like "revolutionary," "reformist," or "conservative" to precapitalist situations.

For all that, the fact remains that, in comparison with the popular political movements of his day, Francis stands out as positively lamblike: He showed no anger at the oppressors of the peasantry, the overseers and tax collectors, the crooked prelates, insolent counts, and usurious merchants. Francis had a simple—and in our eyes rather naïve—prescription for converting dangerous people: good example, unwavering love, humility. And he applied it to highwaymen and bishops, without distinction.

Francis preached and lived the principle of nonviolence. At the same time he insisted, just as stubbornly, on opposing the dominant social forces of his day. This basic political ambiguity has its roots in the Bible, where we find the same peculiar mesh of acquiescence and protest, of reckless denial of the status quo and humble compliance with the powers and authorities of heaven and earth. It would be hard to find a more concise formula for the contradictoriness of bourgeois aspirations down through the ages.

AN EARLY MASS

February 24, 1208, was a special day for Francis.[11] He had just recently completed the restoration of the "little plot," the chapel of Santa Maria degli Angeli. The monks of the Benedictine monastery on Mount Subasio, to whom the little church belonged, had heard of the repairs going on and sent down a priest to celebrate Mass. That was a discreet Benedictine way of thanking Francis, and a delicate reminder that the building was theirs. The quiet service took place on the feast day of the holy Apostle St. Matthew. One imagines Francis as a devout acolyte. He was doubtless excited, and wide awake in any case. When the priest read out the Gospel from the holy book he had brought with him, Francis experienced the text as a divine revelation: He felt a profound assent to it, as though it were a personal message. Over the long history of Christianity, there is a recurrent pattern of people being moved by the Gospel in this way, and such experiences always lead to something—as it did with Francis.

The priest read: "At that time Jesus sent out the twelve, charging them, "Go nowhere among the Gentiles, and enter no town of the Samaritans, but go rather to the lost sheep of the house of Israel. And preach as you go, saying, 'The kingdom of heaven is at hand.' Heal the sick, raise the dead, cleanse lepers, cast out demons. You received without paying, give without pay. Take no gold, nor silver, nor copper in your belts, no bag for your journey, nor two tunics, nor sandals, nor a staff; for the laborer deserves his food."[12]

Francis heard: Go and preach! No gold, no silver, no money! No bag of provisions! Only one tunic! No shoes, no staff! People living in comfort like ourselves cannot easily grasp what suggestive power lay in this demand for total renunciation, for someone as predisposed to it as Francis. The strong and lasting emotion—strong enough to shape one's life—that can be unleashed by the appeal to get back to essentials and cut out the superfluous is fundamentally related to the joy of understanding a terse scientific formula that sums up the most complex operations and makes them seem simple. The charm of the essentials recalls—and the linguistic connection is not accidental—those other essences, perfumes, or liqueurs in which thousands of flowers or fruits are changed by evaporation into a valuable luxury.

The passion for essentials, prized by determined men and women for the way it helps them find their bearings, is both deep and narrow. It plunges into psychic depths which the ego can barely reach, down to where dreams are made. But for the person whose spirit has been seized in this fashion, it demands something in exchange for the concentration of power: It narrows the capacities for perceiving reality in its quasi-infinite fullness. "Essential" people have little curiosity.

The overwhelming assent that Francis felt upon listening to the Gospel may be described as a simultaneously deep and narrow passion. The literally crazy stubbornness we have ascribed to Francis reached the final stage of formation during that early-morning Mass in the Portiuncula.

After Mass Francis asked the priest to explain and interpret the text that had made such a strong impression on him. One imagines the pious monk reading it aloud once again, slowly, translating and clarifying hard Latin words, perhaps quoting from memory one or another appropriate passage from the Gospels. Francis trembled with joy and excitement over the clarity and simplicity of Christ's directives. The priest had barely finished speaking when Francis took his shoes off, undid his leather belt, and threw these now useless items, together with his hermit's staff, into a corner. "That's what I want," said Francis. "That's what I'm looking for. That's what I'm longing to do, from the bottom of my heart!" The monk took off on the way home, shaking his head.[13]

One can easily imagine what a modern theologian—of whatever denomination—would have said to Francis. The theologian would have conceded that Jesus' instructions to his disciples were historically credible, that they derived from a very old tradition. But he would have pointed out that a literal adherence to them after so long a time and under such altered cultural conditions would be an anachronism, an exaggeration. He would have added that they were really only practicable in a country like Palestine, with its mild climate: Jesus had only formulated them for his preaching among Palestinian Jews, as was evident from the text itself. He had never intended to fashion a rule that was valid for all times and places. Francis might observe in this regard what Jesus had said on another occasion (cf. Lk. 22:35–36), namely at the Last Supper, just before his death. He had asked the Apostles, "When I sent you out with no purse or bag or sandals, did you lack anything?" The Apostles had answered, "Nothing." To which Jesus replied, "But now, let him who has a purse take it, and likewise a bag. And let him who has no sword sell his mantle and buy one."

Of course, this was a dubious passage, which may have only gotten into the Gospel after Jesus' death. But one could infer from it that even the very first Christians in Palestine had realized that people couldn't always go about anywhere in the world as carefree and unprotected as in Francis' text from Matthew. So clearly Francis was on the wrong track if he meant to guide his life by a single passage from the Gospel. Such one-sidedness was too sectarian; one must keep the totality of the Christian message in mind.

We also know how Francis would have reacted to the theologian's remarks—with the greatest deference. "We ought to honor and revere all theologians . . . as those who minister to us spirit and life."[14] Thus he wrote in his *Testament*, obviously without any reservations. At the same time Francis would never have dreamed of attaching any importance whatsoever to the theological lesson.

He would have listened politely and then given the same reply he gave on a similar occasion to a respected theologian who had joined the Friars Minor and asked Francis whether the clerics in his fellowship were allowed to have books: "I say to you, brother, what is my original and final desire, my first and last word. No Friar Minor shall have anything except a tunic with a cord, and a pair of drawers."[15]

I like to imagine Francis in heaven chatting with all the Christian theologians, with Augustine and Karl Barth, Aquinas and Rudolf Bultmann. Francis asks them what they would be without their books. They can't find a good answer. He tells them, "Without your books, perhaps you might have become Christians."

As we already know, a year after the early Mass in the Portiuncula Francis walked to Rome with a dozen companions to get an official permit to preach and papal endorsement of his chosen way of life. We remember further how in February 1207, a year before that Mass, he was the laughingstock of Assisi—the exact opposite of a person whom others find so fascinating that they want to pattern their lives after his.

The fact is, then, that within two years Francis must have undergone something like a transformation. From an eccentric enthusiast, an outsider, chased by children on the street, he became a man whom respected men chose for a model—and all this in one and the same setting, in Assisi, where everyone knew him from childhood.

Francis' authority, which would surround him like a distinctive atmosphere until his death, is not easily explained. Before February 24, 1208, Francis had merely repaired a few decrepit churches, driven by a purely personal experience: the voice of the Crucified. It is altogether conceivable that Francis might have continued this eremitic existence, restoring one by one all the ruined chapels near and far around Assisi, living on alms. Over the years people would gradually get to like having such a pious hermit in their neighborhood. And he would end his days as the object of general veneration, like Heimrad the priest. Biographies like that, from India to Europe, are as common as sand on the beach, yet none of these saints achieved what Francis did.

The last twist that pulled the cork out of the bottle, finally freed his powers, and let them flow out into society, was something Francis felt had descended from above and beyond him, as the grace and revelation of God. Along with this came the self-confidence and utter certainty that made him a man who knew what he wanted.

Revelation and grace are medieval categories which no longer convey to contemporary men and women the indisputable meaning that the Middle Ages took for granted. We should like to know more precisely how it was that Francis' private development took on a public dimension, how it won attention and got results, and how it became a popular ideal, as it still is.

The creative moment during the Mass at the Portiuncula may be described as a fusion of two previously separated complexes in Francis' ego. We have already discussed the first complex in Chapters IV and V. In his search for tenderness, Francis happens upon the paradoxical law of the transformation of bitterness into sweetness. This made him turn to beggars and lepers, whose supreme epitome, it seemed to him, was in the end the tortured Savior. And so Francis served Jesus, whose body and blood were made present in the churches of the world, working as a caretaker of various chapels, in "religious" fashion.

The second complex has a more or less objective, indeed almost legal character. This was the collection of God's words, preserved for all eternity in the "Holy Writ" of the Bible. The Bible was the final court of appeal for Popes and Emperors in the Christian West, the basis of all legitimate authority in that age. Nowadays only historians can really imagine how important biblical quotations were in Francis' day. Universities taught the technique of their use for clinching arguments as one of their most important subjects. The learning of entire books of the Bible by heart, particularly the four Gospels and the Psalms, was an indispensable prerequisite for an academic career in theology or jurisprudence. Without knowledge of the Bible you were an *idiota*, an uneducated person, a layman. And, of course, the Bible was only read and commented on in Latin. Anyone who had not mastered the language was excluded from knowledge as the road to power. Francis found himself in just this situation.

His skill in Latin was always modest, and at this stage in his life he understood no more of the Bible than any other young bourgeois with a rudimentary education—i.e., practically nothing. At best one or more Gospel texts, sung at High Mass (still in that unfamiliar Latin), had worked their way into his consciousness.

And so the scriptural fragment read at Mass at the Portiuncula—a few verses muttered in Latin from the Gospel of St. Matthew—became a revelation to Francis, because in them the official God of that epoch—the highest authority, in other words—spoke out clearly and demanded what Francis, as a prodigal son and disinherited rebel, was already inclined to do anyway. Francis' private ecstasies, those extraordinary psychic states that up till this point had meaning only for himself, took on an objective sense, received a heavenly certification, became stations on the way now shown to be the only right one, because it was the path of the God-man, of Christ.

From here on in, whenever his way of life was called into question, Francis could appeal to the "Master," who had walked the earth in exemplary poverty and freedom from earthly cares. Francis understood that his behavior, whatever people might say, had God's approval. His follies were a personal imitation of the Savior's folly. The more literally he took Jesus' words, the more unassailable Francis' position became, the more legitimate his plan of life.

In March 1208, barely a month after his enlightenment in the Portiuncula chapel, Francis gave his first public sermon in the church of San Giorgio, up in the city of Assisi.[16]

THE NAKED CHRIST

Not counting the last two or three years of his life, when he was quite sick and feeble, Francis now had roughly fifteen years of intense preaching activity in front of him, with only occasional interruptions for a few weeks of quiet meditation by himself. This makes it all the more surprising that our sources tell us almost nothing about the form, content, themes, and style of Francis' sermons. Celano observes that Francis had a powerful voice and was a fluent speaker.[17] Another contemporary notes how electrifying Francis' preaching was, and how the crowds pressed up against him, trying to touch his robe.[18] The Legend of the Three Companions speaks of the "power and truth" of his rhetoric, which no one had taught him and which nonetheless astonished educated people.[19] None of this really sheds much light on the question.

We are also short on information about the subject matter of Francis' sermons. In stereotypical fashion we are told that Francis preached "repentance," that he called for peaceableness and generosity from his listeners, and warned them of the agonies of hell.[20] We have the verbatim text of a single sermon by Francis, the famous sermon to the birds. "You have much to thank God for," it begins, "birds, my brothers and sisters, and you must therefore praise him always and everywhere. You have the freedom to fly in all directions. You have clothing, twofold and threefold; you have a colorful, handsome dress; you have food without working for it, and the gift of song, given you by the Creator. In Noah's ark God preserved your seed, that you might not decrease." And so forth.[21]

This high-flown text, written down about a hundred years after Francis' death, betrays the sentimental zeal of some pious Franciscan epigone with literary ambitions. But it is hopeless to look for information about Francis' original tone in the sermon to the birds from the *Fioretti*.

Another text from the same collection is more instructive. There we are told that Francis sent one of his first companions—Rufino by name—to Assisi to preach. Rufino put up some resistance, and said to Francis, "But you know I have no gift for speaking. I am a simple and ignorant man!" "Then I order you," said Francis, "to go naked to Assisi, wearing only your underwear, and to go into the church and preach to the people like that."[22] (At that time, in the early years of the society, Francis had temporary quarters in the Portiuncula forest, below Assisi.)

Rufino took off his tunic and marched off. Up in Assisi the children immediately gathered in a crowd—one has to realize that Rufino came from one of the most respected noble families in the city. He walked unswervingly into the church named by Francis, bowed before the altar, and climbed into the pulpit, to the great amusement of the people who greeted him with ridicule: "The way these people carry on with their penance, they go completely crazy!"

"Dear people!" Rufino cried, "Flee the world, abandon your sins! Give back what doesn't belong to you, or you go to hell! Keep the Commandments, love God and men! Do penance, the kingdom of heaven is near!" While Rufino stammered out a handful of edifying phrases amid general laughter, suddenly Francis stood in the church, likewise wearing only his drawers. He had run after Rufino, with another companion, who struggled frantically to keep his wits, as he followed along, carrying both Francis' and Rufino's tunics.

The gay confusion in the church intensified when Francis made his appearance alongside Rufino in the pulpit. "Then Francis spoke so astonishingly of despising the world, of holy penance, voluntary poverty, longing for the kingdom of heaven, and for the nakedness and shame of the crucified Jesus, that all the men and women present were greatly moved and wept continually. The people's sympathy for the sufferings of the Savior that day was heartrending—nothing like that had ever happened in Assisi within human memory.

At this point I would like to quote a modern text, from *Power and the Masses* by Elias Canetti: "Amid the incomprehensible extremes of annihilation and creation that characterize the first half of our century, amid this doubly inexorable infatuation that first goes one way, and then in the opposite direction, religions of mourning, as organized bodies, offer the spectacle of complete helplessness. Whether they eagerly anticipate events, or hold back in hesitation, they give their blessing to everything (with certain exceptions) that happens. Still, their legacy is greater than one might think. The image of the One whose death Christians have mourned for almost two thousand years has entered the consciousness of all thoughtful people. He is a dying man, yet he does not die. With the secularization of the earth his divinity has lost meaning. He has remained, whether one likes it or not, *the* suffering and dying person."[23]

I chose this passage because it expresses the significance of the Christ symbol in the Western world today, in an unobtrusive, broad-minded manner. The collective image of the suffering Christ, in the century of concentration camps and atom bombs, is definitely still with us. Despite the obvious helplessness of the different Christian churches, it is, as Canetti puts it, indestructible.

The emotional identification by which oppressed and injured human beings could recognize themselves in the shattered body of God is by no means as old as Christianity. For almost a thousand years, from the beginning of the union between Church and State under Constantine the Great until the high Middle Ages, the Christ people knew was the Lord and Master. In ancient mosaics and Roman reliefs the Savior always sat on a throne in heaven. Even on the cross he wore the crown of a King.

The first protests against this feudal God were heard among the heretics, who felt a distinct abhorrence for the cross, as in the case of Leuthard.

Francis was the first—this time in keeping with his age, anticipating it, in fact—the first to incarnate the genuine breakthrough . . . to humanity. Himself unclothed, Francis preached a naked Jesus on the cross, with no divine insignias of power and glory, a very human God, in whom the common people could recognize themselves without any trouble. Which is why they began to cry.

By their sudden comprehension of their God in the figure of a slave, Francis' listeners stumbled upon a new category, which heretofore they had only been dimly aware of in the growling of their bellies from time immemorial. Let us call this new category morality, although not in the current sense of social custom backed up by the police. Rather, Christ's suffering is a highly moral process insofar as human evil, rather than a natural catastrophe, appears at work in it. The God-man falls into the hands of wrongdoers; he is not overwhelmed by fire, earthquake, or flood. His fate is inflicted on him by humans, which means that rebellion is possible.

One more leap, this time to Barcelona. On Sunday, July 19, 1936, the civil war had broken out, and there was shooting in the streets. Stores were looted and churches set afire. An eyewitness reported: "I saw a number of churches that had been destroyed. On the Rambla de las Flores stood the Iglesia Belén, the Bethlehem Church. In it there was a crucifix about two meters tall, which was greatly revered by the faithful. Before the church was put to the torch, they got the crucifix and took it outside. In place of the usual INRI over the head of the Crucified someone had put a large piece of cardboard and written on it, *A ti no te quemamos, porque eres uno de los nuestros.* That is, 'We don't burn you, because you are one of us.' "[24]

Evidently during that strange scene in Assisi neither the preacher nor his weeping audience gave any thought to setting churches on fire. But as they mourned the fate of the tortured Savior, and thereby in a certain sense their own fate, they were performing a human act, unheard of "from time immemorial," as the source aptly remarks.

In fact, the sympathy that Francis evoked was something authentically new, a different kind of aspiration.[25] We know that in Francis' century painters first began to represent Christ from the human point of view as the Man of Sorrows, and the "holy countenance." It would surely be too pedestrian to interpret this critical turning point in the history of the Western imagination as a mere reflection of unbearable social and economic conditions. In this new attention to the Savior as a figure of humiliation, morality, not economics, is the essential factor. "When people can no longer bear the fact that there are two kinds of men, masters and slaves, this means they have passed judgment, not economically, but morally. Economically, I can define master and slave quite precisely, but that doesn't get me anywhere. But the realization that I am not to be, am not allowed to be, that we have had enough of this—that is what starts the revolution."[26]

When we reflect that the bourgeois revolution is a child of Europe, and not of Africa or Asia, then we can put Francis' "underwear sermon" in a meaningful context. Francis took a prominent part in the formation of that humane movement of emancipation from the chilling forces of early capitalism that schoolbooks never talk about. We know that Francis behaved neither like a heretic nor like a rebel. But it would be false to make him out to be a harmless bird-watcher or a sweetly pious sermonizer. Rather, by communicating to his contemporaries his own passionate reaction to the image of the poor and wretched Son of Man, Francis actually implanted among the underprivileged a self-consciousness that later produced much more than tears and sighs—as, for example, in Barcelona, in 1936. Among the real conditions of political powerlessness among the common people tears are always better than the traditional apathy.

MONEY IS A POISONOUS SNAKE

Francis had gone begging before the day when he found a plan for the rest of his life in a few short Gospel maxims, which included: no gold, no silver, no money! As soon as Francis recognized this threefold negation as God's will, his *de facto* experience as a beggar became a matter of principle, the expression of a postulate that uniquely characterizes Francis: the radical refusal to own property.

Exactly one hundred years after Francis' spiritual breakthrough—i.e., in 1318—four Franciscans were burned at the stake in Marseille, as we have already noted. Their execution came as the result of a papal bull of excommunication, promulgated in 1317, which closes with the following key sentence: "Poverty is a great thing, but blameless conduct is greater, and the greatest good of all is perfect obedience."[27] The bull was directed against the Franciscan opposition, which had resisted the successful efforts of Bonaventure & Company to adapt the Order to "altered circumstances." These "Spirituals," as people called them, were threatened with burning if they did not abandon certain opinions. In particular they were forbidden, under pain of death, to criticize the wearing of luxurious clothes and the accumulation of food.

In the year 1318 Pope John XXII summoned sixty-five respected Spirituals to the papal court in Avignon. Of these forty recanted, and the remaining twenty-five were handed over to the Inquisition, which imposed the four death sentences. The other Spirituals were imprisoned for life.[28] A few more facts: In Narbonne, in 1319, three unrepentant Spirituals were burned; in 1321, in the same city, another seventeen. In Carcassonne between 1318 and 1350 a total of 113 Spirituals went to their death. Beyond this, there were executions in Toulouse and other cities of France and Spain, up till the middle of the fourteenth century.[29] By that time the authorities managed to eradicate—to some extent—that dangerous tendency among the Franciscans who still clung unconditionally to Francis' vision and took the love of poverty literally.

As we see, Francis' rejection of property, however submissively or politely it might be expressed, contained the purest sociopolitical dynamite.

In the face of this historical fact it is almost amusing to see how much trouble modern experts on Francis' life will take to defuse the explosiveness of their beloved saint. In 1965 a Franciscan named Heribert Roggen did a study on Francis' way of life "in relationship to the feudal and bourgeois society of Italy."[30] In it he repeatedly points out "that St. Francis never intended to change the social structure of his day." It goes

69

without saying that Roggen argues against Sabatier, now long dead. Sabatier, he claims, "distorted the figure of the saint into a sort of rebellious negativism." Roggen insists that Francis' orientation was "always purely religious," and continues: "If then one cannot deny the saint's social influence, the truth remains that he never consciously intended this influence. His entire concern was for souls." And for the dear little birds, we might add.

Diligent Franciscans are not the only ones who have their problems with the notion of poverty. In 1976 an East German scholar named Hubert Mohr likewise expressed his concern over the correct interpretation of the medieval movements championing poverty, only his approach was Marxist-Leninist. He recommends, in the usual Scholastic fashion, "two distinctions": "First the distinction between subjectively honorable efforts to alleviate the plight of the poor, and objectively reactionary reinforcement of the Church's standing as a feudal institution (and therefore reinforcement of the feudal system itself); second, the distinction between the reformers' efforts to promote poverty and asceticism for the sake of the Church and the feudal system, and the heretical movements, which were subjectively and objectively directed against the Church and the feudal system, but whose arguments likewise appealed to ancient Christian ideals. The reformers' endeavors, which objectively served to restore the Church's efficiency—that is, its control of the masses—can on no account be rated progressive."[31]

According to this Procrustean model, Francis can in no way be "rated" progressive, because he was "subjectively" and "objectively" a stooge of the "feudal system." That is not, at least for the Franciscans living in East Germany, especially good news. Their future "rating" must be a matter of some concern to them.

As the two previous examples show, the theoretical issues discussed by contemporary historians in dealing with Francis' desire for total poverty are scholarly-ideological. Depending on the scholar's "intellectual standpoint"—or which side of the Iron Curtain he lives on—Francis is taken to be a "purely religious" figure or an "objectively reactionary" one.

Another interpreter, Walter Dirks, takes a conciliatory position: "Karl Marx says that in wealth man objectifies his being, suffers the loss of himself, and of love. Francis says that wealth habitually injures the love of God and of neighbor. Both analyses are in agreement. Only Karl Marx wants to carry on the class struggle and bring it to a conclusive finish, whereas Francis follows a different line of reasoning: Things being the way they are, let's not have any possessions at all in this world. Because he knows that history is a history of class struggles—and a history of the Holy Spirit."[32]

So Francis of Assisi and Karl Marx exchange a brotherly handshake across the centuries, on paper at least, in the work of a West German leftist Catholic, in the year 1956. The upshot of all this, the reader will note, is that no interpretation of Francis can really be value-free. The principle of voluntary poverty cannot be examined like a microbe under a microscope. It resists so-called scientific objectivity, because it is a moral phenomenon. It expresses the same idealistic, obstinate vision that goes back to the protocommunist early Christians and continues on through the medieval heretics and early modern Anabaptists, all the way up to the *Communist Manifesto* of February 1848: the goal of a classless society and an ethical existence without property.

Francis learned what life is like among the destitute, after he broke with his father in March 1207. He had had to fall back on the cold institutional charity of a monastery. On his trip to Gubbio he had become a burden to a friend, and as a nurse in the leprosarium he had broken his bread in surroundings that were not exactly sumptuous. Upon his return, as we have already seen, Francis began to work on the church of San Damiano, and the priest there seems to have taken care of his meals. The *Legend of the Three Companions* continues the story: "One day when Francis noticed what the priest was doing for him, he reflected and said to himself: 'Shall I always have this priest, who looks after me with such kindness, everywhere I go?' Then Francis took his beggar's sack, went with it into town, and begged for alms from door to door. He put all the food he had collected in a bowl. Naturally, when he sat down to eat it, he found this hodge-podge utterly sickening. In the past he wouldn't even have wanted to look at such stuff, much less eat it. But finally he overcame himself and ate it, and it seemed to him as if he had never tasted such delicious food. He thanked God, who had transformed the bitterness into sweetness for him, and had increased his strength. He asked the priest not to prepare any more food for him in the future."[33]

We can guess what was on Francis' plate: one or two fish heads, perhaps a bacon rind or some tripe, bean soup and turnips, millet gruel, a handful of olives, dried fruit. Along with that some bits of barley and a cheese rind for dessert. (At that time Italian pasta dishes, so popular nowadays, did not exist.)

Thus Francis took his meals at the table of the poor, as God in his infinite goodness had set it. For the rest of his life he kept to the diet of the underprivileged, with black bread and water as his chief nourishment. Often in his later years, when he was constantly sick, he grew weak, and asked for a certain kind of fish or a bunch of parsley.[34] Once Francis requested an almond cake—but then only when he lay on his deathbed.[35] Otherwise Francis stuck to the same bill of fare as the hungry wretches around him, and honored bread got from begging as a holy sacrament.[36]

It would be a misunderstanding to view this way of thinking as conventional religious asceticism. Rather, Francis had made an unyielding resolution to live like the poor. On the occasions when the rich invited him into their houses to dine, he regularly pulled out some bread crusts he had cadged, and amiably distributed them to his embarrassed hosts. This sort of thing happened one time in Cardinal Ugolino's house, where a select group of nobles was dining. Francis had stolen away with his beggar's sack, and by the time he returned, they had already begun eating. Francis calmly dumped all the provisions he had begged out on the table, and then sat down next to his host, who was ready to burst a blood vessel with rage. After Francis had politely taken a few bites of his usual food, he started to offer each of the gentlemen present a piece of barley bread. Some of them ate their share willy-nilly, others hid it away. It must have been awfully quiet.

The source remarks that a few of the dignitaries removed their velvet caps (extrahebant infulas). The cardinal took him aside afterward, and asked, "But, but, my dear, how could you mortify me like that?" "I take more comfort," said Francis, "from being with my companions and seeing the bread we have begged on the table before me, than I do from sitting down to eat with important guests like yours." A rather brusque reply, and the point behind it was obvious.[37]

We come now to the core of the poverty ethics, as Francis presented it: the absolute ban on the use of money: "I firmly order all the brothers not to accept coins or money in any form, either themselves or by an intermediary."[38] So says Francis' Rule, approved by the Pope, from the year 1223. The original text is preserved in the treasure vault of the basilica in Assisi. In the Rule of 1221, which did not get papal authorization, the ban on money is illustrated by two powerful comparisons: Money is like the dust one tramples with one's feet; and it has no more value than gravel.[39]

Celano tells us that one day someone from the outside world left behind a little bag of coins in the Portiuncula chapel as a donation. A brother carried the money from the altar to the embrasure of a window—and in so doing committed a grievous error, because he touched the purse with his hand. Francis ordered him to pick it up with his mouth and to take it out to the dung heap.[40]

As we have already mentioned, both biographies of Francis by Thomas of Celano were outlawed in 1266 by the leadership of the Friars Minor. Stories like the one just quoted, where the taboo on money is so readily apparent, were surely to blame for this. Celano has a number of such stories in stock. In one of them we find a historically credible reflection of the struggles Francis had in the final years of his life against efforts to dilute the ban on money in the rapidly growing Order.

"Once," says Celano, "when Francis' vicar, Brother Peter of Catania, in the face of the crowds of brothers from other regions who flocked to visit the Portiuncula, was contending with the problem of supplying them with the necessities, he said to Francis: 'I beg you, give your consent so we can keep some of the property of the new brothers who keep pouring in on us. That way we'll have something to fall back on in an emergency!' Francis replied: 'Dearest brother, far be it from us to love one another in this way. Instead, remove the precious ornaments from the altar of our church, if you cannot help the needy in any other way. Believe me, the mother of God would rather have us observe the Gospel of her Son and rob her altar than leave her altar adorned but despise her Son.'"[41] (The chapel of the Portiuncula was consecrated to Mary.)

This story does not merely insist upon the strict prohibition of money, in opposition to obvious rational considerations of practical management; it also attacks the subtle temptation of pious Christians to pile up wealth under pretext of beautifying churches and serving God.

Here is yet another story from Celano, fantastic enough, but with an unmistakable moral: One time Francis was traveling on foot through Apulia with a companion. Not far from Bari they saw a money bag full to the brim with money lying in the street. Francis' companion proposed dividing their find among the poor. Francis refused, and they walked on. But the companion kept pressing him and asking him to change his mind. Finally Francis came around, and ordered his companion to pick up the bag. Hardly had he taken it in hand when a large snake crawled out of it and "showed the brother the devil's deceit." "Brother," Francis said, "for the servants of God money is nothing else than the devil, and a poisonous snake."[42]

In reading these sources one gets the impression that after successfully mastering his aversion to lepers, Francis transferred it to money. He repeatedly refers to money as dung, which will surely please psychoanalysts who stress the anal character of acquisitiveness.[43] In stories about Francis money is treated quite explicitly as excrement—one should not dirty one's hands with it.

This kind of revulsion is not so bizarre as one might think at first. Ever since the days of the ancient Romans we have been assuring one another that money doesn't smell—which wouldn't be necessary, if we didn't have to overcome some hidden emotion here. Our subliminal feelings of shame toward money have a long cultural history. They are a pale reflection of the lofty attitude of aristocratic landowners who regarded tradesmen and usurers with utter contempt.

As a matter of fact, there is an honorable tradition rejecting money, which goes back to Sophocles (c. 450 B.C.), who wrote, "For of all the things in use among men, nothing has been as bad as money!"[44] The two leading thinkers of Europe, Plato and Aristotle, protested with one voice against acquisitiveness. In so doing they founded a theory that Western philosophers have professed, with rare unanimity, for two thousand years, all the way down to Rousseau: in a grand gesture of cultural pessimism, they made money the scapegoat for the decay of all our values.

(One need only pick up the nearest newspaper to hear the perennial complaint over the downfall of "basic values" in industrial society, and this in an age when money functions as the criterion for all those values, including the so-called spiritual ones. If my book doesn't sell, it's good for nothing.)

For centuries, from late antiquity into the early modern period, the "dead hand" of the Church conducted a low-key campaign against the demoralizing effects of money. Again and again, Church Fathers and theologians, councils, and Popes thundered against the charging of interest as the embodiment of abject greed, and "usurers" were even occasionally threatened with excommunication. The official Church was thereby pleading on behalf of the circumstances in which she had grown to greatness— i.e., the barter economy of the early Middle Ages between A.D. 500 and 1000. In these times—golden for the Church, but otherwise barbaric—from which we have fewer documents than from the ancient Egyptians or Babylonians, money played a very subordinate role, and even long-distance commerce was minimal.[45] The ruling caste lived off the drudgery of the serfs and devoted itself to the noble occupations of robbing and plundering in the true knightly manner—that is, with ruthless brutality. In accordance with this system all those who created social wealth, including merchants and tradesmen, were treated with scorn. Up until the modern period, the Church, in its universally binding digest of legal texts, the *Corpus Juris Canonici*, labeled every kind of commerce as sinful.[46]

We can see an expression of the almost habitually bad conscience of all the people who engaged in money transactions anyway, in the many donations that flowed into the Church from these groups. (Hatred of the Jews, who were exempted from the ban on interest, was the other side of the picture.) In antiquity and all through the Middle Ages one could not win social prestige simply with a coffer full of money. You had to have landed property to get your oar in, socially speaking.

While all this was going on, the Church wasted no time in doing its part to effect the change-over from a barter economy to a money economy, a transformation that reached a conclusive stage in Francis' century. Papal and episcopal administrators eagerly adopted Arabic numbers from their enemies the Mohammedans (who got them from India), to modernize their accounting. The papal court in Avignon, which took such severe measures against the radical Franciscans, had the most advanced financial management in Europe at the time, with double-entry bookkeeping and cashless money transfers, along with the best connections to the northern Italian banking houses.

While the theologians tinkered with the proofs of God's existence, a fetish began to take shape in people's heads, a noun like any other, and at the same time as mysterious as a veiled painting: money. We are still living with it—with this concrete universal in our wallets, this real abstraction on which so many theoreticians have broken their teeth, with this "dazzling enigma," as Marx once called it.[47]

If we take a bird's-eye view of world history, Francis' fury against the money fetish does not look especially original. It strikes us as naïve—after all, it proved to be a futile gesture by a single individual which had no impact on the course of events.

Of course, we should not forget that these strictures become irrelevant the moment one decides to come down from the philosophical heights of history and follow the way of the world from the standpoint that Francis wanted to take—the perspective of the people who are never asked what they think. Among the underprivileged the hopes for a moneyless Utopia have never been extinguished. We can trace them all the way up to the helpless projection of the Land of Cockaigne. Then, a hundred years ago, as we know, the idea got back on its feet, in epoch-making fashion. "Finally, let us imagine, for a change," wrote Marx, "an association of free people, working with the means of production held in common and self-consciously expending their many individual capacities as a single, social capacity."[48] In such an association money would be superfluous.

Marx was the first European philosopher to write from the perspective of the powerless. Looked at from above, Francis is a lovable fool. Seen from below, his madness was a splendid effort, and as such it encourages fantasy—that is, thinking in the mode of possibility.

VII

THE LIFE OF THE FRIARS
MINOR BEGINS

IN THE year 1170, twelve years before Francis' birth, a rich merchant by the name of Valdes was walking through the city of Lyon, where he lived and looked after his business. He was married, had two daughters, and owned all sorts of properties (woods, farmland, pasture, vineyards, mills, bakeries). A fair was going on, and a balladeer was performing on a street corner. Valdes stopped and listened. The singer sang an old song about the holy man Alexios from far-off Syria. On his wedding night, the ballad began, the young and rich Alexios had not touched his charming bride, had talked seriously with her, and then gone off into the night. He disappeared for many years, and traveled distant roads as a pilgrim and beggar. In the end he came home to his parents' house, grown old and sick. No one recognized him, he was given a miserable lodging, and he finally died without making himself known. Only the miracles worked by his dead body opened people's eyes.

The pious tune cut deeply into Valdes' guilty bourgeois conscience. He consulted with the clergy, paid them good money to translate the Psalms and the Gospels for him, read and pondered a while, until he finally knew what he had to do with his life. He made arrangements for his wife and daughters, and gave away the rest of his wealth. Valdes started, as a barefoot beggar, to proclaim the praises of Christ's holy poverty on the streets and in the squares of Lyon. Soon other rich citizens joined up with him, after renouncing goods and chattels, wives and children. These "poor men of Lyon," as they were called, got into trouble with the bishop on account of their unauthorized preaching. He considered their activity in the city and its environs both superfluous and dangerous. So in the year 1179 they went off to Rome, to ask for permission to preach.[1]

Up till this point the story of Valdes and his companions displays clear parallels to the genesis of Francis' brotherhood. In one case as in the other we have a betrayal of class interests. Acquisitiveness changes into love of poverty. The Jesus of the Bible is taken for a model; theologically uneducated laymen (*idiotae*) begin to preach in public.

But in Rome, unlike Francis, Valdes had no luck at all. In the eternal city a great Church assembly was meeting, the Third Lateran Council. Bishops, abbots, and theology professors had journeyed there from all over Europe, the tavernkeepers had their hands full, and the Roman prostitutes, as usual on such occasions, turned a tidy profit.

The venerable assembly was busy dealing with, among other things, the deadly poison of the Cathars, whose rapid spread greatly alarmed the Council Fathers. Anathemas were formulated, solemnly read out, ratified, and promulgated. (Somebody bungled somewhere, and the Acts of the Council were afterward lost.)

One can imagine what a suspicious reception the barefooted lay preachers from Lyon got from the Roman authorities. Naturally, there was an investigation into the orthodoxy and theological training of the new society. As a precautionary measure, Valdes had brought along his book of translated Bible texts, as proof of his zealous studies. The examination, according to the description of a certain Walter Map, was a terrible disgrace for Valdes and his companions.

"Q.:   Do you believe in God the Father?
A.:   We do.
Q.:   And in the Son?
A.:   We do.
Q.:   And in the Holy Ghost?
A.:   We do.
Q.:   And in the Mother of Christ?
A.:   We do."

General derision from the theologians. (This had been a trick question: Mary is not an object of faith in the same sense as the Holy Trinity.) Were they supposed to allow such ignoramuses to preach?

Finally, the Pope gave Valdes a fatherly embrace, and praised his intention of living in poverty and renunciation, but at the same time forbade him to do any preaching without permission from the local church authorities.[2]

The further story of Valdes and his society, the Waldensians, chronicles how nervous authorities turned to the use of terror against the reform-minded outsiders, with the familiar result: An originally harmless group was increasingly radicalized. In the year 1184, on the occasion of a summit meeting between Pope Lucius III and Emperor Frederick Barbarossa, the poor men of Lyon were solemnly condemned and proscribed, which practically made them outlaws. Nevertheless, their followers quickly multiplied as they came into contact with related movements in Italy (the "Humiliati," the "poor men of Lombardy"). After a relatively short time there were Waldensian communities in Spain, Germany, and Bohemia. The tone of their sermons was sharply anticlerical and critical of the Church. And, three hundred years before Luther, they constantly appealed to the Bible.

Naturally enough, the list of Waldensians put to death for their beliefs is a long one, but despite that they are the only body of medieval heretics who are still around today. For example, in some of the mountain valleys near Turin they meet in bare, unadorned churches and sing their old songs. One Waldensian pastor, Giuseppe Platone, happens to be a personal acquaintance of mine. I have visited him in his village, called Angrona, a little less than an hour by car from Turin. Giuseppe cares for the six hundred farmers of his mountain community. Progress, for the time being, has passed these people by—many of them don't even have a radio. Giuseppe goes to visit them (on foot), explains politics to them, gives them advice in their dealings with banks and the government, and gets them jobs. When I think of Giuseppe, Valdes and the twelfth century don't seem all that far away. I had almost forgotten to mention that Giuseppe is a socialist. He still has not finished his thesis (on Karl Barth), and his wife, as of this writing, is expecting a baby.

It may be that the radically different development of the Waldensians and the Franciscans is due to a series of minor accidents. What would have happened had Valdes found a clever cardinal in Rome, as Francis did, to plead his case? Or the other way around: Would Francis have remained the unshakeably faithful son of the Church if the Pope had strictly forbidden him to preach? Nowadays the Waldensians (seventy thousand)[3] and the Franciscans (forty thousand)[4] belong to separate denominations. They live respectively as Evangelical or Catholic Christians, the ones without a Pope, the others with. The Franciscans practice celibacy, which the Waldensians gave up a long time ago.

As a group the Waldensians surely have only a fraction of the financial resources of the Franciscans. An old Catholic joke claims that one of the few things not even God knows is where the Franciscans get their money from.

THE FIRST COMPANION

Six or seven weeks after the unforgettable Mass at the Portiuncula Francis received a respectful but mysterious invitation to dinner at the home of Lord Bernard of Quintavalle di Bernadello,[5] a well-to-do man of thirty, unmarried and a resident of Assisi. Bernard, whom we briefly met before this, had a question: "Let us assume that a man had been in possession of the goods of a great lord for some time, and no longer wished to keep them. What should he do?" Francis replied, "He must give them back to the lord." "Everything I own," said Bernard, "I have from God. I now intend to give all of it back to him. I need your advice in this matter."

This is, far more clearly than in Francis' case, the Valdes complex. Francis had never faced the decision to give away a substantial amount of wealth here and now: His father's fortune was never at his disposal. But Bernard was really rich—whether through his own efforts or inheritance, we don't know. Perhaps he had been shaken by the death of someone close to him. In any event he sounds like a man who only speaks when his mind is made up. It is remarkable that at this important interview Francis speaks with almost ceremonious restraint. In Celano's presentation, he doesn't burst in to suggest giving everything to the poor. He recommends that they consult an oracle on the following day: "If you want to attest your words with deeds, then let's go to church tomorrow morning, open up the Gospel, and get advice from Christ."

Bernard agreed, and they went to bed. We have already described the events of that night. Early in the morning they both went to church, asked a priest to say Mass for them, and afterward had him consult the holy book. Such a request was not unusual at the time. The priest knew what he had to do: After Mass he took the Gospel, made the sign of the cross over it, and opened it up at three places. The three passages could serve as documentation for Francis' entire program.[6] (Whether they were actually found by this method is of no consequence to us.)

First: "If you would be perfect, go, sell what you possess, and give to the poor." Second: "Take nothing for your journey, no staff, nor bag, nor bread, nor money." Third: "If any man would come after me, let him deny himself and take up his cross and follow me." Then Francis said to Bernard, "You have the advice that Christ gives us."

These three texts recur, thirteen years later, in the first "Rule" of the Friars Minor that we have in writing—proof of their programmatic significance in Francis' philosophy. The second text is the duplicate of the passage that made such a deep impression on Francis in the early Mass at the Portiuncula chapel. The first was evidently the key quotation for the poverty movement in that period; it also appears in Valdes' biography, where it is used to legitimate his position.[7] The third articulates in different words the principle that had been a determining factor in Francis' development: Take bitter for sweet.

The historical core of the oracle story is now clear. Bernard, the well-to-do bourgeois, confronted Francis with his problem in all seriousness. That he did so at all may be ascribed to Francis' charisma. Francis recognized that the man was looking for an unquestionable authority, and so he quoted from the Gospel. He himself sets forth this process in his *Testament* as follows: "And, after the Lord gave me brothers no one showed me what I ought to do, but the Most High himself revealed to me that I ought to live according to the pattern of the Holy Gospel."[8]

We may suppose that Francis used the next few weeks after the Mass at the Portiuncula to have an educated priest introduce him to certain parts of the Gospels, perhaps with a simple question about passages that criticize wealth. It is also conceivable (Celano suggests as much) that a whole series of conversations took place between Francis and Bernard, over a fairly long time. If that were the case, then Francis' Bible study would become all the more plausible: It would have helped him win over the thoughtful Bernard. In any event, it was a couple of passages from the Bible that made Bernard decide to part with all his possessions and to live cheerfully in voluntary poverty like Francis.

These two sons of the bourgeoisie act as if they had found a precious treasure in their attic under a pile of junk. They take hold of the Gospel and make it their own, without asking permission from the authorized executors of God's estate. Both are laymen, from the rising middle class. By waiving their privileges they gain what people from the Establishment in every age vainly claim to have: credibility. That is the moral of the story, and now as then it's worth taking to heart.

For a while Bernard's house became a place of pilgrimage for all the poor devils from Assisi and environs. Naturally, Bernard owned more than just movable goods. Land and real estate had to be sold, and Bernard was certainly not one to let such things go for a song. Whenever he made a sale, there would be a feast day for the needy, who kept the house under siege. In the end Bernard doubtless flung the doors wide open and let everyone help himself to furniture, tableware, and what was left of his wardrobe. Then, already wearing a tunic, he left the empty house with Francis, and went down into the forest of the Portiuncula.

Whatever you get, you owe. This basic principle of all bookkeeping was solidly established by Bernard and Francis' time, and it still confuses apprentice accountants. Incoming monies are listed under debit: What sense does that make?

People seldom observe that bookkeeping and theology have a connection. Bernard realized it because he knew he was in debt to God. All his property, in a mysterious way, was on the debit side of the ledger. After he liquidated his assets by conveying them to the poor, he balanced the account, financially and theologically, with a zero on the bottom line.

Later on, according to the *Fioretti*, Bernard dealt with God as with a friend.[9] This should not surprise us. Economically, Bernard was now clear with God. Psychologically, he had freed himself from the burdensome pressure of the eternally dissatisfied superego. One can imagine with what profound relief this man traveled the little way down into the valley, to the mud hut in the forest, to begin a new life with Francis.

"I'M STARVING TO DEATH!"

Not far from the Portiuncula chapel Francis had built a shelter, a primitive hut out of branches and mud, with a few stones on the roof and certainly no windows.[10] The smoke from the open fire, at which Francis and Bernard cooked their bean soup, escaped through the door into the woods beyond. Along with Bernard and Francis, two other men spent their nights in this smokehouse. They were Peter and Egidio, and they had discovered Francis at almost the same time as Bernard had.

We may assume that Peter was a servant of Bernard's, who decided to follow his master into a new kind of freedom.[11] Egidio was a peasant. Like everyone in and around Assisi, he had heard of Bernard's sensational act of renunciation: On April 23, the feast of St. George, after attending Mass in Assisi, Egidio marched down into the valley, to the Portiuncula.

This is the story they tell: When Brother Egidio came to the crossroads near the leprosarium and did not know which way to go, Francis suddenly came out of the woods. When Brother Egidio saw him, he said: "For the love of God, I wish to live with you!" Francis replied, "The Lord has shown you a great mercy! Imagine that the Emperor came to Assisi and wanted to knight a man from the city. How many would consider themselves fortunate to receive such a favor! Then how thankful must you be that the highest Lord has chosen you to come to his court!" Then Francis took Egidio by the hand, led him to the Portiuncula, called Bernard over, and said: "The Lord has sent us a dear brother!" And full of joy they shared their meal. Then Francis took Egidio with him back to Assisi, to beg a tunic for him. On the way they met a poor woman who asked them for an alms. Francis turned to Egidio and said, "Let's give her your cloak." He did at once as he was bidden, and great joy filled his heart.[12]

As we see, the terms of admission to Francis' brotherhood were as uncomplicated as possible, and up until his death very little changed in this regard.[13] You declared to one of the brothers that you wanted to join, gave away everything you had to the poor, and slipped into a threadbare old tunic. No examinations, no probation period, no documents. Within a few hours anyone could be a Friar Minor.

Occasionally there were people who took out insurance on their risk. This is the story they tell:[14] Once when Francis had preached to the citizens of a town in the Marches of Ancona, a man came up to him and said, "Brother, I would like to leave the world and join your fellowship."[15] Francis replied, "Then you must give away everything you have to the poor." But the man made over his property to his relatives, and then returned to Francis, and announced that he had gotten rid of his possessions. Francis asked him, "And how did you do that?" The man answered, "I left my belongings to some relatives who were in distress." Then Francis spoke to him, "Away with you, you fly! Find yourself another brotherhood, to take advantage of people's charity."

The family of a certain man named John, a peasant's son who lived in a village around Assisi, had better luck with Francis. One day Francis was in the village to sweep out the chapel, as was his custom. John was plowing in the neighborhood of the little church, hurried by, asked Francis for the broom, and finished the job. Then he expressed his wish to lead a life of service to God. Francis explained to him that he had to give his property to the poor, whereupon John went out to the fields, unyoked an ox, and led it to Francis. In the meantime John's parents and his younger brothers and sisters rushed over, greatly worried about the valuable ox. Francis relinquished it—it already belonged to the poor—and gave it back to the peasant family, who were living in misery as it was.[16]

Francis liked John from the first moment and often took him with him on his travels. Whenever Francis spat or cleared his throat, John immediately did the same. He carefully imitated Francis' posture during prayer, his gestures, and his table manners. When at last Francis, more amused than annoyed, tried to restrain him, John was at a loss. "But I promised to live just as you do!" Francis was enchanted with this reply. Brother John died young, and ever afterward Francis spoke of him as a saint, and offered him as a model of a good Friar Minor and the embodiment of simplicity and straightforwardness.

Reading between the lines, it is hard to deny that Brother John was to some degree or other an imbecile. With that in mind, Francis' tenderness for the man looks rather like a deliberate moral choice.

In the year between Bernard's conversion and the journey to Rome (April 1208 till the spring of 1209) Francis' brotherhood grew to the classic dozen, the number of the Apostles.[17] All these men came from Assisi and the surrounding areas. Their social origins were various: The group included both sons of peasants and young noble lords.

Francis saw to it that the time didn't hang heavy on their hands. Shortly after midnight they got up to pray, one Our Father after the other. During the day they helped the peasants with their work in the fields, or cared for the lepers in the nearby leprosarium. In the early evening they had a meal in common (bread, turnips, beans) and soon after sunset they went to sleep.

One time, in the middle of the night, the general snoring of the brethren was interrupted by a piteous groan: "I'm dying!" Gradually everyone woke up. Francis ordered someone to get a light, and then asked who had been complaining so miserably. When the brother identified himself, Francis inquired as to the reason. "I'm starving to death!" he replied.

So as not to put the man to shame, Francis ordered a communal snack, and gave a little speech. "It may happen that one man gets less to eat than another. You have to take your own nature into account. If someone who needs more food imagines he has to vie with someone who needs less, that is nonsense. One should give the body what it needs for life. Gluttony is certainly bad, but exaggerated fasting is even more stupid. So in the future everybody please eat as much as you need."[18]

In this high-strung little group, with its inherent competitiveness, Francis had to speak with the voice of common sense. Note that he lashed out at hysterical asceticism, that strange mode of overcompensating for instinctual repression.[19] Clearly Francis never succumbed to the temptation of viewing "self-denial"—a variety of masochism often confused with heroic piety—as a major goal in life.

SO MAY THIS PIG BE CURSED

This is the story they tell: One time when Francis spent the night in the monastery of St. Verecundus, a newborn lamb was bitten to death in the pen by a pig. When Francis heard of this in the morning, he said, "Ah brother lamb, you innocent animal! May that malicious pig that killed you be cursed!" And in fact the pig fell sick, and died after three days. It was thrown into a ditch, in which it lay for a long time until it was completely shriveled up. The monks of the abbey regarded this as a great miracle and told it to many people.[20]

This is not primarily a story for animal lovers, but for moralists. The innocent lamb represents unprotected meekness, and its arbitrary killing is the quintessence of destructive malice. The pig is cursed vicariously, so to speak, as a sign of rebellion against the ferocity of this wicked world.

Francis lived at a time in which violence was taken for granted, part of everyday life. It belonged to the human scene as much as spitting where one liked. In this connection we need not think just of large military operations where prisoners were mutilated by such popular procedures as cutting off ears and gouging out eyes. In the Middle Ages people lived in a state of permanent guerrilla war, and the knightly upper class behaved like gang leaders, incessantly busy with feuds, raids, and tournaments. Unaccompanied women traveling the highways were unceremoniously raped by stouthearted warriors on horseback. Thrashings were the rule for the slightest infractions, whether by disobedient children or exhausted serfs. The joy of torturing and killing—and this is the crucial point—was a socially accepted joy, which burst forth on market days as well as at public executions.[21] Family feuds, stretching over generations, with bloody vendettas, were familiar to peasants and the urban bourgeoisie alike. In general, the common people were quick to use their knives, and in the absence of a central executive authority, fast-moving robber bands were ever-present plagues. In our emotionally subdued society, with the Red Cross and the SPCA, police squad cars and traffic rules, the entertainment industry, for the most part, takes care of our delight in destruction—unless a world war happens to be running. As well-bred members of the so-called middle class we find it difficult to imagine the degree of untrammeled savagery that marked daily life in Francis' age. One would have to spend a good long time in the black ghettoes of the United States to comprehend how "medieval" ordinary life has remained for rather large segments of modern industrial society.

The moral of this brief digression into the dark side of the Middle Ages is that Francis' sympathy for the dead lamb was a rather exotic sentiment for the period. In one of Celano's stories Francis meets a peasant with two lambs, their legs bound together, on his shoulder. The animals hang head downward and make pitiful cries.

"Why do you tie up these lambs and torment them?"

"I'm bringing them to market, to sell them."

"What will happen to them after that?"

"They'll be slaughtered and eaten."

No, no, that must not be. Shortly before this Francis had borrowed a cloak on account of the cold, and now he suggests a deal to the man. If he gives him the cloak, will the man take the lambs home, feed them, and never harm them? With pleasure! (The lambs are worth much less than the cloak.) We are not told what the peasant thought of the whole thing. One imagines him tapping his forehead as soon as Francis was out of sight.[22]

Francis wrote in his *Testament:* "We used to say a greeting which the Lord revealed to me: 'The Lord give you peace.' "[23] As a matter of fact, Francis made use of this formula from the very beginning. He introduced his sermons with it, and the call to peace and reconciliation made up the core of his public teaching. When Francis sent the first companions off to preach, he directed them to bring the message of peace to the people.

On November 9, 1210, a peace agreement (*carta pacis*) between nobles and commoners was ratified in Assisi, with the co-operation of the Emperor and his partisans.[24] (Otto IV was briefly in Assisi around this time.)

The accommodation reached by the nobles and people of Assisi removed the occasion for war with the city of Perugia. The lords of Sas-sorosso made peace with Assisi, and got their property back. One of them, Leonardo di Gislerio, joined the Friars Minor some years later.

Perugia, as it happened, was the scene of Francis' most colorful sermon on peace. In the year 1213 he spoke in the town square to a large audi-ence. His words were interrupted by a group of young nobles who wanted to work their horses and stage a joust in the piazza. There was a ripple of unrest in the crowd, and people called out to the young lords to stop the disturbance, but to no effect.

Then Francis shouted out, at the top of his voice: "Listen to me now, just this once. Pay close attention, and forget for a moment that I'm from Assisi. We all know that your city has humiliated her neighbors, and so you've become proud and arrogant, a terror to the peasants throughout the region, whose harvests you burn. Haven't you killed enough men already? Do you want to go on playing the mighty lords even here in town? It could well be that the Lord, who lets no evil go unavenged, will kindle riot and war within these walls, to punish you."[25]

As a matter of fact, the story continues, a little later the people of Perugia rose up against the knights and drove them from the city. In their turn the nobles would have—with the help of the Church—laid waste the fields, vineyards, and orchards of the citizens, and there would have been great bloodshed, with numerous victims on either side—had it not been for the peace. Contemporary chronicles tell us that in fact such conflicts did take place in Perugia in the years 1214, 1217, and 1223.

For a pacifist, Francis' tone is remarkably sharp. One need not ponder very long over who are the lambs and who are the pigs to his mind here, or where his anger is aimed, or what is the significance of the name of God in this outburst. The Lord of heaven is not at all well disposed to the earthly lords, he sends them a popular insurrection to punish them for their arrogance.

The Perugia sermon shows us a Francis whose emotional life was evi-dently not limited to pity for little lambs. His profoundly genial tempera-ment is not to be confused with cringing servility, his gentleness is quite compatible with rage. Christian theologians are forever talking about non-violence, and appealing to Jesus, Gandhi, and Martin Luther King to bolster their case.[26] But in the process they suppress a whole dimension of Christian experience, which is as much a part of the Bible as patience in the face of evil: anger over injustice. Tucked away in one's study, one can write learned articles about the precise moment when such anger is enti-tled to take up arms. But in actual experience Christians who have chosen armed resistance after being driven to the limits of their endurance do not greatly trouble themselves about what theology professors have to say—

which is as it should be. The abstract essence of Christianity, as we know, is always being realized in this or that concrete practice. Theologians have stood and, with some exceptions, still prefer to stand on the side of authority. And the practical effect of their plea for meekness has been and is the establishment of a docile and compliant Christianity. We should not be surprised that they claim Francis' peaceable spirit for themselves, as further evidence for the virtue of turning the other cheek.

But the real Francis was no sweet and gentle soul, and his submissiveness was deceptive. In a memorable text which we shall consider in a moment Francis comments on the true meaning of bearing arms. The revealing fashion in which he does this shows us a man much less naïve than the cliché-ridden picture of him so often presented to us.

This is the story they tell: The bishop of Assisi, whom Francis often asked for advice, always gave him a kindly reception. But he liked to tell him, "Your life seems hard to me; it must be burdensome not to have any earthly possessions." Francis would answer, "My lord, if we wanted to possess anything, then we would also need arms to defend ourselves. That is how all the quarrels and conflicts get started, and they are obstacles to love. For this reason we wish to possess nothing."[27]

These few sentences anatomize the god of war with the clarity of an X ray. They show us the skeletal framework of military life, stripped of the pomp and circumstance, as bare-boned economic interest. The grandiose superstructure of armed conflict, with paintings of battles, general staff meetings, wreath-laying for unknown soldiers, marches in review, awarding of medals, and traditional banners—all the splendid display of masculine idiocy collapses before the vision of the meek and amiable Francis.

From the depths of history we hear a man who rode out as a conceited young squire and then suddenly grasped what feeble-minded nonsense he had taken for his goal in life. Francis then passed on the literally disarming power of this insight to his companions and to the people. Poverty and peace imply one another as the two key principles of a kind of Christianity that people have neither thought about nor lived by since Francis' day. Mercury and Mars, the true gods of the Christian West, proved to be stronger, and Francis' more godly God remained a dream. Anyone who still believes in Him, in spite of everything, can see right through the divine comedy of errors that the Church has put on for us since way back when, with its ceremonial swindle on the grand scale. A God who presides over battles and blesses big business is trotted out into the international political arena, and into religious instruction, as the Father of Jesus Christ —for the benefit of Christendom.

Gradually, this spectacle seems to be losing its appeal for the public.

We cannot absolutely rule out the chance that Francis' God might become a functional part of our world after all.

BROTHER JUNIPER

We can never understand the way of life of the first Friars Minor as long as we view it merely as the implementation of certain abstract moral principles. This new manner of living, handed down from Francis to his early companions, never produced that pedantic uniformity so treasured by admirers of order and discipline. Quite the contrary. Among Francis' companions we meet real originals, unique, forthright types with all the rough edges, whose pranks gave rise to many stories. One of these figures was Brother Ginepro, which literally means juniper. Francis said of him, "If only I had a whole forest of such junipers!"[28] The incomparable aroma of the Juniper stories, as we find them in the *Fioretti* and elsewhere, has the lingering flavor of that Franciscan mentality that flourished for a while before it was stifled beneath a flood of papal bulls.

This is the story they tell: When the brothers still lived in the Portiuncula, one day Brother Juniper went to a brother who had fallen sick and asked him if he wanted anything special. The man answered, "A tasty pig's foot, perhaps, would help me recover." No problem—Brother Juniper got a knife from the kitchen, marched out into the forest where many swine were kept for fattening on the acorns, flung himself on one of them, and cut off one of its feet. He washed it, dressed it, cooked it, and then served it, well spiced, to the sick man. He ate it with a vigorous appetite, while Brother Juniper gaily recounted the story of his attack on the piteously squealing beast.

In the meantime the swineherd, who had witnessed the assassination, ran and told the pig's owner all about it. He in turn went immediately to the brothers' settlement, called them thieves, scoundrels, and good-for-nothings, shouting out again and again, "Why did you cut the foot off my pig?" What to do? Francis apologized just to be on the safe side, and insisted that he knew nothing about the whole affair, which naturally did little to appease the man. He swore revenge, and finally disappeared, shouting all kinds of threats, in the direction of Assisi.

This was a serious matter. The man would tell his story everywhere, and the good name of the brothers would be finished. Suddenly, Francis thought of something. He sought out Brother Juniper, and casually asked him if he had by any chance cut the foot off a pig recently. Yes, of course! With a smile of satisfaction Brother Juniper told Francis of his charitable deed. "And if I had had to cut the feet off a hundred pigs, God would surely have approved." Francis replied in a fury, "Now you run as fast as you can after that man, throw yourself at his feet, confess your guilt, and promise him complete restoration!"

Brother Juniper was astounded by this order. He stood there in a state of shock, wondering how anybody could get so excited about a kind-hearted act like that. Then he said: "Have no doubt about it, dear Francis. I'll give the man full satisfaction. But what I can't understand is all this fuss about a pig, which really doesn't belong to the man, but to God, and moreover might well be put to such a good use."

Brother Juniper hurried after the man and caught up to him. But he was still as incensed as ever, the last shred of his patience gone. Brother Juniper tried to make him understand how he had come to cut the pig's foot off, and spoke with such zeal and enthusiasm, as though he had quite seriously done the man a great service, for which he deserved a rich reward. The man's only answer was to fly into another towering rage and to call Brother Juniper a dreamer, a blockhead, a rascal, and a crook. But the brother paid no heed to these insults; he even seemed to take pleasure in them. He thought to himself that the man must not have understood him properly; otherwise he would have had no reason, in Juniper's eyes, for anger, but only for joy. So he repeated the story one more time, threw himself around the man's neck, kissed him, and assured him that he had done everything out of the purest love. Then he asked him for the rest of the pig. His simplicity and sincerity were so great that the man was overwhelmed. And now it was his turn to throw himself to the ground before the brother and declare with tears in his eyes that he had done the brothers wrong. He went and got the pig, slaughtered it, roasted it, and with the greatest emotion carried it to the brothers' table at the Portiuncula, to make up for the injustice that he had done them.[29]

Brother Juniper outlived Francis by more than thirty years. (He died in Rome in the year 1258.)[30] He saw the building of a mighty basilica in Assisi, together with a monastery, in Francis' honor. They let Brother Juniper live in the monastery, an old man who didn't understand the world anymore and as usual gave away everything that wasn't positively nailed down—Mass vestments, expensive books, and church ornaments. Because of him they were in the habit of keeping such valuable objects under lock and key. Once, around Christmastime, Brother Juniper caused yet another scandal.

This is the story they tell: The sacristan had told Brother Juniper to keep an eye on the church while the sacristan went to supper. Hardly had he left when a poor woman came up to Brother Juniper and begged for an alms. Over the altar that Juniper was supposed to be watching the pious Friars Minor had hung a gold ornament with a little silver bell of some value on it, for the Christmas celebration. Brother Juniper cut off the bell and gave it to the woman, who quickly disappeared.

The sacristan immediately noticed that it was missing, and was aghast. "Don't be upset about the pair [sic] of little bells," Juniper calmly told him. "I gave them to a poor woman, who surely can put them to good use." The superior general of the Friars Minor—they already had one of those—was staying in the monastery at the time. The brother sacristan ran to him and told him the whole story. Thereupon all the brothers were summoned together, and the superior general delivered a stern lecture to Brother Juniper. As he spoke, he grew so angry that he shouted louder and louder, and finally grew hoarse.

Brother Juniper hardly troubled himself over his superior's scolding. He paid no attention until the man was too hoarse to continue speaking. Then he left the monastery, went into town, and asked the people at the first house he came to, to cook him a plate of gruel with butter. That took a while, and in the meantime the brothers had long since retired to their cells. Juniper lit a candle and knocked on the superior general's door. "What is it?" "Father, when you rebuked me before on account of my error, you strained your voice and got all hoarse. I've found a remedy for it: I had this good soup made for you. If you have some, it'll clear your chest and throat." The superior was annoyed at being awakened at that hour of the night, and irritated by the request, which must have sounded like mockery, angrily told Brother Juniper to get out. "Father, if you don't want any soup, then at least hold the candle for me. I'll have it in place of you." Then at last the man realized that he was being neither mocked nor mortified, and spooned his soup together with Brother Juniper.[31]

The last Juniper story to be told here took place in Rome. The Friars Minor had a house there, and as soon as they heard that Brother Juniper was on the way, they went out to meet him—one of the few surviving early companions of the now dead Francis. The little procession attracted many curiosity seekers, and when Brother Juniper finally arrived there, he found himself face to face with a reverential mob.

Nearby two children were seesawing on a board they had laid over a beam. Juniper went over and asked if he could play with them. While Brother Juniper swung up and down, the brothers came up and greeted him deferentially. Then they waited, already somewhat embarrassed, to escort him to the monastery. The crowd finally started to get restless, and critical remarks were heard: "What kind of a numskull is he?" After a while the last curious spectators had vanished, and the brothers too began to grasp that they had gone about it the wrong way. Only then did Brother Juniper get off the seesaw and continue on his way, unnoticed and quite alone, until he finally reached the monastery.[32]

He is supposed to have died soon afterward, this legendary Christian and companion of Francis. With him the life of the Friars Minor, as Francis had wanted it to be, came to an end. It was another story with the silent sisterhood, which began at San Damiano, with Clare, the lady of Francis' heart, as the next chapter will relate.

VIII

IN WINTER
WHEN THE ROSES BLOOM

FRANCIS and Clare were lovers.[1] This sentence from my book *Mysticism for Beginners* has been pronounced "a falsehood" by the *Library News* of the Austrian Borromeo Society (Catholic). On one hand, this is immaterial. The bulletins of the Borromeo Society are read chiefly by parochial librarians in Austria. On the other hand, we can learn something from this official reprimand. It's an example of that Western hostility to physical pleasure, still going strong eight hundred years after Francis, which even today bids little girls to sit with their knees pressed together. Francis submitted to it, with altogether rabid enthusiasm. His love story is one of suppressed desire, and for that reason quite up-to-date.

A GIRL OF GOOD FAMILY

Clare spent a good deal of her childhood outside her native town of Assisi.[2] Her father, Favarone di Offreduccio, belonged to the family of the lords of Coriano, and like most of the nobles he fled to Perugia at the beginning of hostilities between the two sides. He could not return to Assisi until 1205. Clare was eleven years old at the time.

When she was fourteen, the great scene took place between father Bernardone and his son, with Francis standing naked in front of the episcopal church. Could Clare have witnessed it? In any case they would have told her all about it, and about the amazing change that had come over Lord Bernard, how he had given away all his worldly goods to the poor and gone off with that strange fellow Francis to live down in the valley in the Portiuncula forest, like the lowliest beggar.

All this happened, as we have already seen, in April 1208. Clare was then fourteen, and hence of marriageable age. Thomas of Celano, who also wrote a "legend" about her life, mentions the plan to betroth her to a young nobleman of her station.[3] But Clare was not interested, Celano adds, and the matter was postponed for one or two years. Had she already fallen in love with Francis? We don't know. But in those days there were certainly a whole series of solid reasons why an intelligent young lady might view the state of holy matrimony with extreme suspicion.

One of the few intimate accounts of the life of a medieval woman comes from a man named Guibert de Nogent.[4] Abbot of a small provincial monastery in France, he wrote his memoirs—a great rarity in that age— around 1115, and in them his mother plays a leading role. This woman had entered into matrimony while "hardly of marriageable age." (According to canon law, girls could be married at twelve, and boys at fourteen.) From her early childhood the girl suffered from an oppressive anxiety over sin, and the fear of an early death. For a few years these prematurely wedded children were unable to consummate the marriage, which brought on continual pressure from their noble relatives. "Certain rich men" made a game of giving the girl practical lessons in sex education, and the relatives of the boyish groom continually threatened to dissolve the marriage and send the girl off to some other family members living far away.

Finally the spell was broken when efforts to initiate the boy-husband into the mysteries of intercourse finally succeeded with the help of a maid. Then a number of children came into the world, in rapid succession. In giving birth to Guibert the young mother underwent such a long and excruciating labor that his father made a pious vow before the delivery: If everything went well, he would have the child enter monastic life.

When Guibert was eight months old, he lost his father, and his mother took good care not to give in to her relatives' demands and marry a second time. As long as she remained a widow, she would have control of her late husband's property and the right to bring up the children as she saw fit. She was something like twenty years old at the time.

From his mother Guibert received a strait-laced, puritanical upbringing with regard to sex, which was no surprise, given her past experience. At the age of six Guibert had to study hard under the supervision of a cleric: "While others of my age wandered everywhere at will . . . I, hedged in by constant restraints and dressed in my clerical garb, would sit and look at the troops of players like a beast awaiting sacrifice."

Needless to say, he was often beaten by the reverend teacher, who went too far, even for his mother: "[Once] she threw off my inner garment and saw my little arms blackened and the skin of my back everywhere puffed with the cuts from the twigs." Weeping hot tears, his mother voiced her horror at this kind of preparation for religious life. Nonetheless, at thirteen Guibert entered the monastery, and his mother, tortured by her dread of sin, chose to live as a hermit, likewise behind monastery walls. Guibert complains of her decision: "She knew that I should be utterly an orphan with no one at all on whom to depend, for . . . there was no one to give me the loving care a little child needs at such an age; . . . Although she knew that I would be condemned to such neglect, yet Thy love and fear, O God, hardened her heart . . . the tenderest in all the world, that it might not be tender to her own soul's harm." With that astonishing statement an aggrieved son recalls his mother, whose only wish at age thirty was never to see a man for the rest of her days.

In the Middle Ages this was by no means an isolated attitude,[5] at least not among upper-class women, who could manage to get into a halfway decent convent by furnishing the required dowry. One might well compare the sense of relief with which this young widow disappeared into a monastery—and thus eluded her importunate noble relatives who were greedy for her fortune and hence pressuring her to remarry—with the feelings of someone who has narrowly escaped death; for every marriage meant a succession of births, and every confinement brought the very real danger of death not only for the newborn child but for the mother as well. The percentage of women who died in childbirth was extremely high then, even among the upper class. And, on the average, one out of every three newborn babies died shortly after birth.

While women found the joys of married life considerably diminished under these circumstances, they were not exactly pampered either when it came to their consorts. Naturally, they were never allowed to choose a husband for themselves, but had to take what was put in front of them. Equally common was marriage at the age of twelve or fourteen, and by no means always to someone the same age or even half as shy. Often it was an older widower, who took possession of the child on the wedding night, after hearty eating and drinking, before the eyes of witnesses. It would surely be an error to speak of an age of courtly romance simply because a number of contemporary artists tried to promote politer behavior toward women. In reality, Francis' period was characterized by considerable masculine brutality, in love as in other things, and we ought not to assume *a priori* that the flight of many upper-class women into the world of divine love was due to the influence of heavenly grace. It was a question rather of simple disgust at the crude assaults of a grunting mate, who probably smelled of horse sweat.

Something like this, we may imagine, lay behind the noble Clare's personal decision not to marry, and the few troubadour songs and chivalric tales that she may have known made no difference to the situation. If anything they sharpened the aristocratic young girl's critical capacity vis-à-vis the holy yoke of matrimony.

In general we are safe in assuming that the noble wives and daughters of Francis' time were as a group more sensitive and cultured than their husbands and brothers. In any case, among the upper class the number of women who could read and write was greater than that of the men, who, unless they were clerics, were busy with more red-blooded activities. All things considered, the fact that Clare took an interest in a life of virginity says more about her intelligence than about her piety.

In the winter of 1210 Rufino di Scipione di Offreduccio exchanged his elegant wardrobe for a patchy tunic, and joined up with Francis. Rufino— we have already heard of him—was a cousin of Clare's. There were no secrets between the two of them, and Rufino told Francis of his beautiful cousin's inclination toward religious life. Clare was in fact extraordinarily beautiful.

At the time of her first interview with Francis she was sixteen years old. Naturally they met quite secretly, and in accordance with the rules of courtly etiquette,[6] Clare came accompanied by a relative, Bona di Guelfuccio, and Francis appeared with a man named Philip, whom the companions called "the tall one" and who was of noble extraction.

In a similar fashion Tristan and Iseult arranged their secret meetings, in all honor, as it were. And there, to be sure, the similarity between these figures of romance and our lovers ends. Francis and Clare did not talk of lofty passion, but of how a woman could live like Jesus Christ.

We shall be careful not to look at Clare from a romantic nineteenth-century point of view, as a dreamy visionary. This young woman knew very well, first of all, that she didn't want under any circumstances to get married. Second, being evidently by nature a radical, she distrusted the traditional way of life in feudal monasteries as an all-too-comfortable compromise between denying the world and the need for security. Third, Clare had gotten enough information about Francis' program to come to their first rendezvous with a well-considered proposal: I want to live the way you do, as your companion.

Endeavors to create a common life, without marriage, for religiously minded men and women are as old as Christianity itself.[7] Even if they were doomed to fail, these attempts are an interesting and informative subject in their own right. I know of no modern monograph that deals with this archetypal Christian alternative to the ordinary sexual games, although it was tried for centuries, from Ireland to Syria. The little one can find on the subject seldom goes beyond voyeuristic remarks about lecherous monks and nymphomaniac nuns, with allusions to the skeletons of babies occasionally exhumed in the neighborhood of convents. Modern scholars repeat all the morbid insinuations against sexually mixed heretical communities that we find in the *Acta* of the Inquisition. They don't make the slightest effort to sympathize with the peculiar group dynamics that inevitably arose in the course of protests against the family mania of Western society.

Similar reports of fellowships of apostolically minded men and women have come down to us from Francis' time. One contemporary of his, named Burchard, wrote a chronicle around 1220 in which he speaks of the Waldensians. In the text that follows, Burchard gives an account of events that took place in Rome around 1210: "We saw at that time some of their number . . . and these petitioned that their sect might be confirmed and privileged by the Holy See. In truth, by their own account, they undertook the way of life of the apostles, wishing to possess nothing and to have no settled home, traveling about through the villages and towns. But the lord Pope (Innocent III) took exception to them as there were some superstitious elements in their way of life: They cut off their shoes above their feet and walked, as it were, barefoot; also, while they wore a kind of hood as if they were members of a religious order, they did not shave the hair of their head other than in the way laymen do. This also seemed reprehensible in them, that men and women walked together along the road and often lodged in the same house, and it was said of them that they sometimes slept together in bed; yet they asserted that all they did was derived from the apostles."[8]

Francis had been very fortunate that his fellowship consisted only of men, when he walked to Rome in 1209 to get papal approval for the group. Had there been a few enthusiastic virgins like Clare among his followers, not even Jesus in person could have gotten him a permit to preach.

But now, two years later, Francis stood face to face with total feminine determination in the shape of a young noblewoman. Francis could easily conjure up a vivid picture of the beating he would get from Clare's relatives if he tried to admit the girl without more ado into his fellowship. Francis also knew that in this case he couldn't hope for any kind of support from the Church.

Yet we can't imagine Francis being so narrow-minded as to reject out of hand the idea of a woman realizing his vision. Didn't Jesus have women among his followers?

All that provided Clare and Francis with quite a lot of material for conversation. They had to get together more often, and as time went on Clare doubtless grew more urgent. Thus the year 1211 passed, and it was winter again.

This is the story they tell: One day Clare and Francis walked from Spello to Assisi, with great unrest in their hearts. For on their way they had entered a house, where they had asked for and been given a little bread and water. While they were there, they had drawn looks of malice from the people, and were forced to endure all sorts of whispering, with jokes and veiled allusions. So they went on their way in silence. It was the cold season of the year, and the land all around was covered with snow. Soon the horizon began to grow dark. Then Francis said: "Did you understand what the people were saying about us?"

Clare gave no answer. Her heart contracted as if pressed by pincers, and she felt close to tears. "It's time to part," Francis said finally. Then Clare fell on her knees in the middle of the road. After a while she got hold of herself, stood up, and went on with her head lowered, leaving Francis behind.

The road led through a forest. All at once she lost the strength to leave him like this, without hope or comfort, without a word of farewell.

She waited.

"When will we see each other again?"

"In summer when the roses bloom."

Then something wonderful happened. All of a sudden it seemed to both of them as if there were countless roses all around—on the branches of the juniper bushes and on the frost-covered hedges. Recovering from her astonishment Clare rushed up, plucked a bunch of roses, and laid them in Francis' hands. From that day Clare and Francis were never separated again.[9]

The moment when Clare and Francis finally recognize that they love one another is presented with a great deal of delicacy in this popular story. The cold wintertime suggests, accurately enough, the circumstances then controlling relationships between men and women. And the roses? What they mean is something one never learns in religion class.

In the spring of 1212, more than a year after the first interview between Clare and Francis, the pace of our story picks up.[10] Clare's decisiveness and Francis' caution reached a sort of compromise, and the bishop of Assisi may also have been consulted before the two made their move. There was no headlong rush; evidently they had planned it all very thoughtfully.

They had chosen Palm Sunday as the date for Clare's running away— the beginning of the holiest week of the year, and a very sensible choice. In the morning Clare went with her family to Solemn High Mass and received a branch of palm, pressed into her hand by Bishop Guido. The rest of the day passed one way or another, as usual, until bedtime.

Pacifica di Guelfuccio, with whom Clare disappeared from her parents' house later that night, was not only her near relative and true friend. She was also a confidante of Clare's mother, Ortolana, with whom she had undertaken a pilgrimage to the Holy Land. The suspicion that Clare's mother was in on the whole thing has something to recommend it. As a matter of fact, Mother Ortolana later joined Clare in the monastery—where we shall also find Pacifica, together with Clare's two sisters, Agnes and Beatrice.

In other words, out of the dark palazzo of the Offreducci in the cathedral quarter of Assisi came an exodus of women, with Clare leading the way. The three noble sisters, with their mother and cousin, gladly left behind their luxurious home, and left alone inside it the lords of creation, to lead, from now on, a comfortless existence. The freedom from males, at table and in bed, which they purchased at this price must have been worth a good deal to them.

Francis and his entire brotherhood were waiting for Clare and Pacifica, as arranged, down in the Portiuncula forest. By torchlight Clare laid aside her various pieces of jewelry, bracelets, and combs, abandoned her hair to the brothers' shears, and finally vanished behind a bush to change clothes. Dressed in a tunic with a rope around her waist, she gave Francis her word of consent, a fine, free choice of the things he stood for.

Then the whole group marched two miles farther to the convent of San Paolo, where Clare was deposited for the time being, with an eye on her good reputation—a clever move, as soon became apparent.

The men of the Offreducci house took four days to figure out where Clare was staying. On Good Friday morning, a day when any kind of feuding or violence was unthinkable, seven men on horseback appeared at the little monastery of San Paolo and asked to speak with Clare. The scene that followed had a certain operatic quality. The abbess of the monastery, which followed the Benedictine rule and was inhabited by noble ladies, was thoroughly versed in questions of aristocratic etiquette. So when the Offreducci delegation tried to get Clare back by representing her nocturnal flight as bad behavior befitting only a servant and an insult to her family's honor, they got an icy response. Had Clare perhaps spent the night in the forest?

Well, not actually.

Then, gentlemen, I think it would be better if you would no longer disturb the peace of the monastery on Good Friday.

In his fury over this rebuff, it seems that one of the men reached for Clare, simply to drag her away. But she broke loose, ran into the convent chapel, and clung to the altar there, thus claiming her right to asylum. When the men followed her and threatened to use force after all, she threw back the hood of her robe to let them see.

She had her hair cut off!

That at long last decided the company in Clare's favor, for with her head cropped she was subject to Church law, and not even the proud Offreducci wanted a serious confrontation with the power of the Church. They rode off, cheated of their quarry.

But Clare too wanted to go somewhere else, to get out of that all too aristocratic environment. Francis, Philip the tall, and Brother Bernard made arrangements with the women of the monastery of Panzo, a modest convent in the neighborhood, on the slopes of Mount Subasio, and brought Clare over there, after the Easter holy days.

Hardly had she gotten there when the next scandal took place. Clare's younger sister, the fourteen-year-old Agnes, also ran away from home, and hid with Clare in the monastery. The worthy Offreducci rode after her, twelve men strong. There was violence. They seized hold of Agnes and carried her off, weeping and screaming. But suddenly, Celano tells us, ready as ever to believe in miracles, her body became so heavy that they had to let her go. Then Clare appeared and ordered the men to leave Agnes alone. Celano reports: "People saw how these rapacious wolves, who a moment before thirsted only for blood and sought to tear the pious virgin from the arms of the Lord, suddenly grew gentle as sheep, released their prey, and went quietly home."[11]

One may well attribute the fact that little Agnes felt so heavy all of a sudden to Mother Ortolana and Cousin Pacifica's successful exertions to get help from Bishop Guido. In any event the bishop was prepared to put the chapel of San Damiano at the Offreducci girl's disposal, as a monastic shelter for the runaway. Clare was obviously informed about the plans that were afoot, and when she cried to her approaching uncles and cousins that a holy society of sisters was being founded, with the bishop's approval and along the lines of Francis' brotherhood (and he was under the Pope's protection), then Agnes was saved.

Francis personally cut Agnes' hair, thus making her Poor Clare No. 2. Pacifica too had her hair cut and slipped like Clare and Agnes into the Franciscan uniform. With the removal to San Damiano the little community of women now had a roof over their head. Francis had his two fundamental principles from the Bible written out on paper, the bishop put his seal on it, and soon everything was in order.

Later Clare's mother, Ortolana, and older sister Beatrice joined the migration to San Damiano. Over the next few years other women and girls from the upper classes of Assisi swelled the ranks of Clare's sisterhood. (For reasons of canon law Clare took the title of abbess.)

The poor women of San Damiano lived by working with their hands and by begging. They took care of the lepers, and they sang their psalms in the chapel Francis had restored. For centuries the handful of rooms in the little monastery kept all their original furnishings unchanged, in keeping with the practice of the "Poor Clares." You can inspect them to this day. One look at the dormitory and the dining room is enough to dispel any doubts about the privations of their life, as Clare first arranged it.

The aura of Francis' presence persists at San Damiano, in contrast to the big Franciscan operation up in Assisi, with its tourist buses and souvenir stands. The visitor sees little of the nuns who live today at San Damiano, but in the church where Francis heard the voice of Christ the flowers are still fresh.

HEAVENLY LOVE

The relationship between Clare and Francis was admired by their contemporaries as a kind of grand drama. We find a good example of this theatricality in a highly sublimated story from the *Fioretti*.

Often, we are told, Francis went to visit St. Clare and imparted pious counsel to her. But he always denied her fondest wish—to share a meal with him. His companions finally spoke to Francis about it: "It seems to us that this severity is incompatible with divine charity, not to grant a trifle such as a meal with Sister Clare, who is such a holy virgin and beloved of God. All the more so seeing as she abandoned the riches and splendor of this world upon hearing your preaching. Truly, even if she were asking a greater favor than this one, you ought not to deny it to the spiritual shoot that you yourself planted." To which Francis said, "So you think that I should grant her request?"

"Yes, it would be well to give her this joy and comfort."

It continues in this vein for a while, until finally Clare is allowed to go on the little excursion from San Damiano, escorted, naturally, by a companion and in broad daylight. Francis set the table on the bare earth, as was the custom. Then they all squatted on the ground, in strict observance of their formal etiquette: "When it was time, Francis sat down with Clare, and Francis' comrade with Clare's companion. Then the other brothers modestly took their places."

Francis, the story goes on, began at once to speak of God, so lovingly, in such a lofty, wonderful way that the entire company immediately fell into ecstasy. "As they sat there in ecstasy, with their eyes and hands lifted up to heaven, the people of Assisi and the surrounding area saw the church, the monastery, and the entire Portiuncula forest burst into flame, as if a mighty fire were burning there. When they ran down to put out the fire, there were no flames at all to be seen. Only Clare and Francis sat there, in a circle with the others, carried away in spirit. Then the people realized that the fire had been divine and not earthly, that God had caused it to appear in wondrous wise, as a visible token of the fire of heavenly love that blazed in the souls of these holy brothers and sisters."

The prejudice here is obvious. The flames of the love between Francis and Clare, clearly seen by the population, are supposed to be taken as a purely heavenly passion, and not as earthly tenderness. The split between spirit and flesh, brought on by the radical denial of the latter, was by Francis' time one of the fundamental principles of the Christian West. Francis and Clare may belong to each other exclusively "in God."

With an edifying glance heavenward we are informed in the end: "When St. Francis and St. Clare after some time recovered their senses, along with the others, they felt so refreshed with spiritual nourishment that they scarcely touched the earthly kind." Clare disappeared in the direction of San Damiano, modestly accompanied by Francis' companions, "full of consolation."[12]

And with an empty stomach, one might add.

Thomas of Celano, too, in his first life of Francis, reaches deep down into his bag of unctuous phrases as soon as he comes to speak of Clare and the good ladies in San Damiano: "This is that blessed and hallowed place, where the glorious society and outstanding Order of poor women and holy virgins made its happy start some six years after the conversion of St. Francis, and through the influence of this very saint. Here in the person of Lady Clare, a native of the town of Assisi, was that most precious and mighty stone, the foundation on which all the other stones were laid. She was of noble lineage, but ennobled still more by divine grace, a virgin according to the flesh, perfectly chaste according to the spirit, in age yet a girl, but a venerable woman in the maturity of her soul."

And so forth. Under seven headings Celano enumerates the precious virtues that bloomed so richly in San Damiano, among which, for example, was silence: "Some of the sisters lost the habit of speaking, to such a degree that when necessity forced them to speak, they could hardly remember how to form the appropriate words."[13]

Celano becomes still more penetrating in his second biography, where he expatiates on Francis' attitude toward women in general; for example: "Women made him so uncomfortable that one might have thought his conduct toward them was not dictated by caution or the desire to set an example, but by horror or fright. When their immoderate loquacity gave him offense, he broke off speaking and with humbly lowered eyes called on silence for help. But sometimes he lifted his eyes to heaven, as though to find an answer there to their earthly chatter."[14]

According to Celano, Francis never even looked at a woman save in exceptional cases, and he never tired of warning his companions against the "honey-sweet" poison of familiarity with women. Even toward the poor women at San Damiano Francis exercised the very greatest restraint, was extremely reluctant to visit them, and established the rule of assigning only outspoken woman-haters to go on the many necessary errands to San Damiano.[15] In Celano's version Francis says that whoever has regular business with the sisters should always be on his guard, "like birds drawing near to snares."[16]

Celano's personal flight from women was quite unequivocal. As clearly behooved a faithful member of the Friars Minor in his day, he held all dealings with women as a pure waste of time. As he summed it up, "Nobody comes to holiness by looking at them."[17]

Of greater weight than Celano's remarks is a passage from Francis' Rule of 1223 (approved by the Pope): "I firmly command all the brothers to have no discussions with women which would arouse suspicion, nor give them counsel; they shall not enter convents of nuns, save only those brothers to whom the Holy See has granted special license. Nor shall they form close friendships with men or women, so that no scandal arise between brothers or on their account for any reason."[18]

Here, three years before his death, Francis himself lays down the law like Moses, with solemnly lifted finger. As we can tell from its style, the final wording of the text owes something to the gentle pressure and generous editorial assistance of the papal Curia. But, when all is said and done, Francis did agree to insert the monastic taboo against women into his Rule. Perhaps people told him one or other scandalous story of the all too friendly behavior of some friars with sweet-tempered nuns and ladies in need of comforting. Then too, a legal lock had to be put on that ancient temptation threatening friendships between cloistered males, if only on the basis of Church administrators' thousand years of experience with monastic life.

The only interesting question in this connection is: Did Francis—a middle-aged man who was impartial in matters of love—authorize the legalistic ban on physical contact purely out of political calculation and a pragmatic estimate of the situation? Or did he himself fall captive to these prohibitions, led astray by his innate erotic timidity? The whole character of his relationship with Clare makes the second choice much more likely.

Celano would have us believe that his saint had carried on wildly in his younger days: "While this man, with youthful passion, waxed hot in his sins, and the promptings of this dangerous age drove him with unusual force to indulge his youthful desires, which he, aroused as he was by the poison of the ancient serpent, could not subdue, the vengeance of God, or rather God's mercy, suddenly came upon him."[19]

We could allow Francis the modest pleasures of a hasty coupling with some peasant girl, without making a fuss over it, if Celano were a reliable chronicler on this point. But this is surely not the case. His description of the sins of Francis' youth follows a preconceived pattern: first the falling away from God, then a sudden conversion, then superior holiness.[20] (Celano may possibly have been inspired by Augustine's *Confessions*, which was much read at the time.) Celano needs a depraved young man for theological purposes—to be able to paint Francis' miraculous transformation into a true prodigy of virtue with all the more striking colors. From this imaginative reconstruction we learn, unfortunately, nothing at all about Francis' real desires.

Celano's stories about Francis' "carnal temptations" provide scarcely any more help in this regard. Here is a sample: "The devil also visited him with an especially strong temptation to unchastity. But, as soon as he was aware of it, the blessed Father laid aside his habit, scourged himself most severely with a rope, and said: 'There now, Brother Ass, it serves you right, you have to cringe beneath the whip!' But when despite the flogging the temptation would not go away, although all his limbs were marked with welts, he opened the door to his cell, went out into the garden, and threw himself naked into the deep snow. Then he took some snow and formed seven clumps out of it. He laid these before him and began to speak to his body in this fashion: 'See here, this large clump is your wife. Two of these four are your sons and two are your daughters. The other two are your servant and maid whom you need to work for you. And now hurry up and clothe them all, otherwise they must die of cold. But if caring for all of them is too much of a burden for you, then bend all your zeal to serve the one Lord!' At once the devil left in shame, and the saint returned to his cell, praising God. A companion, who just then was saying his prayers, managed to observe the entire scene, because the moon was shining rather brightly. When the saint later learned that the brother had watched him in the night, it grieved him greatly, and he ordered the man not to tell anyone about it as long as he lived."[21]

This episode has a certain sociological interest in that it shows that masturbation was already strongly tabooed for persons consecrated to God, but that is about all. Francis had undoubtedly internalized this prohibition. He saves himself from lust by his game with the snow family.

Did he think of Clare that time?

Probably not. When he first met her, he had already decided against family life, and Clare didn't want to get married either. Even had they been inclined to seek the joys of love, there was, outside of marriage, no socially accepted arrangement for free affection between two independent people. Above all, however, both of them were searching for a tenderness they could not find in the bourgeois models of so-called love. In this they resembled the troubadours and their ladies, who really existed in Francis' time, and not just in books.

Francis' rage against "Brother Ass" (i.e., his own physical nature), with its marked aggressiveness toward sexual appetites, this ferocity toward himself, had no connection with his feelings for Clare. It was one of the possible reflexes on the part of a bourgeois individual whose capacity for pleasure had been impaired to begin with. We shall have to restrain our curiosity about the unsublimated remnants of Francis' masculinity.

This is the story they tell: One day Francis and Leo came to Siena and got a very cool reception there. Francis was not bothered by this: As he walked on after dusk, he thought of sweet Assisi, where he had left Clare and his companions behind. He knew that the pious virgin was exposed to great adversity because of her love for poverty. His concern that Clare might not persist in her good intentions so depressed him that he felt as if his feet were sinking into the earth. Exhausted, he walked over to a spring by the side of the road. The fresh water gushed out of a pipe into a trough, where it formed a clear, smooth surface. For a long time Francis stood bent over the water. Then he suddenly raised his head and spoke joyfully to Brother Leo:

"What do you think I've seen in the water?"

"The reflection of the moon."

"No, Leo. I didn't see the moon in the spring. But by the grace of the Lord I caught sight of the true face of our Sister Clare, and it was so pure and shining with holy joy that all my cares vanished at once, and I am certain that at this very hour Clare is savoring the deep joy God gives to his favorites."[22]

Francis' tenderness for Clare radiates from this story. Here is a man who knows that he is loved, without a doubt, and this knowledge brings him happiness. Their zeal for a common cause—namely, the radical appropriation of the Gospel—lifts Francis and Clare's relationship out of the sphere of purely private happiness, without letting it be swallowed up in the dreariness of sheer practicality. To be sure, the pair saw little of each other once Clare disappeared into San Damiano. But Francis did spend the next-to-last summer of his life with Clare, when he was a seriously ill man beyond the reach of slander. In the song that he wrote then and sang to the poor women in San Damiano, the word *amore* appears but once, and there it means divine love, manifested in forgiveness.

Clare was surely not offended by this.

AS A STRANGER AND PILGRIM

Francis' concern that Clare might one day weaken and submit to the discreet coercion of Church authorities in the matter of absolute poverty proved to be unfounded. Till the day she died Clare defended the principle of an unsecured life against the realism of her papal and episcopal protectors, who wanted to insure the sisters at least the minimum for subsistence, by having them keep the right to collect income from real estate.

In the year 1228 the Pope came to Assisi for the ceremonies of Francis' canonization. This Holy Father, already familiar to us as the cardinal protector of the Friars Minor, sat on the chair of Peter from 1227 to 1241, under the name of Gregory IX.

He visited Clare in San Damiano. By this time there were already twenty-four convents of Poor Clares in Italy. They lived according to a rule from the year 1218, written by that very Cardinal Ugolino, who now wished to chat a bit with Clare "about heavenly things and the way of salvation," as the *Fioretti* piously notes.[23]

Clare was not at all in agreement with the Ugolinian rule. It had a Benedictine formulation, and hence was clearly feudalistic in character.

The following passage comes from Celano's account of Clare's conversation with the Pope: "When the Pope advised her, on account of the troubled times, to accept certain properties, which he himself generously offered her, she bravely resisted and refused to give her consent under any circumstances. The Pope asked, 'If you have misgivings on account of your vow, then we shall release you from it.' "[24]

Clare: "Holy Father, for the last time, I have no wish to be dispensed from following Christ." Then she went on the attack, and asked for the official privilege never to have to make use of guaranteed revenues. The Pope laughed and said he thought no one had ever requested such a privilege from him.[25]

But the Pope found Clare was made of adamant. The text of the bull she obtained from him has been preserved. Since the formulary in the papal chancellery contained no models for the unusual text, the Pope dictated it himself: "As it is clear that being deprived of the most necessary things does not frighten you, and that He who feeds the birds of heaven and clothes the lilies of the fields will not fail to give you food and clothing, We accede to your request and authorize you, by Apostolic Grace, to live in extreme poverty. You are further authorized by this brief never to be forced to accept any possessions whatsoever."[26] In exceptional cases, as we see, one may actually manage to obtain papal permission to live as a Christian.

Clare was by no means satisfied with this limited victory. She waited for the next Pope.[27] This was Innocent IV, a restlessly busy man, absolutely unscrupulous in politics, and a brilliant legal mind. The new Rule, which Clare got from his chancellery in 1247, did free the Poor Clares from certain Benedictine principles, but otherwise it did not suit Clare's taste.[28] So she wrote a Rule of her own. In it we read: "The Sisters are not to acquire houses, lands, nor anything else, for their use, but they are to serve

God as strangers and pilgrims on this earth, in humility and poverty, confidently having recourse to alms. Let them take good care not to be ashamed of this! The Lord himself became a poor man for our sake here on earth."[29]

Innocent IV also paid his respects to Clare. When she asked him to grant her absolution for her sins, he said, "Would to God I needed it as little as you do."[30] On August 9, 1253, in Perugia, the Pope signed a bull confirming Clare's Rule.[31] The next day she held it in her hands.

Then she died, almost immediately afterward, on August 11. She had gotten what she wanted. Her determination is evident from the fact that during the last twenty years of her life she was often sick and confined to bed. Her last words were: "Lord God, praise be to You for creating me."[32]

IX

TEN HAPPY YEARS

IN THE operetta *Die Fledermaus* (music by Johann Strauss; it was first performed in Vienna, 1874) we find the following lines explaining the prerequisite for happiness in modern industrial society:

> *Glücklich ist,*
> *wer vergisst,*
> *was nicht mehr zu ändern ist.*

(Happy is he who forgets what can no longer be changed.) This remarkable refrain had its première at the beginning of a twenty-one-year economic crisis. (The slump lasted from 1873 to 1895, with Germany and Austria especially hard hit.)

Further crises have occurred since that time, and the suspicion that they are as much a part of our economic system as the "Amen" at the end of a prayer has now hardened into certainty. Nevertheless, the message is continually pounded into our heads that the peculiar kind of prosperity enjoyed by the "Western world" must be construed as real happiness.

We have been trained to look upon "security"—a pension plan, yearly vacations, health insurance, a car, a comfortably furnished home, and thirty-five hundred calories a day—as the quintessence of what is worth striving for in this life. Because of this the idea that Francis, who had none of that, might have been happy is rather hard to believe.

A Japanese TV journalist, whom the police recently ejected from her jungle hiding place on a South Seas island because her residency permit had run out, would not have had this difficulty. She had gotten so tired of her old life that she fled from the big city to the loneliness of the forest, where for several months she was completely content. Her only contact with the outside world was a farmer who occasionally brought her food.[1]

This Japanese woman is not the only one. Children, adolescents, and adults are forever running away from home. The impulse that sends them off is related to Francis' own mentality. Francis expressly praised a companion who never wanted to stay in one place longer than a month, and he himself consistently avoided setting himself up in a house anywhere.[2] In the ten years discussed in this and the following chapter Francis spent most of the time on the road. His gaiety is connected to the fact that he had no house to put in order.

This is the story they tell: Once Francis was walking through Tuscany with Brother Masseo. As they went on their way, they came to a crossroads whence one could continue on either to Siena or to Florence or to Arezzo.

"Which way should we go?"

Francis answered: "Whichever one God wants."

"And how shall we recognize God's will?"

"Turn around in a circle, the way the children do, and don't stop until I tell you."

So Masseo spun around, and because of the dizziness in his head, which usually sets in from doing this, he fell on the ground several times. But since Francis didn't say anything, Masseo staggered up again and went on spinning in a circle. Finally, after he had spun a tremendously long time, Francis called out: "Stop!"

Masseo immediately stopped.

"What direction are you facing?"

"Siena!"

"Then this is the way that God would have us take."[3]

I would like to borrow the commentary for this key story from the writings of Meister Eckhart (d. 1329): "The worthiest deed of all is the one that proceeds from a free spirit."[4]

In the original text of the story, Brother Masseo is described as follows: "Francis liked to take along Brother Masseo as a traveling companion, in part because of the charm of his conversation and his great intelligence, in part too because, absorbed as he was in God, Francis found him very helpful. For Brother Masseo dealt with the people who met them on the way, and saw to it that Francis remained undisturbed in his silent contemplation."

For this reason Masseo always walked "a little bit ahead of him."

This scene draws our attention to Francis' rapturous absorption in God, which we shall discuss more fully in Chapter XIV. This much may be said here: Francis' attraction to solitude and contemplation was so strong, even at the beginning of his public activity, that he seriously thought of leading a godly life as a hermit, with the little group of his first companions.

It is not at all unlikely that these reflections went through his head after his return from Rome in 1209 (see Chapter V), when the Pope gave his blessing to Francis' plans. Celano says: "As true admirers of justice they considered with one another whether they should live among men or go off into solitude. The saint decided, not trusting in his own powers, but resorting to prayer before taking action, not to live for himself alone, but for him who died on behalf of all men. He knew that he had been sent to win souls for God that the devil sought to seduce."[5]

If we may believe the *Fioretti*, Francis also flirted with the contemplative life later in his career and wondered "whether he ought to devote himself exclusively to prayer or whether he ought to preach from time to time."[6]

Masseo was sent to Clare to ask what her position was on this point. When Masseo returned, Francis washed Masseo's feet and served him lunch. Then Francis took him into the forest, drew back his hood, knelt down, crossed his arms, and asked: "What does my Lord Jesus bid me do?"

"You should go out into the world to preach, for he has not chosen you for yourself alone, but for the salvation of others as well." Francis sprang up. Now he had the certainty he was looking for.

An overview of the events of 1209–19, the best years of Francis' life, looks something like this: Upon returning from the trip to Rome in the spring of 1209, Francis lived with his early companions in a barn near Rivo Torto in the Spoleto Valley beneath Assisi.

In the fall of 1210 the Benedictines leased the Portiuncula (for nothing) to the Friars Minor, thus providing the group with its ancestral home. Francis preached repeatedly in the cathedral of San Rufino in Assisi.

In the year 1211 came the meetings with Clare (see Chapter VIII).

In the spring of 1212 Clare fled from her parents' house. The sisters began living in San Damiano. Francis left for Palestine, but only got as far as the Dalmatian coast, whence he returned home. He wandered preaching through the Marches of Ancona and came to Tuscany. In May 1213 Count Roland of Chiusi (Tuscany) signed a document making over the mountain of La Verna to Francis' group as a place for meditation. There were now a number of new companions, perhaps two dozen altogether. Francis decided, on the model of King Arthur and his round table, to hold a meeting every year at Pentecost, at which all the companions would gather together.

In the summer of 1214 Francis undertook a pilgrimage to Santiago de Compostela in Spain. His intention of crossing over to the Moors in North Africa was frustrated owing to sickness.

The year 1215 saw Francis wandering through central Italy, preaching to the people.

Three hundred Friars Minor appeared at the Pentecost chapter of 1216. In 1217 Cardinal Ugolino arranged a meeting between Francis and Domingo de Guzman (d. 1221), founder of the Dominicans. At the chapter that year it was decided to send companions to France, Germany, Hungary, and Palestine. Italy was divided into five regions, under the direction of "provincial ministers," to co-ordinate better the brothers' preaching activities.

In 1218 Francis preached before the Pope. Reports from the preachers returning home from Germany and Hungary were not especially encouraging.

In May 1219 it was decided to send brothers to preach in southern France. Francis embarked for Acre, arrived there in July, and sailed on to Damietta in Egypt, which was then under siege from the Crusaders.[7]

In November 1219 Damietta fell after a siege of a year and a half. Of the eighty thousand inhabitants perhaps three thousand were alive, and many of them were severely wounded. Francis was a witness of the bloodbath staged by the Crusaders. His reaction to this horror has not come down to us. We are also in the dark about what he did during the next few months in Palestine, until a messenger arrived from Italy with the news that everything was at sixes and sevens with the Order of the Friars Minor.

While he was in the Holy Land, did Francis grasp the fact that the death machine of the Crusades had made all the talk about Christianity into a horrible lie?

I believe he did.

Francis spent the last seven years of his life working at his own destruction. The innocence of those ten years, which will shortly be discussed, was irrevocably gone. We who have long since learned to live with our shame see in these years a sort of reproach, and Francis' happiness strikes us as remote as the first paradise lost.

FORWARD, TO PARADISE

South of Umbria, Francis' homeland, lies the region of Latium, where twenty-seven hundred years ago the Roman politics of conquest got its start, thanks to the kindhearted care given to Romulus and Remus by the Capitoline wolf. In Latium lies the plain of Rieti, one of the loveliest landscapes of Europe, as Sabatier writes: "The highway goes directly toward this town (Rieti), passing between tiny lakes; here and there roads lead off to little villages which you see, on the hillside, between the cultivated fields and the edge of the forests; there are Stroncone, Greccio, Cantalice, Poggio-Bustone, and ten other small towns, which have given more saints to the Church than a whole province of France."[8]

As the Michelin guide to Italy says, the country around Rieti is "full of monasteries and memories of St. Francis of Assisi."

According to an old tradition, in the fall of 1208, in Poggio Bustone, Francis received the certainty of his own salvation during the first long preaching tour he went on with one of his early companions.[9] Celano tells us: "One day, when Francis was marveling at the mercy shown him by God in His many blessings and he wished to know what form his and his brothers' way of life should take henceforth, he sought out a place to pray in, as was his frequent custom. As he continued to stand there with fear and trembling before the master of the whole world, and in the bitterness of his soul thought over the years he had spent in such wickedness, he repeated again and again the phrase, "God be merciful to me, a sinner!" Then unspeakable joy and the greatest delight slowly began to pour into his innermost heart. Step by step he became completely changed. The storm in his soul abated, the darkness fled, which had spread over his soul from his fear of sin. He was granted the certainty that all his sins had been forgiven, and the confidence that he would come to grace awakened in him again. Thereupon he fell into ecstasy and was entirely immersed in a flood of light. The power of his spirit enlarged and he saw in the light what the future would bring. When at last that bliss disappeared, along with the light, he was spiritually renewed and transformed into another man."[10]

Of course, there were no witnesses of Francis' illumination. He may have intimated this or that detail of it to one of his especially trusted companions, who later told Celano the story when he was gathering the material for his first life of Francis.

In spite of the fact that we have the story only thirdhand, it arouses our interest for a specific reason. The parallels between this report and the accounts we have of another important young man's development are quite manifest. The other young man's name was Martin Luther, and for his part he too found a gracious God, in a way that had a remarkable liberating effect on the psychic life of many people three hundred years after Francis.

In Erik H. Erikson's book *Young Man Luther*, a rare (for today) combination of scholarship and practical wisdom, we read: "Of all the ideological systems, however, only religion restores the earliest sense of appeal to a Provider, a Providence. In the Judaeo-Christian tradition, no prayer indicates this more clearly than 'The Lord make His Face to shine upon you and be gracious unto you. The Lord lift up His countenance to you and give you peace'; and no prayerful attitude better than the uplifted face, hopeful of being recognized."[11]

The prayer cited by Erikson has a long history; it is older than the city of Rome, and may be found in the Bible, in the so-called Old Testament.[12] Francis knew it and loved it. He wrote it out with his own hand on that scrap of parchment, which was originally intended for Brother Leo and which the Franciscans guard as a precious relic:

Il Signore ti benedisca, e ti custodisca; ti mostri la sua faccia, et abbia pietà di te. Rivolga a te il suo volto, e diati pace.[13]

The Lord bless you and keep you; may He show you his countenance, full of tenderness. May He turn his face upon you, and give you peace.

The reader should understand why I translate *pietà* as "tenderness," rather than "pity." That "earliest sense," of which Erikson writes, is that of the very small child looking its mother in the face. What meets his eye is called tenderness. How beautiful if the vestiges of religion left in the coldhearted world of contemporary capitalism could restore that quality of tenderness we all so badly miss. After all, that's what religion is for.

Both Francis and Martin Luther required more time than usual for the transition from adolescence to adulthood. The decisive psychic events in their lives took place only after their twentieth year, and they needed seven years or so after that to find themselves. In both cases when their private conversions took on a public dimension, the effect on people was electrifying. The names of Francis and Martin came to stand for a way of life available to everyone.

Nowadays we can hardly imagine how both these young men released such joyous, confident energies among a rapidly growing international body of followers. Since we lack any such models, we make do with a heavy intake of drugs and alcohol, and the few wretched saviors of our day, from the Maharishi to Moon, in comparison with Francis and Martin, look like third-rate movie actors.

Under these circumstances we feel impelled to cast a backward glance into history. We ask ourselves from what depths Francis and Martin drew their energies, and we discover that their point of departure was a "countenance turned away," a state of lonely abandonment in an untender world.

It is noteworthy that neither Francis nor Martin found any effectual help in the religion of their time.

As a result they forged, through year-long labor, a new way to God.

The overwhelming experience in which that countenance "turned toward" them and shone upon them was like a reward for their perseverance. An absent-minded, bored, and otherwise occupied God, a high Lord—and a harsh one to boot—was transformed for Francis and Martin into the most attentive good will and tender kindness. From this moment on, both of them could forgive God for being a father.

The text just quoted from Celano about Francis' recovery from his guilt feelings gets, unfortunately, practically no attention in modern literature on Francis—this despite the fact that it is the only documentation for his overcoming the anxieties that tortured him in the fall of 1208, when he already had several companions and a divine mandate for meaningful action.

But, according to Celano, it was just this mandate that troubled Francis. He wanted to know clearly "what form his and his brothers' way of life should take henceforth." Here we have the archetypal bourgeois problem of planning for the future, intensified by remorse over wasted years in the past.

Francis faced the question of whether he could be a suitable leader for his companions, the ones he already had and the ones who might soon be joining him, and he was frightened by the weight of this task.

Wasn't it presumptuous to hope that his brotherhood would grow?

In this state of soul, in "fear and trembling before the Master of the whole world," Francis transformed himself into a child who begs for love from his strict father.

For a "long time" nothing happened. But then "unspeakable joy and the greatest delight gradually began to pour into his innermost heart." Anxiety over sin gave way to the certainty of forgiveness, and the future appeared in a favorable light. God had shown himself extraordinarily gracious.

Francis will forgive us for asking whether this wasn't purely and simply a neurotic surrender.

At the beginning of this century, when psychologists were less interested in rats and more interested in people, William James delivered his now classic lectures on "the variety of religious experience." James draws upon a rich body of material on the conversion experiences of simple people from the contemporary Anglo-Saxon world, and he makes at one point a remarkably even-handed statement: "Were we writing the story of the mind from the purely natural-history point of view, with no religious interest whatever, we should still have to write down man's liability to sudden and complete conversion as one of his most curious peculiarities."[14]

In answer to the question how such conversions are produced involuntarily and autonomously, from forces at work in the subconscious, Professor James cites the subject's willingness to "relax"[15] as the decisive factor in the accomplishment of this new birth. There we observe a process of giving way and letting go, which follows a period of intense grief work in the soul.

This is just what Francis went through. While he murmurs his "God be merciful to me, a sinner!" he abandons himself to the nascent powers of his ego. One could say that he has acquired the art of waiting properly, if we may allude once more to Samuel Beckett.

Had Francis continued to let himself be tyrannized by the alien God of the superego, then it would be accurate to speak of a neurotic surrender. But as it was, he came to know for a certainty that, as it says in the Bible, "God is love"—still the most daring utopian statement ever made.[16]

From now on Francis would direct his attention forward, to the future. He had no need to bother anymore with the past: That was behind him, and all the guilt feelings with it.

Sometimes he relapsed into self-torment. The *Fioretti:* Once, when Francis was staying with Brother Leo in a place where there were no prayer books, at the hour of morning prayers Francis said: "My dear Leo, we have no breviary to make our devotions with. And so I shall lead you in prayer, and you will answer me, exactly as I tell you to. I shall pray in this manner: 'O Brother Francis, you have sinned and offended so much in this world that you deserve to go to hell.' You must answer: 'That is certainly true, you deserve hell, and the deepest part of it.'"

Leo agreed.

Thus Francis began to pray, saying that he deserved to go to hell.

Leo answered: "God will work so much good through you that you will go to heaven."

"No, no, you are not supposed to say that, Leo. You should say that I belong to the damned."

"Gladly, my dear Francis."

Once more Francis began to pray amid many tears and sighs, and often beat his breast as he prayed, crying out: "O Lord, God of heaven and earth, so greatly have I trespassed against you that I thoroughly deserve to be damned."

Leo answered: "O Brother Francis, so greatly will God exalt you that among the blessed you will be especially blessed."

Then Francis was very angry that Leo said the opposite of what he had been ordered to say. Francis strongly berated him and once again drummed the right answer into him. "Once and for all, you little simpleton, say what you're supposed to say. You're supposed to say that I am absolutely unworthy to find mercy with God."

But as Francis once again bewailed his unworthiness, Leo gave this answer: "God the Father, whose mercy is infinitely greater than your sins, he will show you the fullness of grace and the joys of heaven as well."

Now Francis flew into a real fury. "Will you finally tell me why you always give the wrong answers?"

"But I *did* want to go ahead and say the words you wanted me to. God must have forced me to say what pleases Him."

Francis was perplexed, and made one last try. With tears in his eyes he cried: "Ah you wretched Francis, do you really believe that God will have mercy on you?"

Leo answered: "Yes, Francis, he will have mercy on you and give you eternal glory."

Then they both had to weep, and the dawn came up.[17]

Nowadays it is hard for us to imagine just how profound the fear of hell was in the Middle Ages. It was the normal form of paranoia in those days; neither beggar nor Pope was proof against it. (Of course, the Popes profited from it more than the beggars did.)

Francis got free of this fear.

There is a connection between the way he lived and his confidence of salvation, which becomes transparent if one thinks of that word of Jesus' which in the mouth of priests sounds like mockery, like cheap consolation in the Beyond for those who labor and are heavy laden. But whenever it is spoken without condescension, its bracing truth always comes through:

"Greetings, you poor people! Paradise is yours!"[18]

The secret of Francis' impact on others is that he entered paradise in his lifetime, that he found the kingdom of heaven in ditches and barns. He dimly reminds us of times when there were neither fences nor locks on the door. He gives us the sense of an earth that was truly common to all men, without boundaries and property claims, that willingly poured out its wealth to everyone. The biblical names for this earth are paradise, the kingdom of heaven, world without end. The appointed time for the irrevocable establishment of this state, so the Bible insists.

Two years before his death Francis composed a song, the so-called "Canticle of the Sun." It doesn't describe another world which one can enter only after death. Instead it praises the good earth, with its amiable elements and kindly people.

Francis' paradise was located in central Italy. That was where he especially liked to stay—in Umbria, in the Marches, in the Rieti Valley. For a while these secluded regions became a new Galilee, with Francis as a Jesus *redivivus*, preaching the kingdom of peace. "Thus it happened that the appearance of the whole land was changed in a short time, so that it put aside the old ugliness and everywhere showed a happier countenance."[19] Celano wrote this sentence two years after Francis' death. In spite of his usual effusiveness, this time he may be taken as an authentic witness to a widespread feeling that seemed to people then a foretaste of a new age.

The question arises why Francis' paradise was so short-lived.

From the memoirs of Augustin Souchy (born 1892): "Of greater social-revolutionary relevance was the fact that the peasant farmers who were inspired by the spirit of renewal voluntarily founded *colectividades*—i.e., they no longer cultivated their fields by themselves, but in common. They renounced their titles of ownership, declared the land common property, and worked it in common. The produce was sold by the community, and the profits fairly divided among everyone according to individual need. There had never been anything like this before, neither in the Mexican Revolution of 1910 nor in the Russian Revolution of 1917. It was a special kind of agrarian reform, without laws, without commands from on high, without compulsion, and without theoreticians (!), originated entirely by the rural population itself. Of the more than a thousand *colectividades* founded up to the end of 1936 or the beginning of 1937, I visited about a hundred in Catalonia and Aragon, on the Mediterranean coast and in Murcia, in Old Castille and in the Republican parts of Andalusia. There was no uniform collectivization plan for the whole country. The founders knew neither Marx's theories nor Bakunin's. If we had won the Civil War, today Spanish collectivism would be a concrete alternative to private capitalism on one side and state capitalism on the other."[20]

The Spanish *colectividades* lasted only a little more than two years. Generalissimo Franco put an end to them, with the help of Hitler and Mussolini. Souchy reports the less widely known fact that the anti-Franco Soviet forces in Spain broke up the farming collectives in Aragon at gunpoint, even before Franco marched in.[21]

This moment from the long history of obstructions to the kingdom of peace shows how practical the common people can sometimes be, if they are left alone, in building their paradise. In a certain sense the Spanish *colectividades* are a real commentary on Francis. Francis taught people a very simple gesture—namely, how to open the hand clutching one's own property. The Spanish peasants provide a fruitful lesson in what can come of such a gesture under certain circumstances. One can imagine the pleasure Francis would have had helping them with the harvest.

"COME HERE, BROTHER WOLF"

In a recent interview in *Playboy* magazine William Colby, a member of the CIA since 1947 and its director from 1973 to 1976, made some remarks about Francis of Assisi.

"PLAYBOY: Do you have any heroes?
COLBY: Saint Francis is one.
PLAYBOY: Why Saint Francis?
COLBY: To be very, very honest with you, he was a humble man. . . . Saint Francis was a young, fairly flamboyant, rich, spoiled brat. He was wounded in one of the innumerable struggles then and he began to think about what he really should do. He went home and decided he wasn't going to be a rich, spoiled brat anymore. He was going to live a simple life, to follow the law of love. And he did. . . .
PLAYBOY: Would Saint Francis have joined the CIA?
COLBY: No. Saint Francis was a pacifist. I'm not a pacifist, but I can still say that I admire some people who take a position farther out than mine in certain ideal directions."[22]

It matters very little that Colby is a practicing Catholic (so was Generalissimo Franco). The only interesting thing about Colby's comments is the trick he uses to fashion a sympathetic (to him) image of Francis. Colby passes over the subversive side of Francis, namely his poverty ethic —and thus takes the sting out of his love for peace. Francis, as this practicing Catholic and military expert sees him, may be conveniently filed away under the heading of "humility," ever a useful virtue for the production of cannon fodder. (Humble young men are accustomed to doing what they're told. They don't become draft dodgers.) Francis' pacifism, as Colby presents it, is as harmless as a poem by Rilke or a high-school essay on disarmament.

By contrast, the real Francis stood for a principle that confronts the normal madness of the aggressor in a highly peculiar and on occasion actually disarming fashion: the principle of brotherliness (in French *fraternité*, one of three watchwords, of course, of the Revolution of 1789).

The key story in this context comes from the *Fioretti*: A very wonderful thing, a glorious deed and worthy of remembrance, took place near the town of Gubbio. In those parts a great, ferocious wolf once roamed about, attacking and devouring men. All the citizens were greatly afraid of this terrible creature, and no one went outside the town walls unarmed. Still, nobody unfortunate enough to meet the wolf with its fangs bared was ever a match for its dreadful fury. Finally, the fear became so widespread that hardly anyone felt safe after leaving the town walls behind.

When Francis came to Gubbio one day, he felt pity for the people there and decided to go out to the wolf. The citizens were horrified at this idea and implored Francis not to expose himself deliberately to the danger of certain death. But Francis confidently made the sign of the cross and left the town with a companion to go see the wolf. The people climbed out on the roofs of their houses and followed Francis from there with their eyes.

The terrible wolf was already running toward Francis and his companion with jaws gaping when the holy man's divine power made the wolf come to a halt. Francis made the sign of the cross over the beast, called it over to him, and said: "Come here, brother wolf. In the name of Christ I command you not to harm me or anyone else."

And, astonishingly, the frightful creature at once closed its horrid open maw, lowered its head, and trotted like a lamb up to Francis, where it lay down quietly at his feet.

Then Francis preached to the wolf: "You have been doing a lot of damage in this region, brother wolf! You have done vile deeds and murdered God's creatures. You even dare to kill human beings, who are made after God's image. You have surely deserved to be punished as a robber and murderer with an evil death. But I want to bring peace between you, brother wolf, and the people. You will never again cause harm to anyone. In exchange they will forgive all your misdeeds, and from now on neither people nor dogs are to persecute you."

Then the wolf wagged his tail and nodded his head, in this way showing his agreement.

Francis went on: "I also want to promise you that you will never go hungry anymore. You will get your food each day from the people. For I know you only did all those evil things because of hunger. Now give me a sign that you have truly understood all this, and agree to go along with it."

The wolf obediently raised his right paw and laid it in Francis' outstretched hand. Then it went politely along with Francis to the marketplace, and all the townsfolk hurried there at once.

When Francis had explained everything to the people, and asked them if they would faithfully feed the wolf and observe the peace treaty as carefully as the wolf had promised to, they all cried out, "yes."

The wolf lived for two years in the town, going from door to door to get its food, and never hurt anyone. Amazingly not a single dog ever barked at him. When the wolf finally died of old age, the people were grief-stricken, for its peacefulness and gentle patience had reminded them of the virtue of the man who had tamed its ferocity.[23]

The first thing we notice about this story is that Francis appears in it as a veritable Buddha, a clear counterpart to that godlike man: "The enlightened one speaks: While dwelling on the mountain slope, I drew lions and tigers to me through the power of friendship. Surrounded by lions and tigers, by panthers, bears and wolves, by antelope, deer, and wild boar, I live in the forest. No creature is frightened of me, and I have no fear of any living thing."[24]

One thousand years and ten thousand kilometers separate this Buddhist text from our story of Francis, but the "power of friendship" invoked in both traditions still creates a surprisingly similar effect. At work in both these stories is a broadly democratic dream which has survived the centuries and which transcends the cultural differences between East and West. It is the desire to reconcile animals and men.

But as we consider the fierceness of the beast transformed into gentleness, a still more important topos presents itself—the idea of a world where man is no longer a wolf to his fellow man. Anyone who thinks of such an international comradeship as utopian might just ask himself what makes it seem so utopian after all.

Scholar Johannes Jörgensen, whom we have already mentioned, believes that the wolf of Gubbio is a veiled literary reference to a malicious local tyrant, transformed by Francis into a self-sacrificing *podestà*.[25]

This interpretation is unprovable, but it does provide some help: It focuses our attention on the central theme of the wolf story—the Christian approach to the relationship between aggressor and victim, a truly classic theme that carries us back to the Bible, to the personal command of the Savior: Love your enemies![26]

William Colby, who as an active CIA man and practicing Catholic is a declared admirer of idealists like Jesus and Francis, may wish to pay tribute as well to the maxim of loving one's enemies. The trouble is that his admiration has no practical consequences whatsoever.

In the original sources, Francis' disarming friendliness toward wolfish natures—even if, like Cardinal Ugolino or William Colby, they wear sheep's clothing—is never depicted as passivity or readiness to suffer. We should not look upon Francis' peaceableness as submission, but as action, very much like a force that emanates from him and stops the charging enemy dead in his tracks.

Was Francis a magician?

As a matter of fact, we find in many of the stories about Francis a kind of faint memory of prehistorical cultural life, such as we encounter today in the "savage thought" of the still surviving "primitive" peoples. More specifically, Francis reminds us of those men and women who through natural talent and years of training achieve powers that baffle modern science, such as the deliberate influencing of the nervous vegetative system, the mental transmission of commands over long distances, extrasensory perception, hypnosis technique, and trance states. More or less down-at-the-heel representatives of these ancient pre-Christian arts were still to be met with in the Middle Ages, herb women or purveyors of magical cures for animals, who drew upon Celtic, Slavic, or Germanic traditions. Thus the conceptual gap separating medieval people from this old heritage was not all that great, and the taming of a wild wolf by a holy man was the sort of occurrence that fit perfectly well into their world picture.

Anyone who takes a heartfelt childish delight (as does the writer) in surprising effects, and the porousness of banal reality, will have no difficulty understanding the story of the wicked wolf of Gubbio. Besides, the Bible is full of useful feats of magic, all of them performed in the interest of the populace, especially the hungry, the sick, and the unjustly persecuted.

In other words, Francis faces the wolf not with an air of sweet tolerance but with a fearless vitality that overwhelms the evil, destructive enemy. Soon the monster is wagging its tail, and we realize that the really crazy people aren't in mental institutions: They're still running around with medals pinned to their chest. Many of them are practicing Catholics.

The story of the wolf of Gubbio has a counterpart in the account of the happy conversion of some wicked robbers. In this tale of open fraternization between the Friars Minor and a group of outlaws, *philadelphia* or brotherly love appears as a humane reality, not some merely legendary entity.

This is the story they tell: There was a time when some robbers used to come to the hermitage of the Friars Minor near Borgo San Sepolcro to ask for bread, for the great forests of this region were full of all sorts of scoundrelly robbers who held up travelers on the highways and plundered them. Some of the brothers thought that they shouldn't give the robbers anything, because they did so many wrongs to people. Others, however, sometimes gave the robbers something to eat, because they were in great distress and begged them so urgently. The brothers never failed to encourage the robbers to give up their evil way of life. One time when Francis visited the hermitage, his companions asked him whether or not they should give the robbers bread.

Francis answered: If you do as I tell you, you will win the robbers' souls.

Then Francis gave the brothers precise instructions on how to act.

So the brothers fetched bread and wine, and walked into the forest with them to a place where the robbers often stayed, and cried out:

Come here, brother robbers, for we are Friars Minor and we have brought you bread and wine.

Then the robbers drew near. The brothers spread a cloth out on the ground and served the robbers with food and drink, very graciously and making all sorts of jokes. After the meal was over, the brothers said a short prayer and asked the robbers, in all innocence, to grant them one request: "Will you promise us never to kill or harm anybody during your raids?"

The robbers agreed.

The next day the brothers brought eggs and cheese as well as bread and wine, and served the wicked fellows as they had before, and spoke these words to them:

"Why is it that you insist on dwelling in the woods and living in destitution, despite your crimes? If you lived a religious life, then God would surely clothe and feed you, just as He does for us, and give you eternal bliss besides!"

At first the robbers didn't say either "yes" or "no" to this. But they began to bring wood to the brothers in the hermitage. After a while some of the robbers promised the brothers to live by the work of their hands. Others asked to be accepted into the brotherhood, and from then on led a devout life.[27]

Clearly, to Francis' mind there was no such thing as incorrigible people (although we have already seen one exception to this rule, in the case of Pietro Stacia, whom Francis cursed). In one of the Leo stories we learn how two men of the world as hardboiled as the mayor and the bishop of Assisi, whose bitter antagonism had reached the point of boycott and excommunication, warmly embraced one another as soon as Francis sang his "Canticle of the Sun" to them a year before his death.[28]

Francis' pacifism, although quite capable of rebelling against the injustice of the class structure, rests on the unshakeable conviction that people are by nature inclined to goodness, that they need tender attention. Francis himself, as noted in Chapter IV, had suffered from the harshness and frigidity of bourgeois life in his own family and the circles he moved in as a young man. When he turned to beggars and lepers he experienced a profound happiness, and so he chose the beggar's life for the sake of the very real well-being it brought him—that is, to find lasting satisfaction for his desire for tenderness. From then on Francis lived among the common people like a fish in the water, without condescension and without money, giving and getting. As he learned every day while helping the peasants with their work and sharing their meals, or simply begging for bread from door to door, people would not let him starve. Francis found, if you will, a great family where everyone was brother and sister to one another. He also saw water and fire, the warm sun, fragrant flowers, and harmless animals as brotherly and sisterly creatures. God himself turned a tender face to him: Fear and concern, guilt and despondency now belonged to the past. Francis was a happy man.

So it is understandable that he could also confront human wolves with such unaffected ease, with the magic words: "Come here, brother wolf."

Francis also practiced this method in the presence of the Pope, as we shall now hear.

This is the story they tell: Lord Ugolino, the glorious cardinal bishop of Ostia, had sent a message to Francis, urgently requesting him to come to Rome. When Francis came to see him, the cardinal informed him what a high honor was to be granted him: The Holy Father himself had asked that Francis preach a sermon in his presence. In view of the importance of the occasion Ugolino had taken the liberty of composing a well-planned address. Francis should study it carefully, so as to dispel any suspicion the Pope might be harboring against him and the Friars Minor. Now when Francis was brought before the Pope and his cardinals on the appointed day, and the blessing was given, and it was time to begin, suddenly Francis could no longer remember a word of the speech that Lord Ugolino had so cleverly thought out and provided him with. In his terrible embarrassment Francis reached for his prayer book, opened it up, and happened upon the passage in the Psalms where it says: "All day long my disgrace is before me, and shame has covered my face."

Francis translated the Latin text into the vernacular and then began to speak in his Umbrian dialect about the arrogance of prelates, about their bad example, and what shame they were bringing on Mother Church; for the prelates, he continued, were the face of the Church, and what could God want more than that this countenance should shine forth in all its beauty?

Francis spoke with such ardor that gradually his feet began to move, and by the end of the sermon he seemed to be dancing, inflamed with joy in the truth. And lo, none of the illustrious princes felt any urge to laugh. Rather they were moved to astonishment by the man's candor, and shame and contrition stirred in their hearts.

In the meantime Lord Ugolino felt as if he were walking on burning coals, and prayed fervently to God that the Sacred College might not be enraged by Francis' bluntness.

But on the contrary, when Francis had ended, everyone was touched by his words, and he took his leave of them, having won the favor of the Pope and his cardinals.[29]

"The individual," writes Hegel, "who has not staked his life, may, no doubt, be recognized as a Person; but he has not attained the truth of this recognition as an independent self-consciousness."[30]

The Pope before whom Francis had to preach was the successor to the one from whom Francis had gotten verbal permission to preach, nine years before. In the meantime Francis' fellowship had thrived, going from a dozen to a mighty army of lay preachers, whose thousands had swarmed over half of Europe and all the way to Palestine. There was some very high-level concern that these theologically uneducated men might serve as a ferment for subversive heretical activities. The hammer of the papal In-

quisition had not yet been completely forged, but ever since 1209 the crusade against the heretics of southern France—the first mass murder of
Christians by Christians—had brought a new horror into the West.

Francis preached before murderers.

"In the first instance," Hegel says, "the master is taken to be the essential reality for the state of bondage. . . . For this consciousness was not in
peril and fear for this element or that, nor for this or that moment of time,
it was afraid for its entire being; it felt the fear of death, the sovereign
master. It has been in that experience melted to its inmost soul, has trembled throughout its very fibre, and all that was fixed and steadfast has
quaked within it."[31]

When Francis entered the hall of the Sacred College, he must have
known that his sermon was a matter of life and death. Neither he nor his
Order would have survived a papal anathema. All the same, Francis
dropped the cardinal's plan completely; he spoke freely and showed his
masters their true colors. For one historic moment, while Francis executed
his dance, absolute fear moved from the slave to the masters, and the
wolves in their sheeps' clothing of usurped legitimacy scented the lure of a
life of peace.

Francis told these mighty lords that they had to change. This indispensable condition for the establishment of true brotherliness was of
course not met, as we learn from Francis' own history. Friendly persuasion
alone has never led rulers to step down from their chairs of state. As we
read in the Bible, they have to be overthrown.[32]

"LOOK AT THE LARKS"

Francis said: "Take a corpse and put it wherever you wish. You will see
that it puts up no resistance. It doesn't contradict you, even if you leave it
lying there. If you put it on a throne, it doesn't glance up but down. If
you clothe it in purple, it looks twice as pale.

"We, the Friars Minor, are a small and simple flock. We call ourselves
minor because we refuse to become superiors.

"Look at the larks. Gaily they search for their grains of seed by the side
of the road, without making any fuss. They fly up to heaven singing.
Their garment is the color of the earth, and with their little hoods on their
head they resemble us, the Friars Minor.

"Are we not here to bring men joy, like traveling singers?"[33]

The first official document on the Friars Minor bears the date of June
11, 1219. It is a papal letter of recommendation to "all archbishops, bishops, abbots, deacons, archdeacons, and other Christians," confirming the

fact that the Friars Minor are good Catholics and deserve to be treated with consideration.[34]

For ten years, from Francis' memorable audience with Innocent III in 1209 till the publication of the bull of June 1219, official records are silent about him and his group. These were, as we said, the ten best years of Francis' life.

His fellowship was free to develop without regimentation, without the constraints of solemnly stamped Rules and notarized paragraphs. There can be no doubt that the lightheartedness of those first ten years of the Friars Minor was related to the fact that their fellowship was utterly classless, as we shall now see.

Here is a children's rhyme from Vienna, as the author remembers it:

Kaiser König Edelmann,	Emperor king nobleman,
Bürger Bauer Bettelmann,	Burgher peasant beggarman,
Schneider Schuster Leinenweber,	Tailor cobbler linenweaver,
Kaufmannstochter,	Tradesman's daughter,
Totengräber.	Gravedigger.

This little verse deftly recalls the class structure of medieval European society, and the inequality of men. Although the clergy are left out, the whole thing is viewed hierarchically, running from top to bottom, down to peasants and beggars. The tradesman's daughter, an especially good match, is ironically compared with the despised gravedigger, and the *mediocres* of the lesser handicrafts stand exactly in the middle of the class system.[35]

The under class, the *minores*, who were linked with Francis' group in a brotherhood that was more than just nominal, all the swineherds, unemployed, and journeymen, on down to the beggars and pariahs of the time, the blind, fools, lepers, whores, robbers, hoboes, fortune-tellers, and clowns —Francis chose this pitiable collection of people as his favorite milieu, looking down instead of up, as he clearly puts it in the comparison with the corpse.

One senses that in a world where social outcasts were fully accepted, things would be better by far for everyone.

Francis took the fundamental principle of equality for his brotherhood from the *déclassés*, among whom, naturally, the usual caste distinctions were superfluous.

The fact was that blue-blooded noblemen as well as ex-robbers, village idiots, doctors of theology, and prize-winning troubadours put on Francis' earth-colored tunic—and when they did, farewell to titles, honors, and privileges, with all the business of prestige and the pecking order. Upon entering Francis' fellowship the new brother became a man without a past, he gained a new identity—that of a homeless beggar for Christ, with no special status or insignia of rank.

The sources almost stereotypically use the expression *humilis* (generally translated as "humble") to characterize Francis and his brotherhood. But the focus of Francis' comparison between the Friars Minor and the crested larks (p. 122)—namely, the sameness of their appearance, their inconspicuousness, their smallness, and their frugality—points not to subservience but to lack of importance.

If one remembers which creature Kings and Emperors all the way into the twentieth century chose for their coats of arms—i.e., the eagle—then the polemical significance of Francis' preference for larks becomes immediately clear. We might also reflect that eagles can't sing.

This is the story they tell: One time Francis was traveling with a companion from Assisi, who came from an especially noble and influential family. Since Francis was exhausted and ill, he rode on a donkey. His companion was tired from walking, and, as he thought of his distinguished birth, he grew vexed because he had to plod on foot behind the son of a merchant, while Francis had the use of a mount.

To his amazement Francis all at once got off the donkey and said:

"It occurred to me that it's not right for me to ride while you walk, seeing that you were an important and powerful man in the world."

Then his companion began to cry, and blushed with shame, and admitted to Francis what an idle impulse had passed through his mind.[36]

Between 1208 and 1217, from the earliest beginnings of the Franciscans (see Chapter VII) up until that general chapter when, after a mighty period of growth, they first appointed functionaries, Francis had no particular problems with the principle of classlessness among the Friars Minor.

It goes without saying that Francis had never liked to command. Before very long many people were joining his Order unbeknownst to him, and some recruits didn't even know Francis by name.[37] He consistently avoided building up an inner circle, which might have generated the managerial elite to run a briskly efficient organization. Not one of his first companions ever took on an official function. Francis also went to great pains not to awaken any suspicions that he had special preferences, by always choosing different brothers to accompany him on his travels. (Only in the last years of his life did he grow more flexible on this point.)

Right from the start Francis insisted on his Order's scattering in all directions, in repeated waves, wandering in pairs down the highroads of central Italy, to preach in towns and villages.[38] Francis himself regularly disappeared for weeks and months with one brother or another, stayed in solitary places or walked, for variety's sake, to Apulia or Piedmont.[39]

In contrast to the "old Orders," the almost programmatic homeless and instability of the Franciscans constituted something categorically new. In the first ten years, recruits did not enter any sort of monastery. Instead they joined a movement, with its center of gravity in Umbria, the Marches, and farther south toward Latium, but entirely mobile nonetheless. (Research has not substantiated the thesis that in their first years Francis and his comrades led a predominantly contemplative life of meditation and prayer.)[40]

This new lifestyle, consciously antihierarchical, egalitarian, and decentralized, of theologically untrained laymen with neither Holy Orders nor clerical privileges, is very much reminiscent of the practices of the Cathars and Waldensians, those reform movements that the Popes of Francis' time persecuted with such total savagery. These heretics also used to go about two by two, preaching in the plainest clothes and living by begging or doing odd jobs. No wonder many bishops looked on Francis' vagabonds with distrust and forbade them to preach.

Celano reports: One time Francis came to the city of Imola, spoke with the bishop there, and asked him for permission to preach. The bishop answered:

"It is quite enough that I preach to the people."

Francis took his leave.

After barely half an hour he was back again.

"What do you want now?"

"My Lord, when a father drives his son out by one door, then he must come back through the other."

The bishop admitted he was beaten and gave him the license to preach.[41]

In November 1215 a great assembly of the Church took place in Rome, with the mighty Innocent presiding.[42] From the point of view of Church politics, this "Fourth Lateran Council" was the most important conference in the Middle Ages (71 archbishops, 412 bishops, and 800 abbots came to Rome as full voting participants).

To open the deliberations, the Pope gave a stirring speech. He spoke of Church reform, of making a sinful Christendom over into a virtuous one, and, naturally, of the next Crusade to Palestine, planned for 1217.

Among the ordinances passed were a series of ecclesiastical punishments for unchaste and alcoholic priests. Bishops were required to track down and punish all heretics in their jurisdiction. It was decreed that all Christian people should go to confession once a year. Not to do so was to incur suspicion of heresy. They decided further to make all Jews living among

Christians easily distinguishable by having them wear a special uniform, a practice later revived by Adolf Hitler.

Thus a reign of bureaucratic terror was proclaimed. The heads of the Church, beneath their episcopal scullcaps, were altogether modern in their thinking, and the first long shadow was cast from Rome on Francis' innocent fellowship.

One of the provisions of the Council was a strict and immediate ban on the creation of new Rules for religious Orders. In the future all pious societies would have to follow one of the old, well-tested Rules. New foundations were not wanted.

Many industrious students of Francis' life have tried to determine whether or not he was at the Council.[43] Only one of the relevant old sources mentions, but not in very reliable fashion, that Francis visited Rome when the Fathers were in session. Nevertheless, researchers have stirred up speculation about all sorts of appeals that Francis may have made to the Pope à propos of the new stipulation on the founding of religious Orders.

In reality Francis had other things on his mind at the time. His brotherhood was still relatively small, and besides, he was anything but an architect of institutions, the sort of person who desires more than anything else to produce a tightly structured organization.

On this critical point Francis differed greatly from his Spanish colleague Dominic, founder of the Dominicans.[44] As early as the year 1216, when his followers numbered at most three or four dozen men, Dominic was circumspect enough to work out a detailed "Constitution." In 1220, when there were already thousands of Friars Minor, the Dominicans had barely fifty members. On the other hand, in sharp contrast to the Franciscans, they had an efficient organization, complete with a system for elections and the apportionment of official posts.

When Francis was introduced to Dominic, in the early months of 1217, in Rome, Dominic already had the Pope's approval for the Order in his pocket.[45] The Franciscans, by contrast, were still floating in the air, and we have no reason to believe that Francis found the situation particularly disturbing.

The *Fioretti:* Now when the entire band of five thousand brothers had gathered in the Portiuncula forest, Francis preached to them:

"None of you is to trouble himself over having enough food and drink. Leave to God the care of what the body needs."

Dominic, however, who was there at that time, was dumfounded by this injunction of the blessed Francis, held it to be unwise, and could not imagine how such a great crowd could simply be left to its own devices.

And see! From Perugia, Spoleto, Foligno, Spello, and Assisi people came with mules, horses, and carts, laden with bread and wine, beans and cheese. Even knights and barons came to serve the brothers. Then Dominic was greatly ashamed, and he confessed how small-minded he had been, begged Francis for forgiveness, and vowed to live henceforth for holy poverty.[46]

As previously mentioned (p. 108), Francis had introduced the practice of having all the Friars Minor come together for a yearly meeting, around Pentecost. We can see how informal these general chapters were from the account in the *Fioretti*. The good Dominic's astonishment at Francis' disregard for planning sounds quite authentic. One can easily imagine the gaiety and spontaneity of these Franciscan festivals. As a matter of fact, we have an eyewitness account of one of them by a brother from the Spoleto Valley named Jordan of Giano, who had a rather wild trick played on him at a general chapter.

Brother Jordan tells the story: In the year of Our Lord 1221, when the chapter was about to end, Francis suddenly remembered an important matter. He was feeling quite weak, and since Brother Elias was standing near him, Francis tugged him by the sleeve and told him to make an announcement. Elias called out:

"Brothers, he says that he doesn't want to order anyone to go to Germany, since our companions have been treated so badly there. But if there are any volunteers, they are to stand up and come over to the side."

About ninety brothers jumped up, all fearless men, grouped together, and waited for instructions as to when and by what route they were supposed to march.

But at that chapter there was also a brother who was greatly afraid of the savagery of the Germans. When he saw the volunteers step out together, he was convinced they were all going to suffer martyrdom. He imagined to himself how he could later tell people that he had known all these martyrs by name, and so he went over and began asking one volunteer after another what their names were and where they came from.

One of them, a certain Palmerio, who later worked in Magdeburg, was from Gargano in Apulia and was known as a wag. When that timid brother came up to him and asked his name, he answered:

"I am Palmerio. And you're one of us, and you'll go off with us!" And he seized him by the tunic.

"No, no! I only wanted to meet you. I don't want to go to Germany at all!"

But Palmerio laughed and held him tight, dragged him to the ground, and forced him to remain with the volunteers, for all his wailing.

In the meantime they had assigned this brother to a different mission.

Then when Brother Cesario came—he was to lead the trip to Germany—to select a suitable group, they shouted to him that he absolutely had to take the curious brother along. But he protested loudly, and so finally they brought him to Brother Elias.

Elias said:

"You yourself will decide where you want to go."

What to do now? In his indecision the fearful man ran up to a companion who he knew had already endured a great deal of hardship. (In Hungary they had robbed him of his underwear no fewer than fifteen times, not to mention his tunic.) *He* thought it would be best to ask Brother Elias for an order.

And Elias decided that he should immediately go along with the rest to Germany.

The man to whom this happened was named Jordan of Giano, and he wrote all this down. He arrived in this way in Germany and helped Brother Cesario to found a colony of the Friars Minor in that wild country.[47]

The incident with Brother Jordan occurred at a time when Francis had been under heavy pressure to put together a serviceable Rule in accordance with canon law. (More on this in Chapter XI.) The provisions that were finally agreed upon reveal how tenaciously Francis fought for his principles with regard to official assignments and the order of command, and even today they strike us as remarkably liberating.[48]

Every class distinction among the Friars Minor, even between laymen and ordained priests, was prohibited.

A periodic rotation of superiors and subordinates was unconditionally required.

All posts in the Order were to be viewed as modes of service; hence the introduction of the names *minister* (servant), *custos* (protector), and *guardian*. Functionaries were subject to the supervision of all the brothers, and could be recalled, should this prove necessary.

Brother Jordan tells the story: Francis used to like to tease Peter of Catania in his humorous way. Peter was a brother of noble descent, and a learned jurist besides, and Francis would say to him:

"Ha, my most noble Lord Peter, what shall we do now?"

Brother Peter, who had a ready tongue, liked to say right back:

"Ha, my most noble Lord Francis, just as you will."

And thus they vied to see who could be humbler and show more respect, one to the other.[49]

And so our discussion of distinctions between superiors and inferiors, higher-ups and underlings, the people who give orders and the people who take them, ends, as Francis would have it, with a burst of laughter.

As strongly as he resisted the inveterate human tendency to lord it over others, Francis never became solemn or morose. The brothers who sometimes laughed out loud while at prayer were his best disciples.[50]

Francis himself, when he was in the mood, occasionally took a piece of wood, laid it across his left arm like a fiddle, and then played on it, holding a stick in his right hand for the bow. As he played he sang pious French songs, and danced in time to the music. He would be moved to tears, and in the end completely forgot himself and the world.[51] This kind of religion, which was no more widespread in Francis' day than in ours, cannot simply be created by administrative fiat, as should be clear by now.

X

"SOLDAN! SOLDAN!"

AFTER the Pentecost chapter of 1219 six Friars Minor set out for Morocco, to suffer death there for the Christian faith. They undertook the trip with the clear intention of provoking the Mohammedans into cutting their heads off as soon as possible. The names of these voluntary candidates for death: Vitale (he fell sick on the way and had to stay behind), Otho, Bernardo, Pietro, Accurso, and Adjuto. The chronicle of their sufferings, described by an eyewitness, was discovered in the last century. The writer was a courtier attending the Spanish infante, Don Pedro, who was living in exile in Marrakech.[1]

Report of the sufferings and martyrdom of the five Friars Minor in the land of the Miramolin:[2] As soon as the brothers arrived in Seville, they ran into the mosque and began to preach against the Koran. They were immediately seized by the furious believers and soundly thrashed. On the next day they climbed a high tower and cried out to the people below that Mohammed was a deceiver and a slave of the devil. Thereupon they were put in prison, and soon afterward expelled from the city. They continued on their journey and came to Africa, where they were arrested and brought before the Miramolin in Marrakech. During the interrogation they declared that the Koran contained nothing but lies. At this the Miramolin ordered them to be tortured. They were whipped till they bled, they had boiling oil poured over their bodies, and then they were brought back to the prince. When he asked them if they were still determined to go on defaming the Koran, they replied that only the Gospel of Christ contained the truth. In the meantime the Spanish infante had intervened with the Miramolin. As a result, the five Friars Minor were banished from the country and brought under guard to the coast. But they got away from their guards, hastened back to Marrakech, forced their way at once into the mosques, and preached against Mohammed and his teachings. The Miramolin tried in vain to placate them with generous presents. As a last resort, he threatened them with the death penalty, and that, finally, seemed to satisfy them. So the Miramolin called the executioner and had them beheaded, one after the other, on January 20, 1220. The infante saw to it that the bodies were quietly conveyed to Coimbra, to the Augustinian church, and the faithful immediately flocked there, to venerate the first martyrs from the ranks of the Friars Minor.

All the exotic excess of the age of the Crusades stands out in this story with disturbing clarity. The prince here is rather hesitant in his encounter with the impetuous Friars Minor: These Christian dervishes represent less a threat than an awkward situation. (The title "Miramolin" is a garbling of "emir al Mu'minin," the conventional honorific title for rulers in Morocco at the time. The emir who had the friars decapitated was Abu Yakub Yusuf II.) From a modern standpoint it is not the Muslim but the five Christians wearing Franciscan habits who look like fanatics; they are the aggressors in this crazy affair.

The question that now suggests itself is: Was their behavior inspired by Francis? Was Francis for his part, as Celano puts it, "full of burning desire for martyrdom," and hence a model for those five doomed men?[3]

This much at least is certain: Francis undertook three journeys to preach the Christian faith among the Moors and Saracens. Two of these journeys had to be broken off before he reached his goal. The third trip brought Francis face to face with the Sultan of Egypt (and back again unharmed to Italy).

We may confidently assume that Francis, as a contemporary of the Crusades, was swept up in the general hysteria surrounding them.[4] In this light his longing to preach a powerful sermon to the Muslims doesn't seem especially original, any more than his belligerent attitude or his readiness to die. More important than this typically medieval cast in his personality is the change it underwent, which we can observe after Francis' return from the theater of war. As will be shown, he came back from Egypt suffering from more than an eye complaint.

A SLAUGHTER FOR CHRIST

Here is the account by an anonymous Christian of the capture of Jerusalem by the Crusaders on July 15, 1099 (greatly abbreviated excerpts): On Good Friday, when the hour approached in which Our Lord Jesus Christ deigned to suffer death on the cross for us, one of our men, Laetholdus by name, scaled the city walls. This was a signal for the defenders to flee. Our soldiers followed them to the temple of Solomon, cutting them down on the way. So great was the slaughter that our men walked in blood up to their ankles.

The Saracens entrenched themselves in the temple of Solomon, and put up a bitter resistance all through the day. Their blood flowed in streams, everywhere. When we finally got the upper hand, our men at their discretion killed the surviving men and women among the unbelievers or took them alive as prisoners. But on the roof of the temple was a great crowd of unarmed infidels of both sexes. Lord Tancred had promised to protect them.

Then the men overran the city, carrying off gold and silver as booty, loading horses and mules with every conceivable kind of valuable. Beside themselves with joy and weeping happy tears they went to the tomb of our Redeemer Jesus, to offer due worship.

Next morning our men crept secretly out on the roof of the temple, fell upon the Saracen men and women there, and cut their heads off with their swords. When Lord Tancred saw this, he was greatly vexed.[5]

Tancred was one of the commanders of the Italian contingent, largely made up of Norman knights. His angry reaction had no consequences: The warriors of God were forever staging the most repulsive butcheries among the civilian population of the war zones. According to Church doctrine these people were infidels and heathens anyway, and their damnation was certain, so what difference did it make?

Pope Innocent, whom we have already met, has left us an example of the rabble-rousing speeches that the preachers of the Crusades dinned into knightly ears: "And thus arose in that very place that son of perdition, Mohammed, the false prophet, who seduced many from the truth with worldly allurements and fleshly pleasures. His unbelief (*perfidia*) has indeed gone on spreading till our own day, but we trust in the Lord, who has already given us a sign that the end of this beast has arrived."[6]

The Saracens are also called infidels (*perfidi Sarraceni*) in the following letter from the Pope to the Christian faithful of the ecclesiastical province of Mainz in the year 1213. In it the Holy Father once again announces a crusade, with the promise of complete absolution from sin for everyone who takes part. The papal appeal is naturally legitimated by invoking Jesus in person: "Ah dearly beloved sons, transform your brotherly quarrels and ill will into a treaty of peace and mutual love. Gird yourselves like faithful vassals to do service for the Crucified. You must give your property and life without hesitation for Him who shed His blood for you."[7] For the citizens of Mainz, at any rate: The Pope was certainly not talking about the Saracens.

At the time this memorable document of Christian love for one's enemies was penned, Jerusalem had long since been recaptured by the sons of
Mohammed (in 1187). The first great thrust of the Crusades was past,
and Emperor Barbarossa had miserably drowned in a river in Turkey
(1190). But on the other hand, Venetian business interests were rising to
greater prominence, and the doges urged the Crusaders on to take Constantinople (1204). The (Christian) city was thoroughly plundered, and
in the process countless relics were stolen and brought to the West, among
them such important souvenirs as a piece of the True Cross, an arm of St.
James, and a leftover bit of Mary's milk.

This mass hysteria flared up for the last time in the Children's Crusade
of 1212. (The duped children and adolescents were loaded onto ships at
Marseille and sold as slaves in Alexandria.) Around this time Walther von
der Vogelweide sang a rather melancholy song, compassionately recalling
the loss of Jerusalem: *Jerusalem, nun weine, wie dein vergessen ist.*[8]
(Now weep Jerusalem, for you have been forgotten.)

It obviously never occurred to the good man that the majority of the
population of Jerusalem was overjoyed not to have anything more to do
with the peculiar form of charity practiced by the Crusaders.

In the year 1265, when the rule of the Crusaders in the Near East was
approaching its end, French Templar Ricaut Bonomel wrote some remarkably disillusioned lines: "He is truly a fool who contends against the
Turks, when not even Jesus Christ fights them."[9] Lord Ricaut sees
through the Crusaders' double-talk with no trouble at all; it's always a
question of money: They sell God for money, and forgiveness in exchange
for clinking coins.

In the year 1291 Acre fell, the last Christian bastion, and the whole
nightmare was over.

In 1965 French scholar Jacques Le Goff, one of the most prominent experts on medieval history in his day, wrote: "Alongside the illusions of the
Crusades one must place the illusions of modern Western historians: For
the majority of them the Crusades had a considerable and on the whole
beneficial influence on the cultural and economic development of the
West."[10]

In reality, Le Goff continues, the common scholarly arguments on behalf of the Crusades simply don't stand up to critical scrutiny.

In reality the Crusades were a crude kind of mischief, to put it mildly.
By the time they were over it was high time for the Reformation. But as
history would have it, the Reformation was in fact another two hundred
years away.

Thanks to it, "Christendom" took the leap into modern times, with
Reformed Dutchmen and Englishmen as the vanguard of the industrial

revolution and modern capitalism. In retrospect, the Crusades proved to be the last show of power by the feudal classes of Europe. Soon afterward the nobility and all their knightly games were things of the past.

Also gone, and gone for good, was the innocence of Christendom (the term had already come into use in the Middle Ages). During the Crusades Europe, precisely insofar as it was Christian, compromised itself so badly that one wonders what right its rulers and leading thinkers ever had to appeal to Jesus Christ again.

WHICH RING WAS THE RIGHT ONE?

In the fall of 1212, the year of the Children's Crusade, after Clare had been safely installed in San Damiano, we find Francis for the first time on the high seas. He had managed to embark for Palestine (in Ancona, perhaps, or Brindisi), as a pious pilgrim to the shrines of the Holy Land. But the winds drove the vessel onto the coast of Dalmatia, as Celano relates: "When Francis saw that he had been cheated of his ardent desire, after a short while he begged some sailors who were planning to go to Ancona, to take him along, since it was unlikely that any more ships would be sailing to Syria that year. When the sailors stubbornly refused to take him, because he couldn't pay the fare, the saint of God, full of strong confidence in the Lord's kindness, stowed away on board with his companion."[11]

But the stowaways found, as Celano goes on to inform us, an unknown benefactor who supplied them with provisions during the passage. They shared them with the sailors, and in this way arrived back in their homeland.

Two years later,[12] after the Pentecost chapter, Francis left once more on a long journey, this time to Spain, to Santiago de Compostela, the most important place of pilgrimage in Europe after Rome. Celano insists that Francis wanted to proceed from Spain to Morocco, "to proclaim the gospel of Christ to the Miramolin and his people."[13] The *Fioretti* makes no mention of any such intention.[14] On the other hand, it does tell us the name of his companion on the trip: Bernard of Quintavalle, the first of his comrades.

It has been calculated how long it took Francis to get to Santiago.[15] His route took him first to Arles in Provence, then on to Toulouse, over the Pyrenees to Jaca (the old capital of the kingdom of Aragon) and Puenta la Reina, where the Camino del Sud met the Camino de Santiago, the famous pilgrims' route through Navarre, Leon, and Castille. All in all, Francis would have spent a good two months going from Assisi to Santiago de Compostela. Perhaps he succeeded in reaching the goal of his pilgrimage in time for the feast of St. James (Santiago in Spanish) on July 25.

Then he fell sick, as Celano reports, and was forced to cut short the voyage to Morocco. The Miramolin and the Moors had to forego the pleasure of making Francis' acquaintance. This is regrettable, at least insofar as the Miramolin could have had a discussion with Francis about a certain Ibn Tumart.[16] He had traveled through Morocco around 1120, preaching penance and admonishing people to remember the pure ideals of the Koran and poverty (!), so pleasing to God. The group of followers who joined up with him were called Al-Mowahhidun (the Christians turned this into Almohads), who took over the political leadership of North Africa in 1147. More to the point, the Miramolin, as an Almohad, was by spiritual descent a kind of Muslim Franciscan.

The conversation between Francis and the Miramolin might have dealt with the question of whether a religious (or in modern terms, ideological) reform movement ought to seek political power.

Francis would certainly have said "no."

He had no way of knowing that by the year 1288 the first Franciscan would be ascending the papal throne.[17]

Clearly, the world of politics evolves in accordance with its own internal mechanisms. It makes opportune use, then and now, of various penitential preachers, although the diverse faiths of the people belonging to this or that power block mean very little to their managers.

William Colby, for example, would surely be glad to chat with Francis about such subjects as, say, the relation of faith to politics. The conversation might deal with the necessity of propaganda, and it would develop that there was no essential difference between President Carter (pp. 4–5) and Pope Innocent (p. 132). Francis would probably express the wish to go on a trip to Moscow, for an audience with one of the top officials.

And nothing more would come of that than from Francis' visit to the residence of the Egyptian Sultan.

Let us now turn our attention to that remarkable event.

The year 1217 marked the beginning of methodical missionary activity in foreign countries by the Friars Minor. This was also the year in which Innocent III's most carefully prepared Crusade (partially financed by himself) was scheduled to set out.

Innocent himself had died the year before. His successor, an amiable old gentleman, reigned as Honorius III from 1216 till 1227. He immediately confirmed the Crusade politics of his predecessor, and stuck to the original target date, June 1, 1217, for the embarkation of the military contingents for Palestine.

But, to the distress of the Holy Father, the Crusade machine was having engine trouble.[18] The English, French, and German princes kept finding new excuses to shirk their vows. Palestine itself, after twenty relatively peaceful years, was in no mood for war. To the grandsons of the early Crusaders now settled in the Holy Land, the idea of reconquering Jerusalem seemed like a useless waste of effort. In the ports of Beirut, Tyre, and Acre the warehouses were full. Business was booming. They had more or less come to terms with the Mohammedans, and many an infidel girl carried on successful proselytizing operations in the beds of Christian lords.

Only the King of Hungary, the extravagant Andrew II, came with his contingent to the rendezvous in the spring of 1217, to discuss transport costs with the doge of Venice. Aside from Andrew, the count of Meran (Tyrolia) and Austria's Duke Leopold also appeared with troops. All told, around fifteen thousand men gathered on the shores of the Adriatic. Their numbers were swelled by a few knights from Norway and Pomerania, lead by Prince Sigurd and Duke Casimir. For the time being that was all.

In April 1217 the papal court could draw up an interim balance sheet.[19] The available forces would sail that year for Palestine. But the Emperor, who was detained in Germany on account of dynastic struggles, still hesitated, and like him the high nobility of France and England were holding back. (Frederick II didn't go to Acre until 1228, after he had already been excommunicated for his dilatory habits.) In this situation the papal Curia had an urgent need for propagandists to crank up the morale of knights not only in Germany and France, but in Palestine as well.

We have already mentioned that the cardinals were quite aware of the existence of the Franciscans. The reader will easily guess who the clever soul was who decided to hitch the unsuspecting Friars Minor to the papal wagon: Cardinal Ugolino, bishop of Ostia, later to be protector of the Order, canonizer of Francis, and founder of the papal Inquisition.

This is the story they tell: When the cardinal of Ostia, accompanied by many priests and religious, took part in the general chapter at Pentecost in the Portiuncula forest, all the brothers came out to meet him in a festive procession. As soon as they had all gathered together, he dismounted from his horse and walked with them to the chapel, where he said Mass and preached to them. Francis sang the Gospel. When the cardinal saw afterward how the brothers were sleeping on the bare ground, on thin straw, almost like animals, he was moved to tears, and said to his entourage:

"Look how the brothers are lying out there! How badly will it go with us, who have so many superfluous things for our daily comfort!"

At these words they were all deeply moved, and greatly edified.[20]

Nothing has come down to us concerning the content of the sermon delivered by the softhearted cardinal. We may assume that he said a few words about the Holy Sepulcher in Jerusalem, which was now in the hands of infidels, to the shame and disgrace of all Christendom, and about the pressing need for worthy knights to free it from the power of that supreme villain, Mohammed. And who would undertake to preach the Crusade to the irresolute Frankish knights?

General excitement among the friars. Volunteers came forward, burning with enthusiasm. Several groups of a dozen men were quickly thrown together and marched off to Germany, France, and Palestine; one even headed toward Hungary.[21] The chronicle continues: After that chapter, in which many brothers were sent off to faraway lands, St. Francis stayed behind with a few remaining brothers.[22]

Evidently he wanted to ponder in peace and quiet the consequences of this new development.

The collection of stories that we follow here subsequently tells us of Francis' decision to go to France, "so that the brothers will bear all their adversity more patiently, knowing that I am taking the same thing upon myself."[23] That doesn't sound exactly like wild enthusiasm for the Crusades.

The account later reports that Francis stopped in Florence on the way to France, had a meeting there with Cardinal Ugolino, and was urgently warned to stay in Italy. Francis obeyed and returned to Umbria. The only significant thing in all this is that in May 1217 Francis had no desire to go on a pilgrimage to the Holy Land, although a body of friars had just set out for there, under the leadership of Brother Elias. (We shall have to say a good deal more of him later on. He was made Francis' "vicar general" in the year 1221, and from then till 1239 was the actual head of the Order.)

Francis was in no particular hurry to visit the theater of war in the land of the Jews, Christians, and Muslims.

But two years later Francis leaped ashore in the harbor of Acre. The old collections of stories deal rather cursorily with Francis' experiences in this storm zone of world religions, and even the assiduous Celano forgets his usual volubility. The sources maintain a persistent silence about the most terrible shock in Francis' life.

Let us recall that it was Celano who told us in loving detail the moving story of Francis' concern for the two lambs destined for slaughter (p. 84). But Celano says not a word about the people in Damietta, whom Francis must have watched being butchered by the Crusaders. From the point of view of world history the capture of Damietta was a sort of nonevent. Two years later, in 1221, the city was back in the hands of the Sultan once more. Unless we have completely misunderstood Francis' character, the piles of corpses must have been a memory that haunted him all his days.

The siege of Damietta began in May 1218.[24] In February 1219 the Crusaders succeeded in investing the city on all sides, whereupon the Egyptian Sultan, Melek-al-Kamil, declared a holy war (March). At the same time he proposed peace talks, with the most generous conditions: transfer of the kingdom and city of Jerusalem to the Christians in exchange for the evacuation of Egypt. But the papal legate, Cardinal Pelagius of Santa Lucia, who was first in command, rejected the offer, against the advice of the experienced military personnel in the Christian camp.

In August Francis arrived from Acre and appeared in the camp before Damietta. A contemporary chronicle notes: "This man, who started the Order of the Friars Minor, Brother Francis by name, came to the army at Damietta and there did much good, and remained there until the city was taken. He saw the sin and evil which began to increase among the soldiers, and was displeased by it. For this reason he left there, stayed for a while in Syria, and then returned to his own land."[25]

Celano shows himself better informed here. He relates that Francis tried to dissuade the knights from attacking the beleaguered city. They laughed him to scorn.[26] The assault was a total failure, and the Christians lamented their six thousand dead and captured men.

We know from other sources that this abortive attack actually took place, on August 29, 1219.[27]

A passage from Celano's account may be quoted here verbatim: "They went, they joined battle, they fought, and our army was pressed hard by the enemy. In the very time of the battle, the holy man, in great suspense, made his companion go and watch the battle; and when he saw nothing the first or second time, he made him look a third time. And behold, the whole Christian army was turned to flight, and the battle ended in shame, not triumph."

Francis did not want to watch the carnage with his own eyes.

At the end of September the Sultan, whose camp was located six miles up the Nile, sent two Christian prisoners to the besieging forces with a new peace offer: a thirty-year truce, cession of all of Palestine to the Christians, compensation for the costs of repairing the walls of Jerusalem, relinquishment of a piece of the True Cross as a free gift, and twenty Muslim nobles as hostages.

Cardinal Pelagius refused once more.

Damietta fell on the fifth of November.

When the siege began, this flourishing port city had eighty thousand inhabitants. After it was captured by the Christian troops, only three thousand were left, of whom one hundred were unwounded. Jacques de Vitry,
who was bishop of Acre from 1216 to 1228 and followed the Crusaders'
army to Damietta, managed to save at least the children of the conquered
city from death or slavery by baptizing them on the spot.

He wrote a letter about his experiences in Damietta, and mentioned
Francis in it: "Sire Rainerio, the prior of St. Michael, has just entered the
Order of Friars Minor. They are an Order that is making great strides
throughout the world, and this is so because it expressly follows the way
of life of the primitive Church and its Apostles. . . . The master of these
brothers, who is also the founder of the Order, is called Francis; he is
loved by God and venerated by all men. He came into our camp and,
burning with zeal for the faith, he was not afraid to go into the very camp
of our enemy. For several days he preached the word of God to the
Saracens, but with little success. The Sultan sent for him in particular and
begged him to pray to the Lord for him, the ruler of Egypt, so that God
might show him which religion he should embrace. Colin, the Englishman, our clerk, has also entered this Order along with two other companions of ours: Master Michael and Dom Matthew, to whom I had entrusted the parish of the Holy Cross. . . . And I am having a difficult
time holding onto the chanter, Henry, and a few others."[28]

In this letter from Damietta, written in the spring of 1220, Francis' visit
to the Sultan is mentioned almost incidentally, in between accounts of the
bishop's daily concerns, which makes it sound all the more authentic.

We do not know when exactly Francis talked with the Sultan. But
presumably his visit to the enemy's camp took place after the fall of
Damietta, in an interval of exhaustion in the war between Christians and
Muslims.

The Sultan who took an interest in Francis was by no means a shadowy
figure of legend. We know all sorts of things about him, from the chronicles of Muslim historians. Melek-al-Kamil was a descendant of the Ajjubid
dynasty. Its founder, Saladin (a Kurd), had retaken Jerusalem in 1187.
Our sultan was his nephew, roughly the same age as Francis, highly
educated, with a special predilection for the mystical poetry of the Sufis.
He was also a gifted general: In August 1221 he dealt the Crusaders a
devastating defeat on the Nile, after which Cardinal Pelagius had to sue
for peace. An eight-year truce was signed, the Christians had to evacuate
Damietta and Egypt, and Jerusalem remained in Muslim hands.

The Sufis were Islamic ascetics dressed like Francis in coarse wool (*suf*
in Arabic), whence their name. They prized voluntary poverty. (The
terms for Muslim religious ecstatics, "fakir" and "dervish," are taken from

139

the words, Arabic and Persian, respectively, for poor.) In a remarkable parallel to Christian Europe, Islam in the twelfth century also saw the formation of brotherhoods, something like Orders, on the basis of ideal poverty and personal devotion to God.

From all this we may confidently assume that the Sultan received Francis with respect.

Before their meeting, to be sure, Francis had been beaten, if Bonaventure's account can be trusted. According to this tradition[29] the enemy sentries had seized Francis and his companion, named Illuminato, and grossly mistreated them. Then Francis had cried out: "Soldan! Soldan!"

Thinking they might have come for a parley, the soldiers shackled both men and led them to headquarters.

It is possible that Bonaventure got these details firsthand—that is, from that same Brother Illuminato. There are, in fact, a number of descriptions, Franciscan and otherwise, of Francis' adventures in the Sultan's camp.[30] They are all written from a Christian viewpoint, and are to that extent biased. They also frequently contradict each other, and reading them one sometimes has the feeling of listening to a tale from the *Arabian Nights* rather than a factual report.

For example, the *Fioretti:* The Sultan liked to listen to the blessed Francis, and begged him to return often. He also granted him and his companions permission to preach wherever they wished, and gave them a safe-conduct, so that no harm could befall them. And thus Francis sent his disciples out in pairs to the lands of the heathens, and for his part traveled about with a companion.

And there in an inn he met a woman, fair of face but corrupt of soul, who desired to sin with him. Francis said to her:

"If you want me to do as you wish, then you must do me a favor too."

The woman agreed and pushed him toward the couch. But Francis pulled her toward the huge fireplace, where a mighty blaze was burning. He undressed and laid himself naked on the hearth, as if on a bed, and said to the woman:

"Now, quickly, take your clothes off and enjoy this delightful couch with me!"

When the woman saw that the saint was uninjured by the fire, she was converted at once from the filth of her sins. She left the darkness of paganism behind, turned to Jesus Christ, and later won many souls to the Lord.[31]

When we look for the historical core of this truly medieval story, we may imagine that the Sultan sent a lovely girl to Francis' tent, simply out of politeness or with the arch idea in the back of his head of leading this Christian penitent a little way into temptation.

In any case, we may reasonably assume that Francis spent at least a week in the Sultan's camp, that the cultivated prince took a lively interest in him, and that they had long conversations about the true faith and the best way to live a life pleasing to God. (We should not forget that the Sultan must have been rather bored by day-to-day life in the camp.)

The first meeting between Francis and the Sultan may have gone like this: When Francis was led before the Sultan, the prince first had a splendid carpet brought in, whose design was woven out of many crosses. It was the custom to make deserters from the Christian camp walk over the crosses, to test their willingness to trample on the sign of the cross.

Francis marched without hesitation across the carpet. And then he told the Sultan through an interpreter why he had had no scruples about treading on the little crosses: "Know, O Prince, that thieves were also crucified along with our Lord. We have the True Cross of our Lord and Savior Jesus Christ; we adore it and show it great devotion; if the holy Cross of the Lord has been given to us, the cross of the thieves has been left to you as your share That is why I had no scruple in walking over the symbols of brigands."[32]

The theological wit of this reply delighted the Sultan. He realized that this was no ordinary fool or fanatic standing before him, and gave orders to lodge the peculiar guest as befitted a man of God.

Some time later a kind of religious discussion took place,[33] as we know, not only from Christian accounts, but also from the Muslim chronicler, Al Zajjat. He informs us that in "the affair of the famous monk"[34] the Sultan consulted his theological adviser, the respected mystic Fakr-al-Din. Jurists and judges were also called in on the case.

The judges recommended that the Sultan not engage in any sort of debate with the foreign monk. They said: "Our law, O Sultan, forbids us to listen to those who preach another law than ours. Rather such men should have their heads cut off instantly."

The Sultan, of course, had no intention of foregoing the pleasure of a debate on religion and philosophy. He let Francis have his say: "My position is difficult, O Prince, for I cannot take my arguments from holy Scripture, because your doctors do not believe in it. Furthermore it is our conviction that reason follows faith and does not precede it, so that the light of understanding can only illumine someone who has already come to believe; for faith is superior to all human reason."

Let us not inquire any further into the question of whether Francis really displayed the elegance of a High Scholastic controversialist. It seems more likely that the argument over which was the true religion soon came to a dead end, whereupon Francis made a quite sensational proposal: He declared himself ready to walk through fire.

In Francis' day the judgment of God (to the Christians *ordalia,* to the Muslims *mubahala*) was a generally recognized test of truth, although it was officially forbidden by both Christian and Islamic religious authorities. It has a long history. We find the custom of the ordeal practiced chiefly in societies that lack a fully developed procedure for dealing with disputes. (Hence its absence in Roman law.) The purpose of the ordeal was to ascertain the facts in crimes that had no witnesses (murder by an unknown party, adultery, sorcery, theft). The methods included trial by poison, fire, and water, as well as dueling and casting lots.

To begin with, Francis proposed a double ordeal. He and Brother Illuminato would walk through a large fire, but so would the Muslim doctors. Whichever side remained unharmed would have God's confirmation of the truth of its cause.

We begin to suspect what it was that drove Francis into the Sultan's camp and finally made him suggest the desperate idea of a trial by fire: Since the war between the Christians and the Muslims had been waged in the name of truth, Francis wanted to establish that *his* truth was the real one. Once that was achieved all armed conflict would have no legal standing.

While there can be little doubt that Francis set off on his journey to the "infidels" with all the unquestioning bigotry of the convinced Christian, the conclusion seems equally inescapable that in the Orient his Western prejudices crumbled one after the other. There he would have learned that the Mohammedans had a quite superior religion, even in the Christian sense, with belief in one God, as in the Bible.

Then in the siege of Damietta Francis saw how the Christian priest and commander-in-chief Pelagius had rejected the Sultan's very sensible peace offers. Finally, he had watched as the Christian troops in Damietta massacred their enemies—once more under the leadership of a cardinal of the holy Roman Church. Hence I would interpret Francis' willingness to undergo the trial by fire as proof that he wanted peace at all costs, even if it meant taking the risk that God would favor the Muslims and let him die in the flames.

Fortunately for Francis, the opposition declined his suggestion, because it ran counter to the will of the Prophet; at which Francis declared himself ready to walk through the flames all by himself.

He said to the Sultan: "If I come out of the fire unharmed, then you and your people shall accept the Christian faith. But if I burn, you may ascribe it to my sins."

This wager rightfully struck the Sultan as unfair. Besides, we must keep in mind that he was far more civilized than Francis. He therefore turned down Francis' second proposal as well, and ordered that gold, silver, and magnificent suits of clothing be prepared for the departure of the two guests. And so the Sultan said to Francis: "Pray for me, that God may reveal to me the faith that is most pleasing to him."

This noble reply, suggesting the rising of those twin stars, skepticism and tolerance, reminds us of the parable of the rings from Lessing's *Nathan the Wise*: "Which ring was the right one?"[35]

As a matter of fact, the story of the three rings, of which only one is genuine, goes back beyond Boccaccio's *Decameron* to the court of Frederick II in Sicily, which puts us in Francis' day.

We certainly have no wish to impute to Francis, with his undeniably Catholic convictions, the sort of slightly mocking agnosticism that flourished in the circle of that proto-Enlightenment figure, Frederick. (The line about the "three archdeceivers," Moses, Jesus, and Mohammed,[36] has been attributed to the Hohenstaufen Emperor—though to be sure the attributor was a rabidly angry Pope, Gregory IX, erstwhile Cardinal Ugolino of Ostia.) In the face of Francis' basic sense of identification with Jesus, we cannot suppose that while at the Sultan's court he might have come upon the notion that perhaps his Catholic religion wasn't quite as absolute as he had always believed.

But, then, Catholic literally means "comprehensive," "referring to the totality."[37] One can understand this missionary-fashion, in the sense of an effort to win the whole world for the Pope. That was (and is) the Crusader or *conquistador* mentality. We can be sure that this ideology lost its hold on Francis, down on the Nile, in 1219.

Maybe then a finer kind of Catholicism began to dawn on him, a broad benevolence that renounces particular dogmatic formulae and fanatical credos of every sort.

In any case, Francis went home with the clear consciousness that his beloved Jesus was once more being crucified, this time by the Crusades and all of Christendom.

INFLATIONARY GRACE

To this day Francis' disciples, organized into the Franciscans (O.F.M.), Minorites (O.F.M. Conv.), and Capuchins (O.F.M. Cap.), preside over a custom that strikes outsiders as quite singular. Any Catholic who goes to confession, receives communion, and says three Our Fathers in any Franciscan, Minorite, or Capuchin church on August 2, receives a "plenary indulgence"[38]—that is, in modern terms, an expiation of all "temporal" punishment for sins that have already been nullified, as far as guilt is concerned. Catholics distinguish between *guilt*, which is wiped away in confession, and *punishment* for sins, which remains even after confession and must be atoned for through suffering, either in this life or the next. The extent of the punishment is unknown, but it can be measured in units of time, and is therefore "temporal." (The punishment of hellfire is outside of time, and hence "eternal.")

For everyone who believes in it, a plenary indulgence is an extremely advantageous offer, as far as celestial bookkeeping goes. After confession the soul is indeed clean, but one's account is still charged with a sentence that must be served (e.g., liver cancer). In case the sinner has not suffered all punishment meted out for his or her sins here below, then he or she must burn in the fires of purgatory until everything is straightened out. Then he or she enters heaven. A plenary indulgence, by contrast, immediately cancels all punishment due for sin. The soul of anyone fortunate enough to get hold of a plenary indulgence before death leaps instantly into heaven.

Nowadays many Catholics (including the author) find this arrangement rather comic.

In Francis' age, with its very real fear of hell, a plenary indulgence was such a precious thing that in the beginning it was accorded only to Crusaders (Pope Urban II granted the first one in the year 1095). The subtle distinction between guilt and punishment, mentioned above, did not yet exist. A knight who cleansed his sword of infidel blood and boarded ship for home could feel free of all guilt before God.

In the year 1277, fifty-one years after Francis' death, an astonishing document came to light. A man named Angelo,[39] provincial minister of the Friars Minor in Umbria, on the orders of the minister general, Hieronymus of Ascoli (the future Pope Nicholas IV), compiled a series of notarized depositions confirming the authenticity of a plenary indulgence given to Francis by Pope Honorius. The indulgence had been promised (orally) for all those who said a prayer on the second of August in the Portiuncula chapel. (August 2 was the feast of the consecration of the Portiuncula.)

The witnesses who were produced: Brother Benedict and Brother Regnier state that Brother Masseo (p. 107) explicitly told them several times how the indulgence had been granted. Peter Zalfani states that when he was a young man he was present at the consecration of the Portiuncula and heard the address that Francis gave on that occasion. Jacob Coppoli (from Perugia) states that he had the story of the circumstances in which the Pope mentioned the indulgence, directly from Leo.

The scholarly dispute over the authenticity of this memorandum dating from 1277 is still going on. No one denies that the document itself is authentic; the question is whether the witnesses told the truth, or whether their statements were simply made up to provide retroactive justification for the indulgence (which was already in use then).

Such forgeries were legion in the Middle Ages.

Modern-day Franciscans need not worry about the origins of their indulgence: Over the years several Popes have confirmed it, and extended it to all Franciscan churches; thus the throngs of Catholics on August 2, which Francis' executors must find quite satisfying.

For us, however, the question of whether Francis himself requested and obtained a plenary indulgence from the Pope has a particular interest in that the indulgence constitutes an artful act of sabotage against the idiocy of the Crusades.

In any event, for sinful knights from London, Paris, or Cologne, Assisi was at all events closer to home than Jerusalem, and a couple of Our Fathers less dangerous than an open battle in Syria or Egypt.

As a matter of fact, there are reports that in the latter half of the thirteenth century the Franciscans who were occupied in preaching and gathering funds for the Crusades strongly protested against the Portiuncula indulgence, as a manifest interference in their own business of marketing grace.

It's also quite possible, of course, that Minister Elias, who was in the process of erecting the enormous basilica of St. Francis in Assisi, was looking for an extra attraction to draw large numbers of pilgrims from all over the world. In that case he may have pushed the wondrous indulgence through the papal Curia, which allowed him to make use of it "unofficially," somewhere around 1230.

In any case, a few decades after Francis' death the Portiuncula indulgence was famous throughout Europe, and every year pilgrims poured into Assisi from all over.

Perhaps Francis was behind the whole business after all.

Neither Celano nor the *Fioretti* tell us anything about the Portiuncula indulgence. But in the Leo stories we find a clear reference to the disputed act of grace: "We who were with St. Francis bear witness that he made special claims for this church, on account of the great privilege which the Lord made manifest there, and because it was revealed to him in this place that among all the other churches in the world which the Virgin loved, she loved this church."[40]

(The Latin of the original is as clumsy as the translation. The "Lord" of the text is God, the "Virgin" is Mary, "this church" is the Portiuncula, and the divine revelation concerning the supreme importance of the Portiuncula, including its great privilege, is granted to Francis.)

This text, the beginning of a long passage dealing with various remarks by Francis on the Portiuncula, dates from the year 1246. That makes it thirty-one years older than the notarized document previously mentioned (p. 144), and so enhances its authenticity.

The story of how Francis talked the Pope into giving him the indulgence may actually have happened.

This is the story they tell:[41] Now when Francis had walked to Perugia with Masseo and paid his respects to the lord Pope Honorius, he said: "There is a tiny chapel in the neighborhood of Assisi that I myself restored some years ago. It has grown very dear to my brothers and me, and now it is to be reconsecrated, to the honor of the holy Virgin, and given over to the regular devotions of the Friars Minor, which is as it should be. This is what brings me here. I beg of you an indulgence for everyone who devoutly visits this chapel on the feast of its consecration, without any further conditions."

The Pope: "If I understand you rightly, you wish the Church to grant a remission of punishment, although dispensing with gift offerings is contrary to custom. Perhaps we might consider granting a year's indulgence."

"Holy Father, what is a single year?"

"Well, do you want three years, or even seven?"

"Dearest Lord Pope, I don't want years, I want souls!"

(A stir in the audience chamber. Honorius, who is known to have given his property to the poor, remains well disposed to Francis.)

"What does that mean, my son?"

"That everyone who enters this humble chapel on the feast of its consecration and piously goes to confession should be released from all penance and punishment for his sins, both in this world and the next."

"Come, come, my friend! That would be absolutely inconsistent with the practice of the Roman Curia."

"Christ told me that there should be a new practice."

(The Pope turns to his attendants. They plead with him. Francis throws himself on his knees, slides nearer to the Pope, and embraces his legs. The Pope stands up.)

"Plenam suorum peccaminum veniam indulgemus."[42]

(Francis understands enough Latin to grasp the meaning of the statement. The Pope has actually granted a plenary indulgence. Now Francis is in a hurry. He makes a rudimentary gesture of kissing the Pope's foot, as prescribed by ceremony, and heads for the exit.)

"Stop! Aren't you going to wait till they draw up the bull, you strange little man?"

"My witness is the holy Virgin, Christ is my notary, and for guarantors I take the holy angels of God!"

(The secretaries entreat the Pope to define the indulgence clearly and thereby limit it.)

"Know then that this indulgence holds good only from the hour of vespers on the day before till vespers on the day of consecration."

And Francis was dismissed. He walked with Masseo back to Assisi. On the way he got very tired, and so near the village of Colle he lay down for a little while in the shade, fell asleep, and had a dream. When he awoke refreshed, he said to Masseo:

"God's dear Son just told me that the indulgence has been recognized in heaven too."

The story goes on: Now when the day of the reconsecration of the Portiuncula arrived (the second of August), and the bishops of Assisi, Perugia, Todi, Spoleto, Gubbio, Nocera, and Foligno came to the festive occasion, at the brothers' invitation, Francis got up on a chair and spoke to the crowd:

"I want to send you all to paradise, now, at this very hour. Know that the lord Pope has granted me a plenary indulgence for all of you who have come today, but also forever after, to everyone who says his prayers in this chapel on its consecration day. All his sins and penances will be canceled. But take note that this only holds good for this one day in August, up till the hour of vespers."

Thus, say the witnesses, the celebrated Portiuncula indulgence had its origin at that time, to the praise and glory of Our Lord Jesus Christ and His blessed Mother.[43]

The grace inflation that began in Assisi didn't reach the Eternal City till a few decades later. When the last bastion of Christendom in the Holy Land had fallen, thereby making the shrines in Palestine almost inaccessible to pilgrims, Pope Boniface VIII in the year 1300 decided to proclaim a plenary indulgence for everyone who visited the city that year and prayed at the tombs of the holy Apostles. (This so-called jubilee indulgence is still granted, at intervals of twenty-five years. The last one was in 1975. The next one will presumably be in the year 2000, provided we don't have a nuclear war before then.)[44]

The destructive capacity of today's "major powers" makes the era of the Crusades look almost idyllic by comparison. The barbarism of two World Wars within fifty years, of Auschwitz, Dresden, and Hiroshima, has compromised the bourgeois faith in progress more seriously than the Christian Crusades ever did.

What can you do with a faith that has been compromised?

Francis spent the last six years of his life struggling with this question, and if he found a conclusive answer he never left us word of it.

XI

AS A MAN IN CHAINS

HERE is a tortured passage—undoubtedly written by Francis himself—from the *Testament* of 1226: "And I firmly wish to obey the minister general of this brotherhood and any guardian whom it may please him to give me. And I wish to be a captive in his hands, that I may neither go nor act without his will and command, because he is my master. And although I am simple and infirm, I want to have a cleric with me always to say the office for me as it is in the Rule.

"All the friars are likewise bound to obey their guardians and to say the office according to the Rule. If any are found who are not saying the office according to the Rule, and want to vary it in any way or are not Catholic, all the friars, wherever they are, are bound by obedience, wherever they may find any such, to bring him before the custodian of the convent nearest to where they find him. And the custodian shall be firmly bound by obedience to keep him strongly guarded as a man in chains day and night so that it is not possible for him to escape from his hands, until he can personally transfer him into the hands of his minister. And the minister shall be firmly bound by obedience to send him in the charge of friars capable of guarding him day and night as a man in chains until they bring him face to face with the bishop of Ostia, who is the lord, protector, and corrector of the whole brotherhood."[1]

The voice that speaks to us in this text belongs to a broken man. The language, with all its recurrent twists and turns, describes a single operation: how a hand lays a powerful grip on its sacrificial offering and refuses to let go. Twice the text speaks openly of hands that clutch their prey. Francis himself wishes, as he says, to be given over "into the hands" of the minister general, without whose permission he cannot make a move. And the disobedient brother—this is the second mention of the word—must be watched so carefully that he cannot "escape from his hands."

On four occasions people are said to be "bound" (*teneantur*). All brothers are bound to obey their guardian and to say the required prayers. All brothers are bound to bring disobedient brothers to the nearest custodian. The custodian is bound to place the guilty party under detention. The minister is bound to send the arrested man to the bishop of Ostia.

Everybody is bound in this text, including the officials. What they are bound to are orders. The orders are written down in the "Rule." The bishop of Ostia is the final link in the chain of command that binds everyone. His is the "master." (The minister general, whom Francis calls his master, is subject to the bishop.)

The bishop of Ostia's master is the Pope.

The Pope's master is God.

Only God is not "bound."

Or is He? What would this God do without men to give orders to? He would be "the absolute form of absolute boredom," as Heidegger says.[2] This closes the circle, and there is no way out.

Francis speaks in his *Testament* like a man under arrest. He seems to be talking to his fellow prisoners.

All brothers, even the "ministers," "guardians," and "custodians" (p. 128), are to understand that they are bound like men in chains. If any one of them breaks away, they must watch him day and night and bring him to the cardinal protector.

And we know who *he* is: Ugolino, of the house of Segni, born a count, nephew of Innocent III, in 1196 cardinal deacon, in 1206 cardinal bishop of Ostia, in 1227 Pope.

We shall be careful not to build him up into the villain of this book. It was just that Francis fell into Ugolino's hands. "The human hand that will no longer loosen its grip is the essential symbol of power."[3] This conclusion (by Elias Canetti) fairly describes the situation that this chapter will deal with.

In the section of the *Testament* on handing over the disobedient brother to the bishop of Ostia, Francis is not making a simple declarative statement. He does not speak in the indicative but in the ought mode (*teneantur*, not *tenentur*). Likewise Francis does not say: "I am a captive in the hands of the minister general." He says instead: "I wish to be a captive in his hands."

In a direct and highly moral fashion Francis affirms his own chains and the chains binding his brotherhood.

He does not say: "That is the way things are, my friends. Conform, or you'll have a bad time of it." He says instead: "The fact that you and I are fettered is good—something to be desired. It is a virtue to live like a man in chains."

That is why this text from Francis' *Testament* strikes us as so tortured, and why one has the impression of listening to the voice of a broken man.

We recall Francis' sermon before the Pope, and his confrontation with Ugolino before the assembled brothers. Both events occurred before 1220.[4] At that point it would have been impossible to call Francis submissive. Six years later the same man inserted in his *Testament* that passage where the chains of slavery rattle away. We wonder what they did to Francis in the final years of his life.

People who themselves belong to the chain of command—university professors, for example, or Catholic priests—will find our question about the change in Francis surprising. They'll say: "Francis recommended obedience all during his lifetime." They have to talk this way because they themselves have obeyed all their lives and trained others in obedience.

The overwhelming majority of modern scholarly experts on Francis consists of university professors and Catholic priests. (Most of the latter belong to one of the three Franciscan Orders.)

When Protestant theologian Paul Sabatier published his book on Francis in 1894, he was a pastor in a tiny corner[5] of the Cévennes in France. (Memories there of the insurrection of the local Huguenots, the "Camisards," against Louis XIV's brutal campaign of forced conversions, from 1702 to 1710, are still very much alive.) Only in 1919 did Sabatier become a professor, at the University of Strasbourg.

"Almost everything," he writes, "which was done in the Order after 1221 was done either without Francis' knowledge or against his will. If one were inclined to doubt this, one need only glance over that most solemn and also most adequate manifesto of his thought—his Will. There he is shown freed from all the temptations which had at times made him hesitate in the expression of his ideas, bravely gathering himself up to summon back the primitive ideal, and set it up in opposition to all the concessions which had been wrung from his weakness.

"The Will is not an appendix to the Rule of 1223, it is almost its revocation. But it would be a mistake to see in it the first attempt made to return to the early ideal. The last five years of his life were only one incessant effort at protest both by his example and his words."[6]

A chorus of learned Franciscans rose up against Sabatier. (He died in 1928, and the Franciscans are still writing against him.) But it was a German professor of history who as early as 1903 furnished the most convenient example of how to obscure the conflict between Francis and the bureaucratic terror of his day. Walter Goetz wrote a study, "The Original

Ideals of St. Francis of Assisi," in which he claimed that Francis had to live through the realization that "his ideal was unattainable."[7] This opinion continues to be repeated even today, along with the equally convenient rhetorical flourish about "the profound tragedy of St. Francis' life"[8] (Goetz).

These scholars have obviously never read a line of Kafka.

Sabatier juxtaposes, quite rightly, two documents that Francis composed: the "Rule" of 1223, approved by the Pope, and the *Testament* of 1226. Francis' *Testament*, in fact, contains evidence to bolster Sabatier's thesis that in the last five years of his life Francis put up a continual fight against the chains binding himself and his fellowship.

But then there is that passage we quoted at the beginning of this chapter. Francis' language there sounds burned out, lifeless. It has an authoritarian structure, of the sort that arises in closed institutions, in monasteries, barracks, prisons, insane asylums, and concentration camps. The latter, those monstrous creations of the twentieth century, have sharpened our ideas of what institutions are really like, and we have come to mistrust them all.

(Michel Foucault, in contrast to the insipid theorizing on the subject by most contemporary sociologists, has revealed the true connection between institutions and internment.[9] All the workhouses, prisons, and reform schools, etc., for the *Lumpenproletariat* which, starting in the seventeenth century, spread over Europe like a net, incarnate the institutional reality of the modern state.)

Between 1220 and 1226 Francis had to watch as his brotherhood (fellowship, society, alliance—*religio* in medieval Latin) was turned into an institution (*ordo*). We shall see how greatly this development made him suffer. The critical question is whether it took possession of him and broke him.

"FROM NOW ON I AM DEAD TO YOU"

In the winter of 1219–20 Francis left Damietta (see Chapter X) and went to Palestine. He spent some months there, but we know nothing more about it.

During his absence from Italy his two representatives ("vicars"), Matthew of Narni and Gregory of Naples, had reached a momentous decision: They agreed to the erection of fixed residences for the Friars Minor in the larger cities.[10] Pietro Stacia's house of studies was built in the period between the summer of 1219 and the summer of 1220, while Francis was away in the Orient.

At Pentecost in 1220 the vicars held a meeting with the Italian officials of the Friars Minor, where stricter regulations for fasting were decreed, to keep in line with the Rules of the "old Orders."

In addition, a certain Brother Philip had obtained a series of privileges from the papal Curia for the Poor Clares—against Clare's will.

And finally there was one more little scandal. A man named Giovanni da Conpello had left the Franciscans and founded a separate Order, made up of men and women lepers.

Francis was dining, possibly in Acre, with Elias, Peter of Catania, and several other companions, when a troubled-looking brother from Italy burst into the peaceful group and laid a paper with the new measures (passed by the vicars) right on the table.

Francis gave the stringent new laws on fasting a leisurely glance, and then asked ironically: "What shall we do now?"

All the men looked thoughtfully at the pieces of meat floating in their soup bowls. Peter of Catania answered in the same ironic tone: "Ah, most noble lord Francis, you still have the power to decide what we may eat."

Francis: "Very well then, let us act in accordance with the Gospel and eat whatever they put in front of us."[11]

In this quite cheerful scene from the summer of 1220 Francis is not in the least panicky. "Some of the brethren have done some stupid things; we'll have to give them a little talking to."

Francis sailed back to Italy (which he probably wanted to do anyway) with Elias and Peter, arriving in Venice in September. His route took him through Bologna, and what happened there shows us Francis in something like a rage. He had the brand-new house of studies vacated on the spot—even the sick had to leave—which was an indication of his anger over a danger he was just beginning to appreciate. He had spotted the first symptoms of the nascent institutionalization of his fellowship.

Francis decided to go immediately to Rome, to see the Pope.

At that point Francis' group was by no means disorganized. Since 1217 the Friars Minor had divided Italy into five regions (or "provinces"), with one friar in each assigned to promote the exchange of information and the co-ordination of activities.[12] These "provincial ministers," we may be sure, were not originally authority figures, much less "superiors." The friars undoubtedly also had several bases of operations by that time: We need only think of the Portiuncula, with its few huts made of branches and clay, in the middle of the forest. Every brother knew about these remote settlements, in the Rieti Valley or in the Marches. They could find a place to sleep and something to eat there, perhaps rest for a few weeks, hear the latest news, and tell their own stories.

At Pentecost everybody would get together in a spot agreed on a year earlier, usually somewhere around Assisi. They would discuss their problems, get to meet new members, argue and laugh together, break up into groups and brotherly gangs, and beg all over the region, till they had picked it clean.

We have absolutely no reason for believing that Francis was disquieted by this turn of events, nor did the vigorous growth of the Order between 1217 and 1220 cause him any real anxiety.[13]

We have no reliable statistics as to the size of the Order in the late autumn of 1220, when Francis went off to Rome.[14] Any number between one thousand and three thousand is acceptable. In Spain, France, and Palestine the Friars Minor had already gotten a firm footing. In Italy, Francis could thank God, they were practically everywhere. It makes no sense to speak of a "serious crisis"[15] among the brethren during Francis' absence, despite the troubles described above. They were inevitable growing pains, Francis may have thought to himself, when he arrived in Rome some time that October. He would have a talk with Ugolino and perhaps with Honorius as well, to get rid of the one or two awkward recent developments, and that would be that.[16]

On the one point that really bothered him—the business of the fixed residences—Francis surely wanted to take vigorous action.

He knocked on the door of the palace where Ugolino lived.

The first thing he got was an unpleasant surprise.[17]

On September 22, 1220, a papal bull, *Cum secundum consilium*, had been promulgated.[18] It was directed to the *priores seu custodes* of the Friars Minor. *Prior* means superior, and it was a word that Francis avoided all his life. He even expressly forbade the use of the word *prior* in the first outline he authorized of a Rule for the Friars Minor.[19]

Francis' name was not mentioned in the bull. The first question he had to ask Ugolino was: "Have I been fired?"

In the bull the following was enacted: Beginning at once, all new candidates had to undergo a year of probation. Once the novice had finished it and taken his vows, he was definitively received into the community and could no longer simply leave it of his own accord. He was obliged to strict obedience to the prior or custodian. In case of any violation of the rules these two had the right to enforce discipline, following the guidelines of canon law.

Finally, there was yet another provision in the bull, a peculiarly vague statement: "No one shall violate the 'complete' poverty of the community."

For Francis a series of further questions arose:

"Why didn't they wait till I got back?

"Why did they introduce the year of probation?

"Why did the requirement of poverty have to be re-emphasized?"

Tradition is silent over what sort of answers Ugolino gave Francis. This much is certain: Francis went to the Pope not to protest against the bull, nor to raise objections to the building of fixed residences, but solely and simply to obtain the appointment of Ugolino as the cardinal protector of the Friars Minor.

This is the story they tell: Francis waited patiently at the entrance of the papal palace so as to speak to the Pope as soon as he came out. Now when the Pope emerged, the saint greeted him and wished him peace. The Pope graciously replied:

"God bless you, my son."

Then St. Francis said:

"My Lord, with your high honor and lofty obligations, it will not do for the common people to be always coming back and begging for an audience, even if it is necessary. I have gotten many fathers from you since the last time. Give me a single one to consult with, whenever the need may arise, so that as your representative he can handle my affairs and those of the Friars Minor and the sisters."

"Whom shall I give you, my son?"

"The reverend lord of Ostia!"

The Holy Father kindly complied with the blessed Francis' request.

Soon after that the cardinal of Ostia arranged so that the new orders for the Poor Clares were countermanded, and Brother Giovanni da Compello, along with his supporters in the Curia, fell into disgrace.[20]

One interesting thing about this text is the allusion to the "many fathers." Francis had realized that he was no match for the papal bureaucrats. Every day bull upon bull went streaming out all over the world, not, to be sure, without bribes and corruption, and one hand often had no idea what the other was doing.

How else could Brother Philip have gone and played that trick on the Poor Clares? And hadn't that ominous bull of September 22 been issued under rather murky circumstances? Hadn't the brothers in France obtained a brief (dated May 29, 1220) from the papal chancellery to French bishops concerning a special license to preach—while Francis was still in the Holy Land?[21] Wasn't Francis' brotherhood characterized in the papal bull as an *ordo* for the first time (a precedent that could later be appealed to)?

Francis, of course, was by nature strictly opposed to bulls and privileges of any sort. Now all of a sudden the papal chancellery was spewing out all kinds of paper at him.

That Francis went to the Pope at this juncture, to secure one of the most powerful men in the Curia as a protector, shows both his political cleverness and his determination to fight a delaying battle against the bureaucracy. It would be false to depict Francis as an unworldly *naïf* with no notion of ordinary reality. At the same time we recognize, as Francis did, the invisible boundary line that he had begun to run up against. The line is extremely elastic; it often yields and recedes, but only for a time and only to soothe the opposition. Over the long run it holds its place unswervingly. Francis wasn't struggling against human beings, but against a pliant, impersonal force that is very old and very patient, that has many ways and means, and that outlives us all.

Up to the present day nothing in this situation has changed.

Francis had to give in on two important points. The house of studies in Bologna stayed. (Ugolino formally took possession of it, as a concession to Francis.) The regulations covering reception into the Order also remained unchanged. Furthermore, Francis was forced to recognize that the Curia would not let his brotherhood continue without permanent, written, officially approved "rules." He himself, naturally, was to write this text, with some friendly assistance from experts schooled in canon law.

In Rome, in the late autumn of 1220, fear entered Francis' life:

He dreamed that a little black hen, with down on her legs like a tame pigeon, wanted to hide her chicks under her wings. But the chicks were too numerous. They hopped about the hen, looking for shelter and not finding it.[22]

Francis knew that he had dreamt of himself.

There was a danger he wanted to protect the Friars Minor from, and painfully, bewilderingly, he sensed his helplessness.

It got cold in Rome, and Francis began to be afraid.

This is the story they tell: At that time Francis went to Rome, to visit Ugolino, the bishop of Ostia and future Pope. Francis stayed at Ugolino's house for several days, and was graciously sent on his way. Then he paid his respects to Lord Leo, cardinal of Santa Croce. The cardinal was a kind man, with very cultivated manners, and an admirer of Francis as well. He was overjoyed at the saint's visit, and respectfully invited him to spend a few days with him. As usual in the winter, it was very cold, and it stormed and rained almost every day.

"This is not a good time, dear brother, to walk along the highways. If you like, you could stay with me and wait for better weather. Besides, I have poor people living in the house with me, and you could take your meals like one of them."

The cardinal said this because he knew that Francis always wanted to be thought of as a beggar, wherever he might be living.

"If you wish," the cardinal added, "you can pray and eat in a distant building that I'd be glad to put at your disposal."

Brother Angelo Tancredi, one of the first twelve companions, was also living in the cardinal's house at that time, and he said to Francis:

"There is a beautiful tower on the city walls, right nearby. It's big inside and spacious, with nine vaulted rooms. You'll be all by yourself, as much as in a hermitage."

So Francis went with Angelo to the tower, had a look at it, and agreed to stay there for a few days. The cardinal was delighted, and Brother Angelo got everything ready so that Francis and his companion would remain undisturbed. It was understood that Angelo himself would deliver the food to the door once a day, because Francis did not wish to leave his retreat.

But on the first night that Francis spent in the tower, the demons came and beat him badly.

Francis cried out to his companion, who was sleeping apart from him.

He said: "Brother, the demons have given me a cruel beating. I am afraid. Please stay by me."

So his companion remained at Francis' side all through the night, for the saint's entire body was trembling, as if in a fever. As they kept watch together, Francis said:

"Why did the demons strike me?

"Why did God give them the power to do me harm?"

Then Francis began to speak of the demons as God's constables.

He said: "Just as the mayor sends his constables to those who have done wrong, so God punishes those he loves by means of the demons, who are his servants.

"It could be that God has sent his constables to me because I accepted the cardinal's hospitality.

"If the brothers hear that I have been staying with a cardinal, they might well murmur against me and say that they were suffering privations while I was making myself comfortable."

Thus the night passed away.

In the early morning Francis left the tower, went to the cardinal, and told him what had happened. Francis said:

"People take me for a pious man, and the demons have already beaten me and thrown me out of my cell!"

The cardinal understood that Francis didn't want to stay any longer.

But Francis withdrew to the hermitage of Fonte Colombo, near Rieti.[23]

The sturdy reality of the demonic beating comes out of a culture that lived as familiarly with its demons and angels as we do with germs and vitamins. Because of our different conventions we can no longer understand the way Francis takes devils for granted. (The cardinal likewise never doubted their existence for a moment.)

But we have no difficulty imagining someone having a severe anxiety attack, and this detailed story from the Leo collection deals with just that. (Leo himself was probably the witness of that night in the cardinal's tower.)

Francis' conjectures as to the meaning of this nocturnal assault reveal both the extent of his insecurity and the depths of his depression after the talks with Ugolino. As he slowly traveled North in the early winter, his state of soul must have fit in perfectly with the season.

On March 10, 1221, Peter of Catania died in Assisi.[24] Francis had designated this man as his "vicar" (representative), probably as early as 1217 or 1218. (We may assume that Francis thought nothing of naming several such vicars in the years before his departure for the Holy Land. Sometimes they were also called "ministers general," and their function, to Francis' mind, was purely administrative. As the number of brothers grew, Francis wanted to be able to disappear completely from the scene. So he made sure that there was always someone around to give advice when it was needed. The fact that he took Peter of Catania with him to Palestine shows his casual attitude to questions of management.

When Francis learned of the death of Peter of Catania, he made Brother Elias his vicar, in a rather informal and offhanded way.

On May 30, 1221, the usual Pentecost chapter of the Friars Minor began in the forest of the Portiuncula.[25]

Thus Francis spoke to a companion: "I see myself speaking to the entire chapter, as I used to before. They listen to my sermon and instructions. I have barely finished when they stand up against me and shout:

" 'We don't want you anymore as our master! You haven't learned how to talk properly. You nobody, you simpleton, you want to dictate to us!'

"And they dismiss me, to my shame and disgrace.

"Must I not rejoice to see this happen?

"Is it not right, if they don't want me as superior?"[26]

This is the story they tell:

At that time Francis resigned the leadership in the presence of all the brothers, with these words:

"From now on I am dead to you."

Then the brothers wept exceedingly, and sighs went up all around.[27]

Francis said: "I had realized that God was daily multiplying the number of the brothers, and the old fervor was growing lukewarm. Therefore I handed over the responsibility for the brotherhood to the ministers, and gave up the duty of directing it, while I pleaded poor health as an excuse. So I withdrew, at the general chapter.

"I know that I would have gladly remained their only minister till my death, if they had lived as I wished them to.

"But in reality I would have had to act like a hangman, smiting and striking like the mighty men of this world.

"But let God's constables take care of that, the invisible executors of his will!

"Yet I shall never stop to show the brothers by my life the way God has shown me, until I die."[28]

We recall Jordan of Giano's report on the Pentecost assembly of the year 1221 (p. 127f.). Elias was in command, while Francis sat alongside him, obviously not in the best of health, occasionally tugging on his habit and telling him something he wanted passed on to the brothers.

This picture comes as close to the historical reality as anything we have.

It is conceivable that one group loudly voiced its opposition to Francis—some of the masters and doctors who had only recently joined the Order and who couldn't understand why Francis had closed down the modern house of studies in Bologna.

It is certain that in some form or other Francis resigned.

It is just as certain that the majority of the brothers was still on his side.

Francis needed their support, because now the real paper war began, the battle over the written version of the Rule.

PLANNING A TRIP

Here is Jacques de Vitry, bishop of Acre (p. 139), on the Friars Minor: "[This Order] seems to us very dangerous in that not only perfect souls (*perfecti*), but young men and far from perfect (*imperfecti*), who ought to be enclosed and proved for some time under conventual discipline are sent out two by two through the whole world."[29]

The bishop, who had hardly any official dealings with the friars, expressed this opinion in the spring of 1220. It is characteristic—hence its interest for us—of the kind of anxiety the Franciscans caused Church bureaucrats.

As if by magic, a few months later the papal bull of September 22, 1220, echoed Lord Jacques' misgivings precisely, although the bishop never contacted the papal Curia. (He remained in Palestine.)

We have all been brought up to cherish the ideals of railroad executives (punctuality, orderliness, etc.), and so the steps taken by the authorities to regulate the Franciscans (year of probation, more discipline, etc.) don't strike us as absurd as, from a Christian viewpoint, they really are. We cannot imagine how a group of three thousand men could exist without rules and regulations.

Francis could.

From the history of the Waldensians and all the harassment they endured from the authorities, we know that this fellowship led an underground existence for three hundred years, with secret schools for preachers and regular gatherings of "clients" (*Kunden,* as they were called in Germany).[30] Despite violent persecution by the Inquisition, papal and episcopal, the Waldensian preachers wandered over Europe, always in pairs, often disguised as doctors, and visited the scattered communities of believers. The Waldensians even had their own hospices, so we may assume that these crypto-Christians were highly organized.

It was organization from below, of the kind that grows out of the real needs of a group of people. It corresponds to the structure of the Friars Minor from 1208 to 1219.

After 1219, the year of the first papal bull concerning the Franciscans, a new type of organization began to be put into effect: the kind that works from above—i.e., from the seat of authority, the structured, prescriptive *ordo* of institutional regularity.

The reason for the change, even if the uneasy Jacques de Vitry did not formulate it very clearly, is quite obvious: control.

As has already been indicated, in Francis' day northern and central Italy was a hotbed of heresy. In a directive from Frederick II, dated November 22, 1220, the various heretical groups are neatly enumerated and made subject to criminal prosecution for violating imperial law.[31] The document bears the date of Frederick II's coronation as Emperor.

The place: Rome.

The Pope, whose stirrup the Emperor held after the coronation ceremony: Honorius III.

Was Francis a witness to this scene? He was, as previously mentioned, in the Eternal City just around this time.

Here is a little sample of imperial prose fulminating the "serpent's brood of unbelief": "Just as, when Our exalted wrath blazes out against those who have reviled Our name, we condemn those guilty of *lèse-majesté* to death and their children to disinheritance, so do We proceed even more justly against the revilers of the divine name and the detractors of the Catholic faith, in depriving, by imperial authority, the heirs and descendants of the protectors, patrons, and defenders of the heretics of all worldly goods, public offices, and honors, unto the second generation, so that they may fade away, living in continual affliction, remembering the crimes of their fathers, and knowing in truth that God is a jealous God, who mightily visits the sins of the fathers. But the heretics, in whatever part of the Empire they may be condemned by the Church and handed over to the secular tribunal, shall have the fitting punishment inflicted upon them. Thus do We ordain."[32] (The punishment was burning at the stake, preceded by torture and mutilation.)

Against this unpleasant background we can well appreciate the ejaculation that Brother Jordan of Giano was accustomed to utter: "O God, let not my faith be corrupted by the heretics of Lombardy!"[33]

Between the "poor men of Lombardy," just mentioned, and the Friars Minor, who appeared on the scene at roughly the same time, we can detect the following programmatic similarities:

1. Orientation toward the primitive Church.
2. Appeal to direct divine inspiration.
3. Emphasis on poverty as the justification for itinerant preaching.
4. Strong convictions about the principle of brotherliness.
5. Rejection of all leadership roles.
6. High estimation of manual work and care for the sick.[34]

The decisive point that clearly distinguishes these renewal movements one from the other is the readiness to submit to the control of Church authorities.

In other words, the "heresy" of the poor men of Lombardy consisted primarily in their reluctance to accept regulation from above.

This same issue was the subject of the negotiations that took place between Francis and the Curia from 1220 to 1223 concerning the creation of a Rule.

Francis was by nature full of artless good intentions toward the hierarchy, but from 1220 on he had a powerful new motive to watch his steps very carefully: fear for his brotherhood.

Francis had seen with his own eyes at Damietta (1219) and Rome (1220) what the Roman Church was capable of.

Modern Franciscan scholarship distinguishes among three "Rules": the *Regula Primitiva*, the *Regula Prima* (1221), and the *Regula Bullata* (1223).[35]

Only the last of these three texts acquired any effective standing. On November 29, 1223, it became law by means of the papal bull *Solet annuere*, which defined the Franciscans as an "Order" in the canon-law sense. (The original text of the bull is kept in the treasury in the basilica of St. Francis in Assisi.) To confuse the reader as little as possible, from now on we shall refer to *Regula Bullata* as the "papal Rule."

The *Regula Prima,* the text of which we still have, was not accepted by the papal Curia. We shall therefore call it the "draft Rule."

The *Regula Primitiva* has disappeared. Francis says of it in his *Testament:* "And, after the Lord gave me brothers no one showed me what I ought to do, but the Most High himself revealed to me that I ought to live according to the pattern of the holy Gospel. And I had it written down simply, in a few words; and the lord Pope confirmed it for me."

Nobody knows whether this took place in 1209, when Francis first paid his respects to Innocent III (see Chapter V), or sometime afterward. In any case, this brief text was no "Rule" in the canonical sense, and hence we shall call it the "life program."

What follows is an attempt to reconstruct this program, or something like it, which Francis and his companions used as a guide during the first ten years of their fellowship:

> In the name of God. This is the life of the Friars Minor.[36]
>
> The life of the Friars Minor takes its bearing from the Gospel of Our Lord Jesus Christ.
>
> If you would be perfect, then go, sell everything you have, and give it to the poor.
>
> Take nothing for your journey, no staff nor bag, nor bread, nor money.
>
> If any man would come after me, let him deny himself, and take up his cross and follow me.
>
> The Friars Minor possess nothing except a tunic with a piece of rope and underwear.
>
> The clerics say the required daily prayers like other clerics. The laymen say the Our Father.
>
> The Friars Minor are to do manual work at all times, and so earn their daily bread. But they are never allowed to accept money.
>
> They are to beg trustfully for alms, and they are not to be ashamed of it.
>
> The preaching of the Friars Minor consists in a short lesson on the virtues and vices, on rewards and punishment, and on conversion from sin.
>
> Francis promises the lord Pope obedience and respect.

A significant point here is that none of the substance of Francis' original life program had to be suppressed either in the "draft Rule" nor in the definitive "papal Rule."

Therein lay Francis' success.

To this day Francis' precepts are still binding, because the Franciscans are obliged to keep the "papal Rule."

The Franciscans have long since given up following Francis' intentions —this is a fact we should simply register, without vindictiveness or spiteful pleasure. The important thing is that Francis' life program did not slip into oblivion.

One can still use it, for example, as an argument against the so-called natural order of things.

Francis could fight quite vigorously for his principles, as we hear from tradition. This is the story they tell:

When Francis had returned from the Orient, a minister came to him to find out exactly what he had in mind with regard to the section on poverty, which had just then been written into the Rule. And in particular he was curious about the sentence, "Take nothing for your journey, no staff, nor bag, nor bread, nor money."

The minister said to Francis:

"What should I do? I own a lot of books, worth more than fifty pounds of silver."

Francis answered:

"Brother, I cannot speak against my conscience!"

This answer troubled the minister.

When Francis noticed his disappointment, he said very resolutely:

"You Friars Minor want to be accounted before men as followers of the Gospel. In reality you are holders of the cash box, just as Judas was."

Later some of the ministers managed to carry the day, so that the sentence, "Take nothing with you for your journey . . ." was stricken from the Rule.

In this regard, Francis once remarked in the presence of several companions:

Do these brothers think then that they can hoodwink God and me? I want it written at the beginning and end of the Rule, that we wish to cling to the Gospel, so that all brothers may know how important it is.[37]

In 1221, Francis finished the draft Rule with the help of Brother Cesario, a German by birth, from Speyer, who had joined the Franciscans in Palestine, and who had the requisite education.[38]

The text is rather long—thirty-nine folio pages, as compared with four in the later papal Rule. The draft Rule is interspersed with edifying passages which to our taste are rather boring.

In its essence the draft Rule closely corresponds to Francis' life program, which it expands to include a number of provisions aimed at the inner workings of the brotherhood (e.g., regulations governing the annual general chapter). The role of officials is categorized as one of service, and the title of superior (*prior*) is strictly forbidden.

A special section deals with robbers, who are to be warmly received if they wish to enter the Order.

Ordained priests are prohibited from owning any books except for the prescribed prayer book ("breviary"). The proper environment for the Friars Minor is to be that of all poor and needy persons, lepers, and beggars.

Francis complied with the wishes of the papal Curia to the extent of incorporating the year of probation for new members into the draft. Otherwise, the text, with all its Bible quotations and pious comments, reveals a dogged determination to stick to the old ways.

The majority of the brothers apparently approved of Francis' draft Rule in the general chapter of 1221. The opposition remained in the minority.

What can the opposition do in such a situation?

It can take its case to a higher court, and discreetly, inconspicuously try to get its way.

This higher court was Cardinal Ugolino.

Between Pentecost of 1221 and the autumn of 1223, conferences took place "at the highest level" behind closed doors. The subject of these meetings was the setting up of the right timetable for the friars' trip to eternity—that is, the editing of a Rule compatible with canon law.

Francis had withdrawn to the hermitage of Fonte Colombo near Rieti, along with Leo and a certain Brother Bonizio from Bologna, a learned canon lawyer.

Leo declares: "We who were with him when he wrote the Rule and almost all his other writings bear witness to the fact that he wished to have certain provisions included in the Rule and his other writings, concerning which some, and especially the superiors (*prelati*), disagreed with him. Thus it happened that, among the issues on which the brothers were opposed to St. Francis in his lifetime, there were points which would have been of real value to the whole Order, now after his death. But because he greatly feared scandal, he gave way, although unwillingly, to the wishes of the friars. But he often made this remark: 'Woe to those brothers who are opposed to me in this.' "[39]

Celano observes: At the time when there was quarreling among the brothers over the confirmation of the Rule, Francis, who was greatly worried about these matters, had a dream. It seemed to him as though he were gathering up little crumbs from the ground, and had to distribute them among many hungry brothers who were standing around him. Fearful that the crumbs might slip through his fingers, he suddenly heard a voice from on high, calling out:

"Francis, make a host out of the crumbs and give it to those who wish to eat of it."

Francis did this in his dream.

The next day he realized that the crumbs were supposed to stand for the words of the Gospel, and the host for the Rule.[40]

This is the story they tell: When Francis was staying on a mountain with Brother Leo and Brother Bonizio of Bologna, to compose the Rule—for the first one, which he had dictated with the help of Christ, had been lost—many of the ministers came to Brother Elias, Francis' vicar, and said:

"We have heard that this Brother Francis is making up a new Rule. We are worried that he'll make it too hard to keep. Go to him and tell him that we don't want to be bound by this Rule. Let him write it for himself, and not for us."

Brother Elias didn't want to go, because he was afraid that Francis would scold him.

But they insisted, and so they all went together to Francis.

When Francis heard of the ministers' request through Brother Elias, he turned his face to heaven.

And suddenly they heard the voice of Christ in the air, crying out:

"Francis! Everything in the Rule comes from me. And I wish to have it followed strictly, to the letter, and without any commentary."

And like an echo, the voice rang out one more time:

"Strictly, to the letter! Strictly, to the letter! Without any commentary! Without any commentary!"

Francis asked the ministers:

"Do you want to hear it all again?"

But they went away confused, arguing with each other.[41]

Of course, stories such as these don't reflect the actual historical situation of 1221–23. Above all else they express the feelings of later generations, more precisely their profound bitterness over the path taken by the Franciscans in the latter half of the thirteenth century. But even in Francis' time the radical majority and the moderate minority of the brotherhood were at odds, and the minority joined a coalition with Ugolino. We have already seen that Francis was by and large able to prevail against it.

But when we take a close look at the papal Rule of 1223, we encounter certain details that were evidently written into that document over Francis' objections. For example: "For the needs of the sick, however, and for clothing other brothers, the ministers and custodians alone shall exercise responsibility, with the help of spiritual friends."[42] These friends of the Order (amici spirituales) were sympathetic outsiders.[43] When ministers or custodians were in a quandary, they could turn to them and ask them to collect a gift of money that had been offered to the brothers (direct acceptance was forbidden), buy tunics with it, and bring them to the community.

This exception to the absolute ban on the use of money surely gave Francis many sleepless nights. Or: "All the brothers are bound always to have one of the brothers of this religious Order as minister general and servant of the whole brotherhood, and are bound firmly to obey him. When he dies, the election of his successor shall be made by the provincial ministers and custodians in the Whitsun chapter . . . and this once in three years or at some other term, greater or less, as the minister general orders."[44]

This provision spelled the end of the gay and turbulent gatherings in the Portiuncula forest. The Rule also called a halt to the friars' unchecked wanderings: Now they had to inform their superior of every step they took. In the future the brothers could preach only after the minister general had tested each aspirant and expressly given him permission.

And so forth. We have already seen how the taboo against dealing with women was introduced (pp. 99–100).

The conclusion of the papal Rule runs as follows: "In addition I order the ministers on obedience to seek from the lord Pope one of the cardinals of the Holy Roman Church, who may be governor, protector, and corrector of this brotherhood, to the end that we be always submissive and subject to the Holy Roman Church, firm in the Catholic faith, and always observe poverty, humility, and the holy Gospel of Our Lord Jesus Christ, as we have firmly promised."[45] It is rather hard to recognize Francis of Assisi in the author of this passage.

Francis subjected himself to the despotism of his masters—that was the price he had to pay for preserving the substance of his life program. Had he done otherwise, he and his brotherhood would have been classed as heretics. We can understand why he didn't want that.

This is the answer to the question posed by this chapter: Francis internalized his submission to authority so thoroughly that he himself believed in the rightness of it. He reacted to this very real insult, injury, one could even say shattering of his personality in a sensational manner that held a special significance for his own epoch. In the depths of his being, where body and ego met, where no Pope and no Ugolino could reach him, powerful forces of protest gathered together in a way that Francis himself could not grasp, forces that would show to all the world what had been done to him.

The passage cited at the beginning of this chapter was spoken by a man with the stigmata.

XII

"THEY WILL THROW
THEIR BOOKS
OUT THE WINDOW"

TEN years after Francis' death, in the year 1236, the most famous theologian of the age, Alexander of Hales, entered the Franciscans in Paris.[1]
This "great doctor" and "monarch of theologians," as he was called by his
contemporaries, was the holder of a university chair. This was the first theological chair (of a total of twelve that Paris had at the time) to go to the
Friars Minor, and from then on they filled it with one of their own people. This coup brought the young Order immense prestige, and it showed
how systematically the Franciscans had been working in the universities.

The Friars Minor had been active in Paris ever since 1219, the year of
the first papal bull in their favor. We find them in Bologna, the second
great center of European academic life, from 1213 on.[2] This means that a
healthy appetite for education had developed in the brotherhood even in
Francis' lifetime.

All over Europe students, masters, and doctors began talking about the
friars. Their rules were looked on as excitingly modern, free of the pon-
derousness of the "old Orders," with their long hours of common prayer
and their vow of stability. Once we realize that in the Middle Ages all the
professors (and students too) with practically no exceptions had to be
clerics, we can understand the attraction felt in academic circles for the
Friars Minor: Entering the Order guaranteed one a certain small amount
of freedom.

In the first chapter we characterized Francis as a man who wore himself
out struggling against the forces of modernity, behaving, so to speak, like a
madman. Now, eleven chapters later, this assessment takes on a new and
noteworthy sense. The very impetus that carried Francis away from his
wealthy father—and from the most powerful class of that period—achieved

the direct opposite of what it was supposed to: Francis became the driving force of a fellowship that drew the most ambitious status seekers in Europe the way light draws moths.

Much as he wanted not to, Francis and his brotherhood of beggars gave vital support to the university system, which was just then bursting into bloom. His portrait belongs in the gallery of the founding fathers of modern science.

Within ten years, between 1214 and 1224, the papal Curia secured control over the three most important new universities in Europe:[3] In 1214 Cardinal Legate Nicholas of Tusculum settled the conflict between the city of Oxford and the schools that had grown up there, gave the university special privileges, and put it under the control of the bishop of Lincoln. In the year 1215 Cardinal Legate Robert Curson imposed a series of statutes on the University of Paris and placed it under the control of the Roman Curia. In 1224 the Curia took over the University of Bologna.

This decade, so important in the history of education, is the same one that saw Francis in the bright light of publicity, one of the most influential figures of his age.

The aura of unworldly piety that the stories of Francis spread over their hero is deceptive, insofar as it smudges the outlines of his political thought and activity. Anyone who fights, as Francis did, for every plank of his platform (see Chapter XI) cannot be described as apolitical.

In the last ten years of his life Francis found himself in the middle of the argument over what was then the most exciting innovation of early modern European society: the universities, which were cropping up all over Europe. Their rise—a necessary condition for the birth of modern science—will be the subject of the following section.

WE OUGHT TO HONOR ALL THEOLOGIANS

Here is an assortment of theses taught at the University of Paris during Francis' century:

Theology is based on fables.

Chastity is not in itself a virtue.

Complete continence is harmful to virtue and the human race.

The Christian religion contains errors the same as other religions.

Happiness may be found in this life, not in another.

The resurrection of the body cannot be rationally analyzed.

The Christian teaching is an obstacle to science.[4]

We know about these audacious propositions because they, and a whole batch of further assertions, were officially condemned on March 7, 1277, by the bishop of Paris.[5] At the same time the author and readers of a patently erotic composition (*De deo amoris* [On the god of love]) were threatened with excommunication unless they reported to the authorities within a week.

The liberal, enlightened, and not altogether pious intellectual climate of Paris which the Church's censors were so much against did not suddenly arise in the last quarter of the thirteenth century. The astonishingly modern-sounding heresies that the bishop of Paris wanted to eliminate had a long history behind them before they made headlines, so to speak.

As early as 1210 bonfires were kindled in Paris by way of popular diversion during a dignified synod then taking place.[6] The writings of a man named Amalrich of Bena were consigned to the flames, and just to be sure, fourteen of his disciples were burned along with them. (Amalrich himself had previously been chaplain to Innocent III. Fortunately for Amalrich he had already died of natural causes.) "In the city of Paris," writes a troubled chronicler of this period, "that fountain of all knowledge and source of all godly writings, the seductive art of the devil awoke perverse thoughts in the minds of several learned men."[7] Nowadays one can hear these thoughts—e.g., the idea that God and the world are fundamentally one and the same—in any halfway superior circle of intellectuals. In Francis' day the authorities viewed this sort of secular piety as pure insanity, because it opened the door to an unblushing spirit of free thought, and a sexual ethic that rejected both sin and the sacred institution of marriage.

The heresy of intellectual freedom took its first theoretical steps around this time, and then went on to survive in the European underground in the following centuries. But it was by no means the only attempt of its kind to liberate human thought. In Francis' day old Aristotle came northward to Paris from Islamic Spain, in the form of translations from the Arabic, made for the most part in Toledo (and on the orders of a bishop).[8]

Among Parisian scholars Aristotle was known simply as "the philosopher." Up till then only fragments of his work had been read in the West. Now students and teachers seized on his writings with the rapt devotion of provincials greeting a Nobel Prize winner on his first visit to their little town. His speculations soared over the lowly ratiocinations of medieval monastic writers, and readers found some of his insights quite shocking. For example, the doctrine of the eternity of matter openly and fundamentally contradicted biblical faith in Creation. (Not even Thomas Aquinas, a thinker who was to some extent in Aristotle's class, succeeded in cracking that nut.)

Aristotle's arrival at the new universities was greeted by a hailstorm of papal and episcopal decrees. The Paris synod of 1210, already mentioned, which cost Amalrich's followers their lives, declared a general ban on the study of Aristotle's writings on natural science. These dangerous books were not allowed to be read and commented on, either publicly or privately (*secreto*), under penalty of excommunication. In 1215 Aristotle's *Metaphysics* fell under a like prohibition in the new statutes of the University of Paris, as established by the papal legate.

None of these regulations were particularly effective. In 1228 Gregory IX (our old friend, Ugolino of Ostia) had to send a letter to the professors of the theological faculty of Paris to remind them discreetly of the nature of their sacred subject. Theology, as everyone knew, dealt with a knowledge that transcends the powers of natural thought. And so, the admonition summed up, it just would not do to pervert the ancillary role of philosophy into a leading one, and to treat the queen of the sciences (as theology must still be regarded) no better than an inferior handmaid.

Hardly had the Pope delivered his evidently much-needed sermon when a new book hit Paris like a bombshell: a Latin translation, produced under the patronage of Frederick II and his court in Sicily, of an Arabic original, a tract *On Heaven* from the pen of the Muslim physician and philosopher Ibn Rushd (or Averroes, in the Latinized form), who had died in Cordoba in 1198.

Averroes was a distinguished commentator on Aristotle. In addition, he had some ideas of his own to propose, such as his claim that mind was a reality that everyone participated in. The logical consequence of this teaching was to deny the immortality of the soul. This notion was promptly adopted by a Parisian *magister*, the renowned Siger of Brabant, and thus found its way into the lecture notes of the students of sacred theology—not the best sort of preparation for a pious career in the Church.

On Mardi Gras of the year 1229 some students in Paris got into a fight with an innkeeper. This petty incident triggered a riot which the student body enthusiastically joined. (Their living conditions were not exactly ideal, with overcrowded and dismal accommodations.) The authorities struck back brutally; the professors took sides with the students and finally shut down all instruction in the University for a period of six years.

Once again the Pope had to intervene. This time he backed down and let it be understood that Aristotle's writings might be suitable after all for promoting sacred studies. He set up a commission to scrutinize and "purify" the controversial texts.

The commission was convened in 1231, but it shuffled papers back and forth without taking any action; and until 1270, when thirteen theses of "heathen" philosophy were solemnly condemned, Paris enjoyed a certain degree of academic freedom.

The years from 1230 to 1270 were, in fact, a sort of high Gothic period for the intellectual life, with a great sunburst from ancient Athens flooding into the backwoods of Europe. The Franciscans were eager participants in all this, and Minister General Bonaventure (pp. 10–11) inscribed his name at the head of the scholarly elite.[9] Another friar, John Peckham, successively rector and professor in Paris and Oxford, wrote a series of famous philosophical and theological works, and served from 1279 till his death in 1292 as archbishop of Canterbury and primate of England.[10]

Peckham published a treatise on optics, at the same time that people in Tuscany were wearing the first eyeglasses.[11] Not long afterward they were perched on the noses of learned Franciscans who had grown nearsighted from so much reading.

In Francis' century, as we said (p. 17), the foundations were laid for the world in which we live. The importance of the new universities in this process, it should be clear by now, cannot easily be underestimated. And here, in turn, the systematic appropriation of Aristotelian thought played a crucial role. All this was taking place on the grand scale in Francis' century, under the guidance of the new intelligentsia of the leading countries in Europe, at French, Italian, and English universities.

In Aristotle, the early bourgeois self-consciousness of the West (cf. Chapter III), which had been shaped along monastic-Christian and urban lines, found just the sort of theoretical structure it needed. It came along, as vital and fresh as it had been in the days of ancient Greece when, centuries before Christ, the bourgeoisie had just gotten started.

The impact of this event on the contemporary avant-garde was exceeded only by the intellectual agitation brought on in Galileo's time (1600–50) by the crystallizing of the modern scientific outlook.[12]

Since then we live in the age of science and technology. Opinions differ as to the meaning of this triumphal rise. Looking back on the last eight hundred years one might say, for example, that the whole development looks from our perspective like a plan without a planner, an idea of nobody in particular; or one could simply, and less confidently, say that Something or other is taking its course.

The one thing certain in all this is that the birth of our era was a unique and unprecedented moment. It is also certain that Francis was one of the midwives—though not as he had intended—at this rather difficult delivery.

We may assume without hesitation that Francis had no idea of the scholastic theology of his day. And he knew nothing more of Aristotle than the name, and perhaps not even that.

Nevertheless, as already mentioned, in his *Testament* he recommended an apparently unreserved deference to professors of theology: "We ought to honor all theologians."

But, as we shall soon see, Francis had a notion of sacred theology that would have qualified him, at most, for a job as beadle at the Sorbonne.

The "divine words" (*parole divine*) touched off the same sort of feelings in Francis as the consecrated host.[13] Celano tells us that Francis picked up every piece of paper with writing on it that he found in the street or elsewhere in the dirt, to put it in a more becoming place—worried that it might have the name of Christ on it.[14] Francis also never allowed, Celano continues, so much as a letter or syllable to be crossed out in the notes and messages he dictated,[15] "even if they were often superfluous or out of place." Celano discreetly hints that because of this many greetings reached their addressees in rather horrible Latin, full of mistakes, and without the slightest trace of stylistic care. (Chronicler Thomas of Eccleston remarks that Francis sent a letter to brothers in the university city of Bologna "in which there was a great deal of bad Latin.")

Written characters had for Francis an altogether sacramental—no other word will do—quality, because they could be formed into the name of God. Consequently they must not under any circumstances be mistreated so recklessly as to be crossed out.

On the other hand, the irritation that anyone brought up with a love for correct Latin might feel toward his unaffectedly vulgar "kitchen Latin" left Francis perfectly cold.

In his *Testament* Francis mentions theologians in the same breath with "ministers of the divine word."[16] Now we understand the reason for Francis' deference to theologians: They lived on intimate terms with those same holy Scriptures in which, Francis was convinced, breathed "spirit and life." They were quite similar to the priests who attended the eucharistic body of God's Son.

Clearly, with our daily diet of trivial verbiage, we have a hard time appreciating Francis' downright worshipful attitude to words.

It ought to be equally clear that Francis' attitude of tender, nurturing care has a great deal to do with culture, in the original sense of the word.

The following is undated. Since Peter of Catania appears in it, we can place it with some security in the time before Francis' journey to the Holy Land, i.e., in the years between 1217 and 1219. The story talks about the book that Francis cultivated with the most affectionate reverence, the words of the holy Gospels of Christ, the New Testament.

This is the story they tell: One time, when Francis was staying in the Portiuncula, an old woman came to him, the mother of two of the companions, and begged him for an alms, since she was completely destitute. Francis said to Peter of Catania, who was his vicar at that time:

"Do we have anything that we can give our mother?"

(This was how Francis used to call the mothers of his companions.)

Peter answered: "We have nothing at all of any value, except for the

New Testament in the chapel, the one we use for the early-morning readings."

(In those days the brothers had no breviaries, and very few psalters.)

Francis said: "Go give our mother the New Testament, so she can sell it. Isn't it written in that book that we should come to the aid of the poor? I believe that God will take more pleasure in our giving the book away than in our reading from it."

And so it was done, and the first and only New Testament that the brotherhood had ever had was thus given away.[17]

We may assume that the Bible Francis gave away was no de luxe parchment copy, but a paper manuscript. Still its value was not trifling, book prices being what they were. (It has been calculated that before the introduction of printing a university professor would need an entire year's salary to buy about ten books.)[18]

We miss the true meaning of Francis' charitable donation of the Gospel, however, if we translate the value of the gift into purely monetary terms. This kind of value (*pretium* in Latin) was what counted for the old woman—the invisible price tag on a given commodity. The Bible became a commodity the moment she accepted it. For Francis, on the other hand, the essence of the gift was his renunciation of another value of that Bible, which derived its splendor and worth (*valor* in Latin) from its daily devotional use. More simply put: Francis prized the divine words because of their value for blissful living, and therefore he wanted theologians to be honored as men in service to those words.

Three years after Francis' death, in the year 1229, immediately after the end of the long, cruel crusade against the heretics of southern France, Ugolino of Ostia founded a university in Toulouse for the ideological welfare of the defeated enemy. Count Raymond VI of Toulouse, as the loser, had to provide the wherewithal.

So Ugolino, now Pope Gregory IX, gave powerful support to the academic life and to sacred theology, and the Franciscans played a major role in this scheme.

We shall now recount how Francis, despite his respect for godly learning, struggled, mostly in vain, against his Order's involvement in the heavily political world of higher education.

"MEA CULPA! MEA CULPA!"

A number of chapters in the Leo stories deal as clearly as one could wish with Francis' attitudes toward books in general and prayer books in particular, to scholarly studies and their usefulness for his brotherhood. These chapters were so important to the radical Franciscans that, despite the ban of 1266 on reading and disseminating the Leo stories, they made separate copies of them and passed them around under the heading, *Intentio Regulae*.[19] Literally translated, this means the intention of the Rule. The point behind the title is clear. The original Francis, with his unadulterated ideas on poverty, simplicity, and plain thinking, would once more have his say against Bonaventure and his ilk, the managerial, professorial, and official elite of the latter half of the thirteenth century.

In these chapters the real Francis speaks, there can be no doubt about it.

The key concept we find here is, in the original Latin, *simplicitas*. The literal translation "simplicity" falls short of its real significance; for, as is evident from many of the stories about Francis, *simplicitas* means, quite fundamentally, the courage to speak clearly and without disguise, the ability to distinguish between the essence and the extras, the passion for going straight to the point, the scorn for theoretical abstractions and intellectual games, the love for terse, precise speech—everything, therefore, that one never learns at a university.[20]

And then, along with the equally basic attitudes of plainness (*humilitas*, generally rendered by the insipid word "humility"—see above p. 124) and frugality, as demanded by the poverty ethic, comes that peculiar identifying trait of the Friars Minor, the common sense and ready wit of people who speak straight from the shoulder.

As a matter of fact, taking the long view, we note that the down-to-earth, unpedantic Franciscan style of preaching[21] did have some red-letter days, to the great pleasure of the common people, if not always to their real benefit.

From this angle, Francis' distrust of the doctors was not so ineffective after all.

This is the story they tell:

In the time after the blessed Francis returned from the Holy Land, there was a novice in the brotherhood who knew how to read the Psalms, though not all that well. His pleasure in this pursuit was so great that he obtained permission from his superior to have a psalter. Still, before making use of it, he wanted to get Francis' personal consent. He had heard that Francis did not like the brothers to be overly eager about study and to crave books.

One day when the novice was staying in a hermitage, Francis came there to visit. After the novice had put his request to him, Francis answered:

"In bygone days Emperor Charles fought with Roland, Oliver, and all the true champions and worthy knights against the infidels with great sweat and toil. Brilliant victories and glorious death in battle were their lot. Later, to be sure, there were people who wished to be honored simply because they had written about the heroic deeds of those men in clever books. Will it get to the point that, like them, we shall boast of muttering over the deeds of the saints?"

The novice was not completely satisfied with this answer, and soon found another opportunity to speak with Francis about the psalter. Francis was sitting right by the fire, warming himself.

He said: "When you finally have a psalter, you won't let up until you get permission for a breviary. As soon as you have that, you'll sit down in an armchair like a high-and-mighty prelate and order your companion to bring you your breviary."

And in great excitement Francis took a handful of ashes and rubbed them into his head while he said to himself:

"I a breviary!"

For a long time he kept at it, saying many times:

"I a breviary! I a breviary!"

The novice was completely nonplussed.

Later Francis said to him: "I too, brother, had to fight the temptation to own books. Then I took the Gospels and opened them. The first passage I happened on was this: 'To you has been given to understand the mysteries of the kingdom of heaven.'"

Francis continued: "When I read this, then I thought to myself that it might be better from then on to avoid the heights of learning."

But the novice brother tried his luck for a third time. It was after some months, when he once again questioned Francis about the psalter.

Francis said: "Go and do what your superior tells you to!"

Hardly had the brother gone off when Francis thought over the answer he had given him, and called after him to stop. Then he ran to him and said:

"Come back with me now, brother, and show me the exact spot where I gave you my answer."

When they got there, Francis went down on his knees before the novice and said:

"*Mea culpa! Mea culpa!* Through my fault I neglected to tell you what a Friar Minor is allowed to have—namely, a tunic with a piece of rope and underwear."

And Francis stuck to this answer, however many brothers might come to question him about owning books.[22]

As we see, Francis' objections to book learning do not arise out of that mixture of backwardness and prejudice which has always nourished anti-intellectualism among the failures and victims of this world.

There is no question, then, of narrow boorishness in Francis. When he said good-by to books, he knew what he was missing.

Francis said: "I would like to have the brothers strong in virtue and not greedy for knowledge, so that in their time of trial they may have the necessary steadfastness. For the hour of trial will surely come, and then books will be useless. They will throw their books out the window.

"There are many brothers who toil day and night over study and in so doing forget their original purpose. Then when they preach, and they notice that their listeners are edified, they become all puffed up and congratulate themselves on their success. But in truth they are empty inside and cold as ice.

"Won't the ordinary brothers be glad if the ministers and preachers of our fellowship do their share of manual work?"[23]

There is a striking similarity between this passage and some lines written by Mao Tse-tung. Francis' concern that the intellectuals in his brotherhood might neglect manual work on account of their studies is echoed in a speech by Mao from 1942: "I acquired at school the ways of a student; I then used to feel it undignified to do even a little manual labor. . . . I felt the intellectuals were the only clean people in the world, while in comparison workers and peasants were dirty."[24]

Things ought not to be this way, Mao thought at the time.

Thirty years later:

"Some figures could be seen silhouetted against the light of the dazzling sky. A man pushing a wheelbarrow turned toward us, his face jovial.

" 'What is he carrying?'

" 'It's human manure,' Kuo Mo-jo said, leaning over my shoulder in the dark. I guessed that he was smiling.

" 'What does he do for a living?'

" 'He's a university professor. He's undergoing his re-education.' "[25]

So writes French politician and anthropologist Alain Peyrefitte in his report from China in 1973.

In 1976 Mao died, and since then China has entered upon a new Long March of the "four modernizations" (industry, agriculture, defense, science). The university professors have gone back to their desks and laboratories—there can be no progress without brainwork.

In the heaven of unrealized ideas Mao asks Francis how things were in the European Middle Ages, and perhaps they both ask the good Lord why progress has to be such an ambiguous business.

If there is an answer to the question, word of it has yet to get around.

Francis, in the papal Rule of 1223: "Those brothers to whom the Lord has given the grace to work, shall work faithfully and devotedly; in such manner that idleness, the soul's enemy, is kept at bay."[26]

Celano, by way of explanation: "Sluggards, who refuse to have anything to do with work, must be quickly spat out of the mouth of God. Francis used to say this, and any idler who appeared before him would be rebuffed with cutting words. He himself liked to work with his hands, as a living example of perfection."[27] He also said:

"I want the brothers to work and to toil heartily. Those who don't know any craft are to learn one!"[28]

Francis, in his *Testament*: "I used to work with my hands and I wish to work. And it is my firm wish that all the brothers work at some good and worthy occupation. Those who are not trained to one shall learn, not through desire to receive pay for their work, but for the example and to repel idleness. And when pay for labor is not given we shall run to the table of the Lord, begging alms from door to door."[29]

Francis' insistence on manual labor for his brotherhood, and his critical attitude toward brainwork, were the crucial points in his quarrel with the papally controlled university system of the period. To get an overview of this situation, a brief glance at the "social function of science" (to quote the title of a relevant book) will be of some use. Ever since the first appearance of literacy five thousand years ago in the so-called high cultures of the Near East, science has always been a privilege of the upper classes and has primarily served their interests. Brain workers always stood (and still stand) on a higher rung of the social ladder than manual workers.

In antiquity and the Middle Ages this class distinction was accompanied by a corresponding dual perspective, from which intellectuals and workers looked at each other: contempt for physical ("servile") labor on one side, deep-seated distrust of book learning on the other.

This opposition, to make a long story short, became sharply aggravated in Francis' day with the rise of the universities.

As the story of the novice shows, Francis saw through this situation. By making it clear to the young man that his desire for a book concealed expectations of using knowledge to command others, he laid bare the social-climbing impulse behind his studiousness.

At the same time Francis continued to revere the "divine words," so vitally useful in everyday life, and to esteem the men who dispensed them. This contradiction between ideal and actuality need not surprise us. Francis had to live with it just as we do, and his attempts to reconcile the brain workers and the "ordinary brothers" in his Order had to remain fragmentary, because he lacked the means to make them succeed.

PERFECT JOY

After the events in Bologna in the fall of 1220, Francis was fully aware of the trend to book learning in his Order. At the same time he recognized that more and more ordained priests were joining up, among whom were not a few clerics with academic training. The brother who had scruples over his expensive books would have been one of these, and he was surely not an isolated case.

Ordained priests and educated people increasingly set the pace among the Franciscans, who had begun as a group of uneducated laymen.

During the last years of his life, Francis himself seems to have felt like something of a stranger in his own brotherhood.

The *Fioretti:* "As St. Francis went once on a time from Perugia to the Portiuncula with Brother Leo, in the winter, they suffered greatly from the severity of the cold, and Francis called to Brother Leo, who was going on a little in advance: 'O Brother Leo, although the Friars Minor in these parts give a great example of sanctity and good edification, write it down and note it well that this is not perfect joy.' And having gone a little further, he called to him a second time: 'O Brother Leo, even though the Friars Minor should give sight to the blind, and loose the limbs of the paralyzed, and though they should cast out devils, and . . . they should raise to life those who had been dead four days, write that in all this there is not perfect joy.' And going on a little while, he cried aloud: 'O Brother Leo, if the Friars Minor knew all languages, and all the sciences, and all the Scriptures; and if they could prophesy, and reveal, not only things in the future, but the secrets of consciences, and of men's souls, write that in all this there is not perfect joy.' Going still a little further, Francis called aloud again: '. . . even though the Friars Minor spoke with the tongues of angels, and knew the courses of the stars, and the virtues of herbs, and though to them were revealed all the treasures of the earth, and though they knew the virtues of birds and of fishes and of all animals . . . and of stones, and roots and waters, write that not in this is perfect joy. . . .'

"And as he spoke in this manner for two good miles, Brother Leo in great astonishment asked of him, and said: 'Father, I pray thee, for God's sake, tell me wherein is perfect joy.'

"And Francis replied to him: 'When we shall have come to the Portiuncula, soaked as we are with the rain, and frozen with the cold, encrusted with mud, and afflicted with hunger, and shall knock at the door, if the porter should come and ask angrily, "Who are you?" . . . and if he would not open the door to us, but left us without, exposed till night to the snow, and the wind and the torrents of rain, in cold and hunger; then if we should bear so much abuse and cruelty . . . patiently and without murmuring at him . . . O Brother Leo, write that this would be perfect joy.

"'And if we . . . should continue to knock, and he should come out in a rage, and drive us away as importunate villains, with rudeness and with buffetings . . . if we should sustain this with patience, and with joy, and with love, O Brother Leo, write that this would be perfect joy. . . .

" 'And if constrained by hunger, and the cold, and the night, we should knock again, and beg him with many tears . . . and he should come out furiously with a knotted stick . . . and beat us all over our bodies; if we should bear all these things patiently . . . O Brother Leo, write that it is in this that there is perfect joy.' "[30]

The rhetorical structure and moralizing tone of this story lead us to attribute the narrative as we now have it to an epigone with literary training. Still, beneath these later layers of paint we can make out the original colors.

Francis imagines himself standing before his beloved Portiuncula, a stranger, unrecognized and rejected by his companions, who take him for a tramp. This story, so full of serene irony, sounds authentic. As a matter of fact, Francis could not resist the temptation, at least on one occasion, to play the part of an unknown beggar before his companions when the opportunity offered.

This is the story they tell: On a high feast day a minister was visiting at the hermitage near Greccio. Francis was there too. To honor the minister the brothers had provided white tablecloths and even drinking glasses, and had prepared a splendid dinner. When Francis came down from his cell for mealtime and saw how exquisitely the table was laid, he silently left the house, found a begging pilgrim who was right nearby, and borrowed his hat and staff. In the meantime the brothers had begun to eat without waiting for Francis. (They used to do this anyway, at Francis' specific request, as he didn't like to keep people waiting.) Then Francis knocked at the door, disguised as a poor pilgrim. One of the companions whom Francis had let in on the plan opened up at once, and Francis cried: "For the love of God, give alms to a poor sick pilgrim!"

The minister and the other brothers recognized Francis immediately.

The minister said: "Brother, we are as poor as you are. And as there are many of us, the alms on our table are just enough to appease our hunger. But since you have invoked the love of God, we will gladly share our alms with you."

When Francis came to the table, the minister gave him a helping of the dish that he himself was eating, along with a piece of bread.

Francis took the gift, sat down on the floor near the table, sighed, and said:

"Had I not known that poor Friars Minor were living here, men who have to beg for their daily needs from door to door, at the sight of this splendid table I would not have dared to disturb your meal."

Then the brothers were all deeply ashamed.[31]

Francis had staged this scene with affable malice to make the worthy brothers uncomfortable, and he surely enjoyed their embarrassment.

We are not told how the interrupted meal ended. Perhaps Francis went along with the flustered brethren after all, and sat down at table after his little comedy. In any case, tablecloths and glasses were certainly never brought out again, not while he was around.

XIII

THE FLAME WAS GOD

THIS chapter will discuss occurrences that seem to us—normal bourgeois consumers in the industrial nations—"a bit much": trances and ecstasies, raptures and transports, visions and miracles of every sort.

Because we middle-class people find such phenomena rather disturbing, as painful and unpleasant as the contortions of lunatics; because we have no idea what to make of them, and on the whole take them for a sort of humbug, we feel tempted to dismiss this dimension of Francis' life as mere exoticism, with no real significance for us.

But we should be careful. Doesn't the growing number of depressed individuals in our society indicate the presence of needs that mass consumption cannot satisfy? Haven't the back-to-the-landers, conservationists, and apostles of the counterculture already grown so numerous that their many-voiced (and sometimes dissonant) chorus can be heard everywhere? Don't we all have friends and acquaintances who have rejected the one-dimensional dreariness of the stimulants prescribed by the prevailing wisdom of the social engineers, and are now trying to heighten their sensitivity to experience in one way or another, through meditation, drugs, vegetarianism, etc.? And we ourselves, though we remain skeptical as ever, mistrusting our own reactions, are we not plagued by doubts about the virtues of what its propagandists call technological progress?

We begin to suspect that our brains are good for more than just addition and subtraction; that we could learn to do more than answer idiotic, pointless questions—at school and on quiz shows; that the cultivation of logic as money for the mind goes hand in hand with the neglect of the side of the brain whose use we admire in musicians and filmmakers.

In brief: Our narrow-minded resistance to everything once discarded by the instrumental rationality of the natural sciences has now begun to crumble. Because of this, the prospects that we may pay some attention to Francis, even in his role as ecstatic visionary, are really not too bad.

Altered states of consciousness, as the latest Anglo-American research calls them,[1] are experienced by their subjects—whether African medicine men or working-class women from the American Midwest—as, first of all, a withdrawal of the normal field of perception. At the same time the usual psychosomatic threshold of excitement shifts up or down, toward violent activity or imperturbable apathy. (The whirling dervish and the meditating yogi are, each in his way, classic examples of this displacement of nervous excitement.)

The most useful term for situations like this is a trance.

The intensity of trances ranges from brief fits of distraction to the complete loss of external sensation. Their duration varies from a few minutes to hours and days.

The many reports concerning altered states of consciousness, from past and present, across an immense gamut of societies and cultures, suggest a common denominator. The capacity for this kind of behavior is more widespread than people think. In many cultures it is actively stimulated and socially acceptable—e.g., in South America, and by no means only in the rain forests but in the cities as well. In others it is tabooed and repressed, as is the rule in industrial societies.

Anyone with enough self-confidence to view his existence as a member of the white middle class living in one of the major cities of Europe or North America as the pinnacle of evolution may skip this chapter.

The following are selected passages from a letter that the author received in 1977 from a woman who had read his books. They fit rather well into the subject under discussion:

"I was born in 1939. As soon as I could quit school I went to work in a factory. We grew up without any kind of religious background. I have to say that from the age of twelve I wrote poems about everything that moved me. When I was nineteen I met my husband. We lived together, and got married when the first child was on the way. I had a baby every year, I was very happy and completely absorbed with my life. Since my husband's first wife had died, and there was one child by that marriage, a boy, I brought him up with the others, and so I had six children to take care of.

"In the meantime there was no subject that I didn't write poems about in all those years: death, birth, life, war, love, spring, etc., even politics. Only God was taboo.

"First of all, I had a strange argument with a woman Jehovah's Witness, who was trying to talk me and the other people in the house into believing that only 144 [sic] people would be saved, that God was a God of anger, etc. Any other time I would have laughed and slammed the door, but suddenly I began to speak to this woman about God and to tell her that he was love. Something inside me forced me to say words that were completely strange to me. I was on fire inside, and this woman looked at me flabbergasted, and went away without saying a word, just leaving me her pamphlets. I was horrified at myself.

"And then something happened to me that made me wonder if I was in my right mind. A voice called me, at first just begging, and then when I dismissed it as craziness, really demanding. My children heard it too, so that I had to pay attention to this voice. I meant to go to the psychiatrist. The voice became embodied in the shape of something like a shining light, which seemed to come out of me and force its way back into me, and yet was entirely different from me, and spoke in a language that was all my own. I asked this voice what did it want, who it was. It said, word for word, 'You shall be called daughter of love, because you have borne love to me.' Then it was silent, and it left me completely at a loss.

"This shining thing came back, when I wasn't thinking of it at all. I was just then writing a poem about my one-year-old son, who was trying to take his first steps. It was December 25, 1968. First came the call that I had already heard before, then the voice. This time it showed me a flower, like a lily; it gave it to me. It wasn't anything material, but symbolic. The flower disappeared in me and the voice said: 'Guard the faithful flower of your head!' It was just as unintelligible as the first sentence it had said.

"I was horrified at myself, at my thoughts: What had become of the emancipated, self-confident woman? What should I do? They'll put me in an institution if I go to a doctor, I told myself. It was at once the most terrible and the most beautiful time of my life.

"I confided in my husband. He is very much in love with me, and around fourteen years older. He said I was overworked, I ought to relax. He made me take heart again.

"Then this voice came a third time.

"An indescribable feeling of happiness came over me when the voice said, 'Trust me and your courage, tomorrow you will experience something terrible, but at the same time you will learn everything about yourself.' And that's just what happened! I suddenly got an abscess in my mouth overnight. The dentist sent me to the hospital on January 14. While I was there I suffered what they call a cardiac arrest. I was even clinically dead, the nurse told me afterward.

"The voice had kept its word. I discovered my meaning, my name, who I was to God.

"Since then many years have passed. My fear is gone, only joy and hope have remained.

"Pardon the handwriting, short on time!"

What does this letter (a matter for the neurologist, most of us would say) have to do with Francis? It serves to document the fact that in 1968 a middle-class housewife in central Europe could spontaneously have experiences of the sort we shall be discussing in this chapter on the basis of seven-hundred-year-old stories.

In the Middle Ages, this housewife's experiences would have probably led to her being revered as a saint or reviled as a witch, depending on the time, place, and customs in question. In modern-day Rio de Janeiro in all likelihood she would surround herself with a community, small or large, of believers. She would regularly hear her voice and work cures. In Hamburg or Zürich she would possibly end up in a mental hospital and be given drugs to calm her down.

In our society hyperarousals, to use the technical term, fall under the jurisdiction of psychiatrists. It is important that we recognize this as a mere convention, as a practical regulation with no special claim to truth. In fact, contemporary scientific investigation of altered states of consciousness approaches its subject with a good deal of modesty. We have only recently begun to observe these phenomena impartially, without writing them all off before the fact as part of some psychopathological syndrome. We are on the verge, in other words, of rediscovering exceptional states, from a scientific point of view, as an autonomous dimension of human psychosomatic behavior, past and present.

This approach has much to recommend it as well in dealing with the ecstatic, visionary side of Francis. And it fits our initial motto: to reveal what Francis the man was really like.

LONELY PLACES

From the time he returned from the East (1220) up till his death (1226) Francis lived a very quiet life. Some of the hermitages he lived in during these years are still standing: Poggio Bustone and Fonte Colombo in the Rieti Valley, Greccio (likewise near Rieti), La Verna in Tuscany.

In Francis' day the Friars Minor called these settlements simply "places" (loci).[2] A few huts of clay and wood, and a little stone chapel in the middle of the forest, an hour's walk from the nearest village—that is how we ought to imagine these hermitages.

Today one visits these shrines by car. With their silence and remoteness they are pleasantly different from the pious hustle and bustle in Assisi, and sometimes one even searches in vain for a poor box to drop a donation in. "Le Celle" is one such place, a little monastery above Cortona, in the province of Arezzo, where visitors are shown the tiny room Francis is supposed to have lived in. One cannot help but wonder what he did all day long there.

In these last years Francis was scarcely strong enough to work in the peasants' fields anymore. Apart from the eye disease that he contracted in Egypt, his liver and stomach were giving him a lot of trouble.[3]

As far as his daily schedule in the hermitages can be reconstructed, Francis got up before daybreak. (On Mount La Verna he was awakened by the cry of a falcon, or so the story goes.) Then he prayed the Psalms with the other companions, and after that an ordained brother celebrated Mass for them. Francis often received communion on these occasions, as Celano notes.[4] In the meantime the sun had risen, they had a little something to eat, and thereafter Francis disappeared into the woods until lunch.

"He filled the forest with sighs, moistened the earth with his tears, and beat his breast. Often he spoke aloud in conversation with his Lord. There he gave an account to his Judge, there he besought the Father, there conferred with the friend, there he made merry with the Bridegroom—thus he represented to himself in many guises the One who is supremely simple."[5]

Celano's mannered style should not mislead us into assessing this passage as pure literature. It is easy enough to believe that Francis spoke out loud to God, when he knew he was alone.

Afternoons too we must picture Francis in lonely places—perhaps in a cave during wintertime, protected from the wet and cold. Romantic biographers of Francis (there are many) like to show Francis the hermit lost in contemplation of the beauties of nature. They favor sunsets and broad vistas over the gentle hills of Umbria. Amid their effusions they completely overlook the fact that Francis lived several centuries before Rousseau.

In the evening we find Francis by the fire with his companions, for a while. Then he went off again to be alone with himself (and God), and seldom went to sleep before midnight.

Francis was, to use the technical term, a contemplative. His inner life began to develop quite early in this direction, a sign of deep psychic energies.

The first trance condition that Francis had came, as mentioned in Chapter IV, as a complete surprise to him. His next ecstasy, which occurred shortly afterward, was likewise unexpected. These experiences—Francis was twenty-two at the time—undoubtedly made a profound impression on the man; they must have seemed like revelations of a new dimension of life. The deep feeling of happiness he sensed during the brief moments of the "swoon" survived as a precious memory. Francis went off by himself during the period when he was making up his mind, and this was surely due to his longing for the return of such sweet rapture.

Over the course of time Francis learned (he was, one might say, an autodidact) to put himself voluntarily in such exceptional states. Presumably he had made considerable progress by the time he began his public activity. At that stage Francis was thinking of becoming a hermit, which shows a strong inclination to ecstatic training.

He decided otherwise, as we know.

But that in no way means that he neglected his meditative practices. Even on his wanderings along the streets and roads of Italy, from one sermon to the next, Francis was in the habit of losing himself in God, and twice a year, during Lent and in the autumn fast,[6] he withdrew to one of the hermitages for prayer and contemplation.

Occasionally, in the early days of the Franciscans, there were regular group trances, triggered by Francis himself.[7] We have already described one such incident where Francis appears in the role of animator and guiding spirit, as he leads the little band of brothers at the Portiuncula (including Clare, who had come to visit) in the posture of ecstasy (pupils turned up, lifted arms).

This phenomenon did not disappear from Western society with the Middle Ages. It is remarkable how again and again (from the days of Cromwell right up to the present) collective ecstasies continue to take place, in both little groups and mass meetings, among—of all people—the supposedly sober Evangelical Christians in Anglo-Saxon cultures. The latest of these waves is Pentecostalism, which has grown particularly strong in recent years, and spread to the Continent, with large numbers of adherents even in Catholic Italy.

By the way, in this context we should not forget the roar of mass enthusiasm from Hitler's day. The energy from exceptional states does not always and unconditionally have to serve the purposes of peace.

Here is a report by an American university professor (linguistics, cultural anthropology), who in 1969 visited a small Pentecostal community on the Yucatán Peninsula, in a village 100 kilometers east of the state capital, Mérida: "6 July 1969. Sunday-morning services, *matutin*, start at six. I am up early enough to get up and dress, but before I have a chance to light my gasoline stove . . . Eusebia (my informant) knocks. . . . I hastily swallow a raw egg, then grab my equipment, and we leave.

"In the church Eusebia goes to kneel at the altar. The last conscious memory I have of the episode to follow is that of thinking, 'At home when I was a child, we were taught a little prayer to say before we sat down in church.' Then someplace in the church, I do not remember where, I leaned against something, I do not know what. I saw light, but then again I was surrounded by light, or perhaps not, because the light was in me, and I was the light. In this light I saw words in black outline . . . descending upside down as if on a waterfall of light. And at the same time I was full of a gaiety as if my entire being were resounding with silver bells. Never before had I ever felt this kind of luminous, ethereal, delightful happiness.

"I recovered with the thought: Now I finally know what joy is."[8]

As we see, nowadays under the right circumstances even a woman professor making scientific observations of trance conditions can unexpectedly experience a psychic high.

Professor Goodman, dropping back again into a cool, scientific tone, remarks in the notes she took after her trance that first, people can fall into trances spontaneously; second, that "people can be taught to go into a trance"; and third, that trances can be consciously induced at will. Her profound feeling of happiness falls into the first category, which belongs to the unforeseen gifts occasionally met with in exceptional states. The meaning of the word "grace" among the early Christians could be tied in with such experiences: The early Christians were thoroughly familiar with trances.

The conceptual (ideological) link between exceptional psychic states and specific thought structures—for example, Christian ones—is of course a product of culture. Given his spiritual makeup, Francis would have become a mystic had he lived among Muslims or Hindus. The thoughts, ideas, and feelings in his head would in that case have taken a different turn, without, however, lessening his capacity for going into trance states.

Accordingly, the stories of Francis' ecstasies could also be read in an atheistic sense—that is, without recourse to a transcendent God in personal contact with Francis. Francis' God then would be viewed, for instance—and Sartre would take this stance—as the totality of all other human beings; and Francis' raptures would become transitory reconciliations between the self and the not-self.

All the same we have to bear in mind that the (analytical) separation between exceptional psychic states and their cultural context never occurs in the real world. Individual or collective ecstasies always and everywhere occur within a specific conceptual pattern mediated by society. There is no such thing as a pure trance.

In contrast to bourgeois members of industrial society like ourselves, with our apparent freedom to choose whatever kind of psychic excitement we wish, whether Christian, spiritualist, socialist, Buddhist, etc. (when in fact what we really do is run after money), Francis made a decision that changed his life. Without this intrinsic, lived seriousness, Francis' raptures become little more than petty incidents of only modest entertainment value.

We are already familiar with the central importance that the battered and bruised figure of Christ held for Francis (pp. 64–65). We have described the formation of this basic feeling (pp. 40–41), and now we shall deal with its culmination in the appearance of Christ's wounds on Francis' body. It is clear that Francis' inner life revolved around the image of Christ, and that his tendency to identify with the Savior kept growing stronger. During Francis' many lonely hours of contemplation, he went over the life and especially the passion of Christ, as told in the Gospels, again and again, with great tenderness and tearful emotion. He was moved by the fate of the Son of Man, as the Bible calls him—no remote, celestial God, but a very present one—present, that is, in the "least of the brethren," to whom he transferred forever the aura of divinity, with the word that shattered all archaic religion: "As you did it to one of the least of these my brethren, you did it to me."[9]

"NEXT TO THE OX AND THE ASS"

On November 29, 1223, Pope Honorius III confirmed the definitive Franciscan Rule (see Chapter XI). That meant for Francis that the three-year paper war with the papal Curia and the Friars Minor in league with it was now over, and for a while the demons gave him some rest. Francis began to think about Christmas.

The idea that occurred to him was an epiphany of his interior life. Over the centuries its annual repetition continues to bring happiness, and not just to children.

Francis was staying at the time in a settlement near the little town of Greccio. There was a little dwelling there, shabby and off the beaten track, where Francis often put up. The people of Greccio were so entranced by him that many of them lived like Franciscan brothers and sisters, without leaving the world (their homes and families). "They entered religion" (*intrauerunt religionem*),[10] as the Leo stories put it. And in so doing they provide us with a rare and certainly authentic glimpse of the original form of Francis' fellowship.

For this reason the Christmas celebration of 1223 was a memorable one, apart from the devotion to the crèche. It shows us a collection of people who have discovered a new form of community spirit, by renouncing the old hierarchies and class distinctions, and not just at Christmastime.

Even John, the noble lord of Greccio, seems to have fallen under Francis' spell and hung his weapons up on a hook—no empty gesture for a knight at that time.

Francis spoke to him: "I would like to celebrate with all of you the memory of the child who was born in Bethlehem. I would like to see with my eyes the distress he had to suffer, as he was laid in a manger and bedded on hay, next to the ox and the ass."

And where is the celebration to take place?

In the woods, of course.

Celano continues: On Christmas Eve men and women from all over the region came with torches and lights to the appointed place, and the brothers from various hermitages appeared there as well. They found a manger filled with hay, and an ox and an ass had been led up to it. Francis sang the Gospel of the birth of Christ, and afterward he began to speak. The subject of his sermon was the child of Bethlehem, and he was overcome by such ardor that in saying the name of Jesus he licked his lips, like someone enjoying delicious food. And several times ordinary language failed him, and his voice came out sounding like the bleating of a lamb. While he spoke, a man in that devout congregation suddenly saw a baby in the manger; it lay there as if lifeless, until Francis woke it from its deep sleep.

Afterward people took bunches of hay from the manger back to their houses and gave it to their sick animals as medicine, whereupon they all got better. Some women, too, who were just about to give birth, placed this hay on their bodies and had a fortunate delivery. Later an altar was erected at the site of the manger, and a church was built in honor of the blessed Francis, so that the people could partake of the body of Christ there.[11]

In the story of Christmas in Greccio we find all the ingredients, in their original freshness, for the reality that we vainly try to capture with the insipid name of religion:

A relatively small, relatively homogeneous group of people with distinct and unfulfilled desires. One of them who has a special openness to extraordinary levels of reality, temporarily liberates the group self, lifting it up on a joyful collective flight. In the course of this, individual men and women spontaneously leave their banal everyday consciousness behind, take off, "flip out," and thereby increase the general excitement.

Miraculous cures take place.

Nevertheless, the whole process has a stable structure all its own, and afterward the people all feel relieved.

When such meetings take place nowadays, whether in Mexico City or Columbus, Ohio, the believers always come from the lower classes (blue collar, as they say in America). Naturally, ever since the days of slavery blacks have been the supreme experts in group ecstasy, where their music plays an important part.

So to this day, overburdened and injured people help each other to bear up with everyday life amid the real conditions of political and economic powerlessness, just as in Francis' time. And they improvise their own highly useful kind of transcendence, earthy and nondogmatic, and sometimes they get carried away, as they have every right to.

Even fussy old Celano, who ends the first book of his biography of Francis with the story of Christmas at Greccio, lets his feelings run away with him as he records this scene. The last word in his manuscript is "Hallelujah."

Francis' talent for ecstasy, as the Greccio story shows, was not some merely private affair. It would be a misunderstanding to ascribe his lonesome ascensions into heaven to the sort of inwardness that goes off to explore its own soul after getting a sharp rap on the knuckles from the outside world. Francis did not vent his psychic energies in the woods, but among men. In the woods he restored his exhausted nervous forces so he could expend them in front of the public gathered in the piazzas of towns and villages, or in the presence of the Sultan in Egypt or the Pope in Rome.

Hence it is misleading to make Francis into a nature mystic on the strength of his "Canticle of the Sun" and his friendly relations with all sorts of animals.

In the "Canticle of the Sun" (*Cantico di Frate Sole*), it is true that people appear only once, as creatures capable of forgiveness. Otherwise Francis hymns the sun, the moon, and the stars, the wind, the clouds, the delicious spring of water and the warmth of fire, the flowers of Mother Earth and bodily death.

But Francis calls all these natural objects "brother" and "sister," obviously a human form of address. And this fraternization significantly alters his view of what nature is. His idealized sense of humanity becomes a possible answer to the eternal question posed by the world—that puzzle that stares out at us from the icy emptiness of galactic space. He sees the worldly creatively, in the sense of a human reality rather than a problem in math or physics.

Francis also calls animals, whether they be cicadas or wolves, his brother and his sister, and thereby incorporates them into the broad cohumanity as he views it and lives it.

This is the story they tell: Once while Francis was staying in the Portiuncula, he happened to see a cicada sitting on the branch of a fig tree. The fig tree was near his hut, which was the last one along the garden hedge behind the house where Rainerio the gardener lived after Francis' death.

Francis stretched out his hand and said to the cicada:

"Come here, sister cicada."

Then the cicada began to chirr, and Francis was happy. A good hour passed in this way, till Francis put the cicada back in its place on the fig tree.

Whenever Francis left his hut, the cicada would always be sitting in the same place, and Francis would do as he had the first time.

After eight days Francis spoke to his companions:

"Now let's say good-by to sister cicada, so she can be on her way."

No sooner had he said this than the cicada disappeared and was never seen again.

Francis took joy in every creature.

He often begged the brothers who went into the forest to cut firewood, never to fell a whole tree. He bade the brother who took care of the garden not just to plant vegetables, but also to lay out a plot for aromatic herbs and flowers.

Francis didn't like to snuff out candles or lamps, out of reverence for brother fire. Once when he was sitting close to the fire, his tunic began to burn without his noticing it. Little by little he started to feel the heat, when a companion came up to him to put out the flames. But Francis would not let him, and said:

"We shouldn't do any harm to brother fire."

It took the combined persuasive powers of the brothers to change Francis' mind and stamp out the flames.

We who were with him observed how he spoke to fire and to other creatures, as if they understood him, and how he fell into a rapture as he did so.[12]

In his first biography Celano dedicates a special chapter to Francis' tenderness toward animals: One time in Greccio a companion came to Francis and brought him a hare which had been caught in a trap. Francis spoke to the animal, and said:

"Come here, brother hare. Why did you let yourself be duped that way?"

The companion, who had been holding the animal till then, set it free. It immediately ran to Francis and jumped into his lap, as if that were the safest place. After Francis had petted the hare for a while, he wanted to let it go, and put it down on the ground. But the hare wouldn't go away and leapt up into Francis' lap once more. This happened several times till Francis asked the brother to take the hare into the nearest woods and set it free there.

One day Francis was sitting in a fisherman's boat on the lake of Rieti, near the shore. The fisherman had just caught a large tench and gave it to

Francis as a present. Francis took the fish, addressed it as brother, and then put it back in the water near the boat. For quite a while the fish frolicked about in the place where Francis had put it, while he sank into contemplation. Only when Francis said good-by did the fish swim away.

In the little town of Alviano, Francis was giving a sermon when a great flock of swallows that nested there disturbed the devotions with their twittering. Then Francis talked to the swallows and said: "My sister swallows! You have now said enough, and I would like to get a word in edgewise. Be still now and hear the word of God."

At once the swallows were quiet, and the people were struck with wonder.[13]

A line from the "Canticle of the Sun" might be used as the motto for the many stories about Francis' loving relations with stones, plants, and animals, with the earth and the wind, with fire and water:

Laudato si, mi Signore, cum tucte le tue creature.[14] (Praised be you, my Lord, with all your creatures.)

The Leo stories likewise stress that Francis rejoiced in creatures because of his love for the Creator.[15]

And Celano reports that Francis addressed a pheasant, which was actually destined for the brothers' stewpot, as follows: "Praised be Creator, brother pheasant!"[16]

Francis' reverence for the earth, this profound feeling of human brotherliness toward animate and inanimate nature, had a medieval cast to it, insofar as it looked to "the most high, almighty, good Lord" (the beginning of the "Canticle of the Sun").

Philosophically speaking, Francis' God was the *summum bonum* (highest good) as the essential goal of all striving. That does not mean the supreme moral authority, the ultimate court of appeals. Francis had gotten beyond that kind of superego religion, as we've seen. Francis experienced his God as total attachment, as a passage from the *Fioretti* which goes back to Brother Leo makes revealingly clear:

The *Fioretti*: While Francis was staying on Mount La Verna, Brother Leo came at the usual hour to pray the Psalms with Francis, but Francis was not in his hut. As Leo looked about him in the forest he discovered Francis on his knees in the moonlight, with outstretched arms. Francis said:

"Who are you, most kind God, and who am I, a worm, your little slave?"

Francis said these words over and over again.

Then Leo, who was standing there motionless, saw a light of wondrous beauty, like a glittering flame that was pleasing to the eyes, floating down from heaven and hovering over Francis. It also seemed to him as if a voice were coming out of the flame and speaking to Francis.

After a while Leo wanted to withdraw discreetly, when Francis heard a rustling noise and cried out at once:

"Whoever you are, don't move!"

Leo stood still, and cried:

"It's me."

Later Brother Leo related that he was so terrified he wanted to crawl right under the ground.

Francis said:

"How often have I told you not to listen in on me? Now tell me whether you saw anything."

Leo reported what he had observed, and asked Francis to explain the words he had spoken so repeatedly, and the meaning of the flame.

Francis greatly loved Leo for the simplicity and gentleness of his character, and so he told him:

"I have been granted a twofold revelation. I have seen the abyss of God's kindness, as well as the abyss of my own nothingness. That is why I had to utter the words you heard. But the flame that you saw was God. Now be careful not to come following after me again!"

Then Leo went back to his hut and experienced a deep joy.[17]

Abyss calls to abyss, as Psalm 44 says.[18] It is possible that Francis, who knew the Psalms well, had this passage in mind when he spoke of the two abysses. Like many other reflective people, before and since, Francis recognized his own nothingness by becoming conscious of the transiency and fortuitousness of his existence.

His happy surprise, upon learning that he was nonetheless called by name, in loving kindness, from the depths of God's eternity, sent him into raptures. A sentence of Francis', which we omitted just now from the passage of the *Fioretti* just quoted, may now claim our attention: "Who are you," he says, speaking to God, "that you come down to me?"

Sixteen years separate Francis' nocturnal prayer in Bernard of Quintavalle's bedroom and his devotions by moonlight on Mount La Verna. Francis' descent into the depths of his bourgeois self, to the very ground of his loneliness, has taken a long while. Now that he has arrived at the bottom, he gets his reward.

THE FIVE WOUNDS OF CHRIST

The oldest account of Francis' stigmatization, bearing a papal *imprimatur* dated February 25, 1229, comes from Celano: "Two years before Francis gave his soul back to heaven,[19] while he was living in the hermitage which was called La Verna, after the place on which it stood, he saw in a vision a man standing above him, like a seraph with six wings, his hands extended and his feet joined together and fixed to a cross. Two of the wings were extended above his head, two were extended as if for flight, and two were wrapped around the whole body. When the blessed servant of the Most High saw these things, he was filled with the greatest wonder, but he could not understand what this vision should mean. Still, he was filled with happiness . . . because of the kind and gracious look with which he saw himself regarded by the seraph, whose beauty was beyond estimation; but the fact that the seraph was fixed to a cross and the sharpness of his suffering filled Francis with fear. And so he arose, if I may so speak, sorrowful and joyful, and joy and grief were in him alternately. Solicitously he thought what this vision could mean, and his soul was in great anxiety to find its meaning. And while he was thus unable to come to any understanding of it and the strangeness of the vision perplexed his heart, the marks of the nails began to appear in his hands and feet, just as he had seen them a little before in the crucified man above him.

"His hands and feet seemed to be pierced through the middle by nails, with the heads of the nails appearing in the inner side of the hands and on the upper sides of the feet and their pointed ends on the opposite sides. The marks in the hands were round on the inner side, but on the outer side they were elongated; and some small pieces of flesh took on the appearance of the ends of the nails, bent and driven back and rising above the rest of the flesh. In the same way the marks of the nails were impressed upon the feet and raised in a similar way above the rest of the flesh. Furthermore, his right side was as though it had been pierced by a lance and had a wound in it that frequently bled so that his tunic and trousers were very often covered with his . . . blood."

The *Fioretti*, in the original Latin version, reports the story quite laconically: "During those same forty days, around the feast of the Exaltation of the Holy Cross, Christ appeared to Francis on the mountain in the form of a crucified seraph with wings, and imprinted the marks of the nails in his hands and feet and the wound in his side, as the legend tells us. The apparition came at night and was so bright that the mountains and valleys all around were lit up and stood out as clearly as if it had been broad daylight. The shepherds of that region, who were out with their herds, bear witness to that. The reason why the marks of the wounds were imprinted on the blessed Francis is not yet fully understood."[20]

(The "forty days" refer to the autumn fasting season, from the day after the Assumption till the twenty-ninth of September, the feast of the Archangel Michael. The feast of the Exaltation of the Cross is celebrated on September 14. The seraphim are the biblical angels from the books of the prophets Isaiah and Ezekiel. The "legend" is Celano's, in the sense then current of "reading material.")

The Leo stories mention a small detail that informs us whom Francis told his vision of the crucified angel to: "Among many other consolations both secret and open which God gave him, the vision of the seraphim was shown him by God, from which he received much comfort in his soul in communion with God for the whole of his life. When his companion brought him food that day he told him all that had happened."[21]

The companion was Brother Leo.

Leo always carried a sheet of parchment with him, because Francis had written a blessing for him on it. Then in his own hand Leo added a note, and before he died he left the sheet to the convent of the Friars Minor in Assisi. It reads: "Two years before his death St. Francis kept Lent in the house on La Verna in honor of the blessed Virgin Mary, the mother of God, and of the Archangel Michael, from the feast of the Assumption of the blessed Virgin Mary until the feast of St. Michael in September. And the hand of God was upon him. After the vision and speech of the seraphim and the impression of Christ's stigmata on his body he composed these praises that are written on the other side of the leaf, and wrote them with his own hand, giving thanks to God for the benefit conferred on him. St. Francis wrote this blessing with his own hand for me, Brother Leo."[22]

The genuineness of this document is beyond doubt.

Francis himself wrote down the act of thanksgiving on the opposite side of the sheet.[23] It is a mixture of personal piety and conventional prayers. Addressed directly to God, it has an untroubled assurance about it. The last word of this long litany calls upon God by the name of Savior: *Salvatore.*

In reality, ever since September 1224, Francis himself had become a savior, a second Christ, with visible certification of his likeness to Jesus engraved in his hands and feet, in a manner never seen before. The Franciscan coat of arms has proudly mirrored this lofty claim for centuries: It shows two crossed forearms, the naked one belonging to Christ and the one clothed in the sleeve of a monk's tunic belonging to Francis. Both hands are marked with the wound of the Crucified.[24]

This representation is extremely daring from the standpoint of Church dogma. Contrary to the usual stress on Christ's divine superiority, it suggests an equality between the two stigmatics.

As a matter of fact, after he died many of Francis' contemporaries began to conceive of Francis as the Messiah of the third (and last) age of world history—a quite subversive and dangerous interpretation, as far as the official Church was concerned (see Chapter XVI).

The first traces of this heterodox theology of the stigmatized Francis appear in Celano, writing five years after the vision on Mount La Verna.

Celano: "Indeed the glorious life of this man sheds a more brilliant light upon the perfection of the saints who preceded him. The passion of Jesus Christ proves this and his cross shows it most clearly. For in truth the venerable father was marked in five parts of his body with the marks of the passion as though he had hung upon the cross with the Son of God. This is a great mystery and shows forth the majesty of the prerogative of love (*praerogativa dilectio*). But a secret counsel lies hidden therein and therein is concealed an awe-inspiring mystery which we believe is known to God alone."[25]

Celano is careful. For safety's sake he buries the question of Francis' uniqueness and its theological consequences in the depths of divinity. For all that, Francis, on account of the stigmata, immediately takes his place at the head of all the saints in existence. In Celano's mind he has no peer in the canonical heaven.

That makes sense, to the extent that Francis' stigmatization does in fact constitute something new in the history of culture. Francis heads a series of people who followed his example by bearing the wounds of the Crucified on their bodies. (The total number of European stigmatics is somewhere in between 100 and 330. The last case to date was the Capuchin Padre Pio of Pietrelcina, who died in 1968.)

For the modern reader, the story of how Francis received the stigmata raises two questions: Did it actually happen, and how can it be explained?

The oldest account of how Francis' stigmata became publicly known comes from Celano. It is found in his first biography of Francis from the year 1229, along with his description of the events following Francis' death in the year 1226.

According to Celano, Francis' body was first laid out in the Portiuncula chapel, and the population of Assisi and the surrounding area streamed out there in a crowd. What they got to see caused a sensation: "He seemed as though he had been recently taken down from the cross, his hands and feet were pierced as though by nails and his side wounded as though by a lance."

The body, Celano continues, looked very beautiful. The limbs moved freely, and the skin color was white (in contrast to Francis' rather dark skin tone during his lifetime). Then he adds, in an obvious effort to be precise: ". . . it was wonderful to see in the middle of his hands and feet, not only the holes made by the nails, but the nails themselves formed out of his flesh and retaining the blackness of iron, and his side was red with blood."[26]

The crush of the crowds was overwhelming: Every one in the multitude thought he had received the greatest grace, if he were allowed at least to see the holy wounds that Francis bore on his body, or, better still, to kiss them.

The reasons for believing this account are evident. The inspection of Francis' body, as Celano describes it, was a public event, with hundreds of witnesses. Not even in the Middle Ages, when people believed in miracles, could a chronicler, still less an official chronicler, get away with an open fabrication so soon after an episode so widely known. The facts of Francis' stigmata rest on solid historical ground.

Nonetheless, many details in the reports of the stigmatization are easily recognizable as later embellishments, as, for example, the brightly illumined night of the *Fioretti*. On the whole, however, the (relatively few) texts from the old Franciscan sources that relate to the stigmata take a remarkably objective approach. That is especially true of the Leo stories, whose historical value modern Franciscan scholarship does not dispute. They are conspicuously casual in their references to the stigmata, as if Leo and his fellow authors Rufino and Angelo were reluctant to publicize Francis' wounds. That makes sense, since all the accounts stress how carefully Francis hid the stigmata from view. As true brothers, Francis' three companions wished to respect his wish to treat the matter with discretion, even after his death.

A characteristic instance of this attitude is a Leo story in which a man from a village around Rieti got the idea (during an outbreak of rinderpest) to go to the friars' hermitage at Fonte Colombo and get some water that had been used to wash Francis' hands and feet. (By this time he had already become something of an invalid.) The man sprinkled this water over the sick cattle, and they recovered immediately. There is a lapidary explanation for the miracle: "At this time St. Francis had scars (*cicatrices*) on his hands and feet and in his side."[27]

All told, we may believe in Francis' wounds with an easy conscience. The question still remains whether we can find a reasonably satisfying scientific explanation for them.

Here is an example of the sort of prose one encounters in searching for an answer to this question: "The combined medical and psychoreligious explanation (of stigmatization) is based on analogous clinical cases. Judging from such cases, stigmatization would appear to be psychogenic subcutaneous bleeding from seemingly intact blood vessels by virtue of a general neurovegetative tendency. People with a neuropathic constitution, a complex of symptoms resembling hysteria, heightened sensibility and porous skin, with the sort of faith that all but divests itself of the body, and a pious cult of Christ's passion that borders on the miraculous, are capable of converting an imaginative conception of the crucifixion into physical realities. On the issue of how the psychic mechanisms operate during the ideopathic transfer, opinions differ quite widely."[28]

Let them go on differing.

In reality, the sciences hide their ignorance of psychosomatic phenomena behind learned jargon (a not unheard-of procedure elsewhere). Notice the heavy-handed ideological manner of the text quoted above, which consigns stigmatization (seldom seen nowadays) to the madhouse ("analogous clinical cases," "complex of symptoms resembling hysteria")—especially charming in a Catholic lexicon.

The irritating thing about such scientific tunnel vision, still so widespread in our day, is not so much its inability to make sense of an outstanding historical figure like Francis. We can ignore that easily enough. It is rather its incompetence in dealing with the pattern of psychosomatic complaints now manifesting itself in society.

So we shall have to rescue Francis' stigmata from the waxworks of incomprehension and see them for what they really were: an unusual but understandable reaction of a suffering individual (genuinely suffering, for obvious reasons) to noxious forces, which he was helplessly subjected to through no fault of his own.

After his return from Palestine Francis suffered increasingly from fits of depression. (That is how we put it nowadays. Back then people spoke of "temptations," "dryness" of soul, spiritual "sluggishness." Demonic interference was given a major share of the blame for these gloomy, irritable psychic states.)

The story of the beating by demons in Rome is only one of many describing more or less at length how Francis was harassed by devils in the last years of his life.[29] Even on Mount La Verna—i.e., immediately before the stigmatization—Francis had to endure many battles with demons (according to the *Fioretti*), which greatly sapped his strength.[30]

The devil is the enemy of joy. This notion derives from a saying of Francis' handed down to us in the Leo stories: "The devil exults when he can extinguish . . . the joy at heart of God's servant."[31]

And the *Scripta Leonis* go on to emphasize the point: "This was St. Francis' chief and principal concern: He was always anxious to preserve spiritual joy (*laetitiam spiritalem*) in himself."[32]

Almost universally in the Middle Ages (and in the early Franciscan sources as well) the opposite of this joy was termed *acedia*,[33] which literally means laziness. In point of fact it stood for a complex syndrome of bitterness, melancholy, weariness, self-torment, existential anxiety, dejection: everything up to and including blank despair.

Francis was quite familiar with this condition; otherwise he would not have had to fight it.

We find a further reference to Francis' depression in Celano. He speaks of an "especially severe temptation of the spirit"[34] which hung over Francis for "several years" and which he finally overcame through an act of confidence.

These rather obscure hints become clearer when we recall the traumatic experiences Francis had to go through in the Holy Land and the Eternal City (see Chapters X and XI) in the years 1219 and 1220.

To put it rather emotionally, Francis had looked into the blind eye of coldhearted power; had seen two shapes of terror—one military, one bureaucratic.

The causes, therefore, of Francis' depressive states are not to be sought in a metabolic disturbance. They are not at all, as they say, endogenous.

What made Francis psychically ill, what caused him to suffer, was not a matter of biochemistry or neurophysiology, but of politics.

We have seen what damage was done to Francis' psyche by the *Realpolitik* of his day. His sustained contact with what would later be called institutions brought on the stigmata, even before the wounds of Christ broke out on his body.

What is an institution? An arrangement for separating people into "tolerable" and "intolerable" elements. The latter are labeled as such.

The history of the labeling is a long one, from the branding of slaves in antiquity to the Jewish caps in the Middle Ages to the bad marks in modern schools.

This kind of stigmatization, once one gets a good view of it, proves to be a rich subject. (One could write entire books on it—as has already been done.)[35]

We have broached it because of Francis' striking predilection for the true stigmatics of his day. His overcoming of disgust at the lepers marked the decisive turning point in his life. From then on he moved by preference among social outcasts and the lowest classes. He chose the stigma of poverty.

Then all this was taken away from him when they transformed his fellowship of beggars to an officially recognized Order. Francis knew that doctoral robes and cardinals' capes would be awaiting the Friars Minor as soon as he was dead and buried.

What could he do?

The five wounds that Francis bore were a body sermon which proclaimed two things: first, his abiding desire to stay on the side of the people who went about their whole lives with various stigmas—beggars, criminals, or lepers; second, Francis' body revealed how much he himself had been injured and humiliated against his will, branded as a loser in his contest with the powerful, and clearly conscious of his impotence.

Of course, Francis' final countermove in this struggle was not a deliberate response of his nervous system. We have seen how confused he was by the appearance of the angel and the breaking open of his wounds, how carefully he strove to hide them from the people around him.

Nevertheless, the stigmata are entirely his creation. They belong to him as the finished work of art belongs to the artist who made it.

At the end of this determinedly factual discussion of Francis' stigmatization we see something that lies beyond the reach of purely objective thought: the real goodness of a man.

The gesture with which Francis surrenders to the fiery angel is the abandonment of his subjectivity. The protective armor surrounding his ego is blasted away, and thereafter he need hold back nothing of himself.

Francis has now finally become like the figure of Christ at the Last Supper that filled him with such tenderness and blissful eucharistic devotion. The Savior's gesture of self-donation in offering himself as food to the community of brothers signifies precisely that unlimited openness to others which we find so difficult and at the same time so desirable. Bourgeois loneliness, with its acquisitive ego, found an ideal image "in those days," and since then it carries it around everywhere, looking for redemption like the wandering Jew.

There is no way of knowing whether there will ever be a world where people won't have to hold anything back from others. But, obviously, it would be much more harmonious than the one we're used to. That is why we sense a special kind of warmth radiating from Francis—without it we would have long since gone completely cold.

XIV

IL SANTO

Brother Jordan of Giano tells us: "When I was returning to Germany I called on Brother Thomas of Celano, who was delighted to see me and gave me some relics of St. Francis. When I reached Würzburg I sent word to the brothers of my custody that if they needed to contact me they were to meet me in Eisenach. . . . Delighted, the brothers gathered at the convent there and gave orders to the porter that when I arrived he was not to admit me but was first to let them know. When I came to the door and knocked I was not admitted, but the porter hurried to the friars with the news that I was at the door. They instructed him not to let me in by the door, but through the church. The friars, exulting in spirit, went into the choir and entered the nave in procession, two by two, bearing crosses and censers and palm branches and lighted candles in their hands. When they were all drawn up in line they opened the doors of the church to admit me, welcoming me with joy and gladness. . . . Astonished at this novel reception, I held up my hand for them to be quiet, but they finished with joy what they had begun. As I in amazement wondered at this, it came into my mind that I had with me the relics of St. Francis, which in my astonishment I had forgotten. When the chant was finished I said, rejoicing in spirit: 'Rejoice, brothers, for I know that it is not for me myself, but our blessed father, Francis, in me that you are praising. I have his relics with me and without my saying anything his presence roused your spirits to his praise.'

"Taking the relics from my breast, I placed them on the altar. I had seen St. Francis while he was alive and so had the impression that he was thoroughly human; but from then on I held him in greater reverence and honor."[1]

What the worthy Brother Jordan discovered by accident after Francis' death, the men and women of Umbria and Latium had already grasped while Francis was alive. It is an open question at just what point Francis became the object of public veneration, but he was already beloved by the populace before his journey to the Holy Land. Yet only in the last two years of his life, when he said good-by to Mount La Verna and rode off on a donkey, like Jesus, through central Italy, did he begin to radiate his unique aura. Francis, we should not forget, was forty-two years old at the time and still quite capable of "having sons and daughters,"[2] as he occasionally remarked, when people's eagerness to do him homage got on his nerves.

But all the cured epileptics,[3] possessed,[4] blind,[5] and lame individuals[6] whom he left in his wake spoke out unmistakably. Francis' fingernail clippings, his bath water, the bandages on his hands and feet all became coveted medications, and every now and then someone in the crowd would cut off a piece of Francis' tunic for future use as a home remedy.

By a free plebiscite, as it were, Francis became a walking relic. The cry the people greeted him with in his lifetime was the title the Pope officially and belatedly conferred on him two years after his death: *il santo* (the saint).

"SINCE I AM HERE FOR EVERYONE"

We are well informed about the last years of Francis' life (October 1224 to October 1226).[7] No other period gets such extensive and detailed treatment in the sources, and so we can reconstruct the chronology with relative precision:

On September 30, 1224, Francis left Mount La Verna, riding on a donkey, accompanied by Brother Leo. Their path led them via Borgo San Sepolcro to Mount Casale, then farther on to Città di Castello, where Francis spent October.

In November 1224 Francis arrived at the Portiuncula.

During the winter of 1224–25 Francis traveled through the villages of Umbria, preaching as he went along. He had to cut his activity short because of severe eye pains, and return to Assisi. He was practically blind and suffered from continual headaches.

Cardinal Ugolino invited Francis to come to Rieti to get medical treatment there. Francis put off his departure, and spent the summer of 1225 in the garden of San Damiano, where he was nursed by Clare. Here he wrote the "Canticle of the Sun."

In the early autumn of 1225, Francis went to Rieti, where he was lodged at first in the bishop's palace. (The Pope was likewise in residence in Rieti at this time.) He began to get medical attention, which proved fruitless. Francis moved to the hermitage at Fonte Colombo, where he underwent an unsuccessful eye operation.

Francis celebrated Christmas at the hermitage of Poggio Bustone (also in the Rieti Valley).

In the spring of 1226 Francis went, at the instigation of Cardinal Ugolino, to Siena to consult the doctors there. His health deteriorated further: his stomach, liver, and diaphragm were affected. He suffered a severe hemorrhage. Brother Elias, as minister general, ordered Francis brought to Assisi. The route was chosen so as to avoid Perugia. (It was feared that the citizens might take possession of Francis because of the high value of his person as a source of relics.)

In April 1226, Francis was brought to Assisi by way of Cortona, Gubbio, Nocera, and Satrino. Over the last stages of the trip he was given a military escort. Francis was now suffering from dropsy as well. For security reasons he was housed in the episcopal palace, where he stayed from May till September. There he composed his *Testament*.

At the end of September, Francis was taken by his own request to the Portiuncula, where he died on the evening of October 3, 1226.

During his final years four of Francis' companions were with him almost continually: Leo, Masseo, Angelo, and Rufino. Three fifths of the Leo stories relate to the events of the years 1223–26, and they are not free from a certain bias. They document Francis' words and deeds after the passage of the papal Rule, and they were written for the benefit of the friars who resisted the official party line taken after Francis' death.

As opposed to Celano, who wrote regular paeans to Ugolino,[8] the Leo stories treat the cardinal of Ostia and eventual Pope rather coolly, and the influential Brother Elias is never, except on one occasion,[9] called anything but "the minister general" when he makes an appearance. Francis himself is not presented as "the saint," but as a mortally ill human being whose willpower remains strong nonetheless till the very end.

This picture of Francis surely comes the closest to the real man.

This is the story they tell: One day when Francis was being treated in Rieti for his eye trouble, the doctor came and told him of a poor woman from the area who had seen him about pain in her eyes. He would probably have to treat her without charge, the doctor added.

Francis immediately felt sympathy for the woman; he called a companion over and said:

"Brother, we have to give back what doesn't belong to us."

"What is that?"

"Ah, this cloak, which we got from the poor woman with the eye disease. It was a gift on loan, and we must give it back."

The companion who was responsible for Francis at that time had no idea what he meant, and said only that Francis could do whatever seemed right to him.

Thereupon Francis sent for a pious man who was a friend of his, and said to him:

"Take the cloak here, and get twelve loaves of bread, and bring them both to the woman whom the doctor will lead you to. Say to her that the poor man she lent them to now returns them with thanks."

The man did what Francis asked him to.

The woman thought someone was playing a practical joke on her and begged to be left alone. Only when the messenger made her take the cloak and the loaves, and went away, did she begin to believe in her good fortune. For fear the whole thing would turn out to be a misunderstanding, she left at night and went back to her village.[10]

Giving away the relatively valuable cloak was only one of the peculiarities that the honored patient took pleasure in—not always to the delight of the staff around him. Brother Elias had to order him by holy obedience, for reasons given, not to trade tunics with any of the brothers without explicit permission.[11] Francis liked to do this whenever he had the impression that a brother was worse clothed than himself. Word of this got around, and so many of the friars managed to get a precious keepsake.

Two French brothers, for example, were lucky enough to exchange a few words with Francis and to ask him *"per amore di dio"*[12] for his tunic.

Francis immediately took it off and gave it to them, and then, we are explicitly told, stood around in his underwear for an hour, until somebody got him some new clothes.

Francis, it seems, had the habit of always giving away his tunic or rope belt whenever anyone invoked the love of God. As soon as he heard this phrase, Celano says, "he would become excited, stirred, and inflamed, as though an inner chord of his heart had been plucked by the plectrum of the outward voice of the speaker"[13]—as Celano quaintly puts it.

Accordingly, the turnover in tunics and belts was high, and Francis' companions were kept fairly busy just looking after his wardrobe—all the more so because Francis wore a new tunic only with the greatest reluctance. He preferred to wear robes that had long been worn by other brothers and were inevitably patched and threadbare. Sometimes he went so far as to make a new tunic for himself by sewing together the more or less intact parts of useless old ones. Francis seems to have been especially gifted at mending,[14] despite his bad eyes. He even managed to write this mania into the papal Rule,[15] where he recommends that the friars repair their clothing with burlap. Every attempt to force a cloak on Francis became a major production.[16] First his companions had to be careful to choose the right words. The most successful formula seems to have been that Francis really ought—on account of the extreme cold, for example—to let somebody lend him a cloak for the time being. Thereupon Francis would ask if he could always give it away if he felt that somebody needed it more than he did. Only when they told him "yes" would he finally take the cloak.

In his effort really to be the least of the Friars Minor, Francis always wanted (theoretically, anyhow) to have a companion with him, whom he promised to obey in absolutely everything—his so-called guardian.[17] (One can imagine after what has been said that the job was not particularly sought after.) In fact, he naturally found ways of getting around the prohibitions placed upon him by this guardian, when he had once more driven his companions to distraction by giving away his belongings.

This is the story they tell: Once a very poor man, clad only in rags, came to a hermitage and begged the brothers for the love of God to give him an old piece of cloth so that he could cover his nakedness. The companion whom he talked to searched all through the house but could find nothing.

At that Francis began to cut a large patch out of the lining of his tunic with his knife—secretly, so his guardian wouldn't notice. But the guardian immediately saw what he was up to, and forbade him to do it, because he was sick, and it was terribly cold.

Then Francis grew sad. He begged the brothers at least to tear off a patch here and there from their tunics and give it to the poor devil. And this they did.[18]

Only against the background of such practices do we clearly appreciate what Francis meant by the "loving service of our holy Lady Poverty (*ut semper diligant et obseruent dominam nostram sanctam paupertatem*).[19]

In the Leo stories there is a collection of sayings by Francis on this subject.[20] They come from the spring of 1226, when Francis was living in Siena, and they have the character of a last will and testament. The occasion for these little speeches was provided by a Lord Bonaventure (not to be confused with the later general of the Order), who had made a plot of land available to the brothers in Siena, on which they built a shelter. Francis was lodged there too in one of the "cells."

Lord Bonaventure paid Francis a visit and asked him whether he was satisfied.

Francis answered: "May I tell you how I think the brothers' shelters ought to be built?"

The benefactor answered, "Yes, of course," and Francis began to speak.

This is what he said: "Let us suppose that the brothers come to a city where they have no shelter (*locum*). When they find someone who puts some land at their disposal, then they must first ask how large a site it will take, lest they offend against holy poverty. They should constantly recall that we are obliged to set a good example, so that they never live otherwise than as strangers and pilgrims among men, without any right to property.

"Then the brothers are to go to the bishop of the town and ask his permission to build a shelter.

"Once they have the bishop's blessing, they should first of all plant a hedge around the plot, instead of a wall. Then they can set up simple huts out of wood and clay, then workshops, and a little church. The brothers are never to build large churches, of the kind they have for preaching. It is better that the brothers go to other churches to preach, so that they always observe holy poverty. Besides, the unpretentiousness of the shelters will be a continual and powerful sermon for the prelates and clerics of the town.

"I know that the brothers already have erected big buildings, and thus offended against poverty and given a bad example.

"The brothers' shelters should be small and shabby, and there shouldn't be too many companions in one place, because then it's harder for them to observe holy poverty."[21]

This is the story they tell: One day after he had spoken these words to Lord Bonaventure, Francis got violently sick in the evening, so that he had to vomit. He retched, and spat up blood all through the night, and was so weak that the companions thought he was on his deathbed. Then they said to Francis:

"Father, what shall we do? Don't you wish to make known your last will (*memoriale tue voluntatis*), so that your companions may always have something to remember you by?"

Francis whispered that they might call Brother Benedict of Piratro, a wise and holy man, who had long been a member of the fellowship, and was a priest. When he came, Francis said to him:

"Write down that I bless all the brothers, those who are now in our fellowship, and those who will come afterward, till the end of the world. May they remember my last words, always love one another, honor our holy Lady Poverty, and be true to the prelates of the Church."

Then he enjoined the brothers one more time to be careful not to give bad example, and he cursed all the companions who caused men to speak ill of the fellowship and brought shame down on the zealous brothers.[22]

Owing to his hemorrhage Francis' speech about the humble shelters acquired a sacred testamentary quality in the eyes of his faithful companions. Although their stories were not written down until twenty years after

Francis' death, he speaks in them with an unmistakable voice. One point that catches the eye is that the Leo stories consistently call Francis' brotherhood a "fellowship" (*religio*) and not an "Order" (*ordo*), thereby contradicting the official terminology of the papal Rule, in which the Friars Minor are adjudged to be an Order.

One is free to believe or disbelieve that Francis qualified his words of blessing with a powerful curse against the destroyers of holy poverty. We can be sure in any case that despite a heavy loss of blood he was not in the least disposed to resignation.

We hear Francis speaking, not as authentically as in the Leo stories, but with a similarly powerful self-consciousness, in a number of letters sent out in his name during the last years of his life. Their genuineness is not always above suspicion,[23] and it is quite conceivable that many of these pieces were not drafted till after Francis' death—a not uncommon practice in the Middle Ages.

No matter what, four of these letters merit our interest.[24]

Brother Francis to the minister general:

God bless you. I shall be able to tell whether you love God, and myself as well, by the way that you treat the brothers. No companion who comes before you, no matter how serious his fault, ought to leave without your compassion. You must give him proof of your love, and more than you would show to me, and in this way you will get him back on the right path again.[25]

Brother Francis to the officials of the Friars Minor:

With all the love I can muster I beg you to show all honor and reverence to the body and blood of the Lord Jesus Christ. How worthy must the priest be who is permitted to touch the Son of God with his hands! What wretchedness if other things occupy him while Christ comes down to the altar in his hands![26]

Brother Francis to all heads of cities, consuls, judges, and regents throughout the world:

Remember that the hour of your death comes closer every day. All men who slight God's Commandments are cursed. They will fall into oblivion, and everything they thought to possess will be taken away from them on the day of their death. The wiser and mightier they were, the more bitter their torments in hell will be.[27]

Brother Francis to all Christian people:

Since I am here for everyone, I must be useful to everyone, and bring them the words of my Lord. No one should desire to be placed over another. Whoever is deemed greater is to behave as if he were lesser and serve the others. Remember what it is like when a rich man dies impenitent. His money, his titles, his knowledge are taken away from him. His relatives divide up his property among them, and are vexed because he did not leave them more. The worms will sate themselves on his body, and the demons will gnaw his soul.

Accept these words and all other words of Our Lord Jesus Christ with love, and pay close heed to them. Blessed are those who persevere in the good until their end![28]

We cannot miss the note of determination in Francis' last letters. He knew his wishes still carried weight with the public. The papal Curia, to begin with, would consider him the real head of the Friars Minor until his death.[29] Within the Order, although he had laid aside all leadership functions and named Brother Elias minister general, Francis remained the real authority. Above and beyond that, Francis spoke out, as if it were the most natural thing in the world, to the powerful men of his age and, finally, even to all of Christendom.

He proclaimed, in rather radical fashion, the principle of an end to all privileges, which in our day is generally damned as anarchy on both sides of the Iron Curtain.

Francis persevered in his vision of a society where nobody would be subordinate to anyone else. His key to the realization of this condition was, paradoxically, the postulate of a general willingness to serve. When nobody wanted to give orders anymore, then the domination of man over man would be at an end.

There, in all its bedrock simplicity, is Francis' idea of obedience. Its goal is not the introduction of a universal serf mentality, but a mode of understanding among men that is not based on the giving of orders. One might call it, if the expression made more sense, the mode of courtesy in social intercourse.

Francis consistently put himself in the lowest place. He wished to be everyone's servant, to kiss the feet of all the people.

Since this was not possible, he sent them a letter, as though he were the secret Pope of his time.

At the same time he knew that for Lord Ugolino and his kind he was a mortally ill and powerless anachronism who no longer posed any threat, that his freedom to speak out was the freedom of a fool.[30]

"YOU TAKE ME FOR A HOLY MAN"

When we think about the behavior of the throngs of mourners who paid their last respects to their idol Elvis Presley in Memphis in 1977, the historical distance separating us from the origins of the cult surrounding Francis shrinks considerably. Then as now, people's readiness to adore, once they find a suitable object, seems almost unlimited, and the energies released in such situations are tremendous.

We know that Mussolini, Stalin, Hitler, and Franco in their day enjoyed a high degree of veneration, and the shouts of enthusiastic men and women have become, to our way of thinking, a questionable form of the voice of God. In our century we may well have our doubts whether the people's endorsement constitutes the ultimate guarantee for the worthiness of the conquering hero, and this salutary skepticism governs our attitude toward the so-called great men of history. It is a point in Francis' favor that he resisted the adulation of the people.

This is the story they tell: Once, when Peter of Catania was minister general, Francis had just recovered somewhat from an illness. He was still suffering from a quartan ague, but he insisted on getting up and speaking to the citizens of Assisi out on the piazza. After the sermon he asked the people to wait a little. Then he went with Peter of Catania and some other companions into the church of San Rufino, confessed his sins to Peter, and begged to be allowed to choose his own penance. Peter answered:

"Of course. I leave it up to you."

Then Francis took off his tunic, tied the rope around his neck, and had Peter lead him around in front of the assembled populace. Brother Peter and the other companions had tears in their eyes. But Francis said to the crowd:

"You take me for a holy man, and many people have followed my example and entered religion. But now I must confess to you that during my sickness I ate meat. I also had meat broth."

This happened during the wintertime, and it was bitterly cold.[31]

This is the story they tell: Another time, during the Martinmas fast, Francis was staying in the hermitage of Poggio Bustone. Since he could not tolerate food prepared with oil, on account of his illness, the brothers cooked special dishes for him with lard. When the fast was over, Francis preached to a great crowd of people who had come for the Christmas festival. He began his address with these words:

"You have come here with great piety to hear me preach, and you take me for a holy man. But I have to confess to you that during the fast I ate food cooked with lard."[32]

The most illuminating story in this series is the one about the fox pelt. The companion who was responsible for Francis at the time had gotten hold of some fox fur and asked Francis to sew it on the inside of his tunic, to protect his ailing spleen and his weakened stomach. Francis answered: "If you want to do that, then you have to sew a piece of fur the same size on the outside of my tunic, so the people can see what I'm wearing on the inside."[33]

Francis lived in a time of deep and widespread resentment over the conduct of prelates, priests, and monks. When the opportunity arose—for example, during the Crusades—the *Lumpenproletariat* might gather in crowds in the rear of the knightly armies and invade Christian towns. When they did, the houses of the priests were the first to be put to the torch. Greed and lecherousness were thought of as characteristic clerical qualities, and numerous contemporary lampoons and satirical songs testify to their prevalence.[34]

People knew very well that the habit doesn't make the monk, and so their initial response to religiously professed persons was mistrust.

In the face of this devaluation of religious life, a serious person like Francis had only one alternative: to strive mightily to make his behavior match his formal status. In this light we can understand Francis' pedantic insistence on publicizing his infractions against the Rule: He wanted at all cost to forestall any suspicion of hypocrisy.

Besides, there was competition from the heretics.

The Catharist saints (pp. 26–27) were still very much in evidence in Italy around Francis' time. They traveled around the country in pairs, wearing various disguises, and met with their followers in secret. As strict vegetarians they lived in some ways a more ascetic life than Francis and his brotherhood, and their frugality undoubtedly set a powerful example.

One of them even makes an appearance, and quite a revealing one, in a story about Francis.

Celano tells us: Once when Francis came to Lombardy and preached in Alessandria, he was received as a guest by a pious and respected man. This man wanted to serve an especially festive meal for him, and so he had a seven-year-old capon roasted. While Francis sat with the family at table, a man appeared at the door and asked for some food in the name of God. Francis immediately took a fat thigh of the bird from the plate and served it to him. But the man saved the delicacy, and brought it with him the next day to the sermon that Francis preached to the people. Then he lifted it high in the air and shouted:

"Now look here and see what kind of a man this Francis is. Look at the meat he gave me yesterday evening!" But the people took him for a madman and didn't believe him. Others thought what he really had in his hand was a fish.[35]

Celano sees in this incident a small miracle, in virtue of which the chicken thigh was metamorphosed into a fish. More important than such ingenious imaginings is the troublemaker's obvious intention of showing Francis up. The names Celano calls the man ("son of Belial," "accursed," "base") suggest that he was a secret apostate who wanted to put Francis (known for his loyalty to the Church) in the wrong. The location of the scene also fits in well with this interpretation—Lombardy was a homeland for heretics at the time.

Last of all we have the words of a peasant, which show us Francis' true value, without any halos or mystification.

The *Fioretti:* One morning, as Francis was on his way with the companions to Mount La Verna, it turned out that he was too weak to walk. And so the brothers went to a peasant who lived nearby and asked him to lend them a donkey. The man asked:

"Do you belong to that Francis of Assisi one hears so many good things about?"

The companions said "yes," and told the man that Francis himself needed the mount.

Then the man harnessed the donkey, helped Francis to get on its back, and went along with the little group up Mount La Verna.

After a while the peasant asked:

"Are you really Francis of Assisi?"

Francis said "Yes."

The man went on: "Then you'd better make sure you're really as good as everybody thinks you are. Because many people have great confidence in you, and that's why I'd like to tell you, I hope you're not any different from what the people expect."

Then Francis dismounted from the donkey, embraced the man, and thanked him for what he had said.[36]

XV

THE SONG OF DEATH

Among the companions from the early years of the Franciscans there was a skillful minstrel and poet who had won the title of "King of Verse" before joining the brotherhood. Celano, who describes the poet's conversion with more than usual unctuousness, gives an embarrassed hint that his repertoire also included all kinds of ribald songs. Francis gave him the name of Pacifico, and from 1215 on he belonged to the inner circle of the Friars Minor.[1] In 1219 we find Pacifico in Paris, the leader of a group of friars. He returned to Italy in 1223. Pacifico kept Francis company at Rieti in the fall of 1223, and went back again to France after Francis' death. He died there around 1230.

It may well be that Pacifico was a Frenchman by birth. In any case he would have been fluent in the language of the troubadours and jongleurs.[2] Francis too had a weakness for this tongue—the so-called *langue d'oc*, which was the literary idiom of southern France and northern Italy around that time. In his youth Francis had certainly learned to sing Provençal songs: With all their romantic languishing and worship of women, they were a favorite mode of emotional expression among the upper class. In comparison with these effusions the service of Lady Poverty to which Francis later devoted himself was a rather prosaic and in any case much more strenuous business. But it gave a new religious substance to his sensibility, without in any way deadening his taste for sweet music and poetry. On the contrary, in the last two years of his life, when Francis was practically blind, exhausted, and seriously ill, suffering from insomnia and all sorts of pain, when he bore the wounds from his ecstatic vision of Christ, *then* he began to write poetry.

This happened in the summer of 1225, in Clare's little garden, and it is noteworthy that in this situation he asked for Pacifico, the gifted singer.

This is the story they tell: At that time Francis was living for fifty days in a little hut made of rushes near San Damiano. He could see neither daylight nor the glow of fire by night, and so he spent the whole time in his dwelling. The sharp pain in his eyes seldom allowed him to sleep. Besides all this the place was infested by mice, who swarmed all over his hut in great numbers, scurried over his body, and disturbed his meals.

One night, when he was beginning to feel sorry for himself because of his sufferings and to reflect longingly on the kingdom of heaven, he had a most cheering thought. He realized that he could enter paradise while he was still alive if he no longer struggled against the troubles that gave him such terrible pain.

The next morning he said to his companions:

"I would like to make up a song in praise of this earth—for without all the gifts it brings us we couldn't live a single day."

Then he began to compose:

"*Altissimo omnipotente bon Segnore!*"

And he made up a song of the things of earth and then taught it to the companions. His soul was so full of happiness that he wished he could have Brother Pacifico there, who had been such an artful master of all songs. He wanted to send him with some clever brothers out into the world, as preachers and musicians combined.

And Francis said:

"Aren't we Friars Minor God's musicians, who should bring glee to the hearts of men?"[3]

There is a clear connection between Francis' song and his blindness. It begins with devout thanksgiving to the sun, which brings on the day and spreads its rays with great splendor (*radiante cum grande splendore*). It praises the moon and the stars, and it hymns "brother fire" too, with his gaiety and strength (*bello e jocondo e robustoso e forte*), who serves to illumine the night.

In the Leo stories Francis is quoted as saying that people should be led to give thanks every morning and every evening for the light of the sun by day and the glow of fire by night.[4] This saying occurs in the immediate context of his composition of the *Cantico del Sole*, and it documents Francis' condition as he thought, in his blindness, of the two most important sources of light. Without them, he adds, we would all be blind, because through both these creatures God brings brightness to our eyes.[5]

By writing his song Francis fought, as others have before and since, against despondency. (People with no problems are not in the habit of writing poetry.) The Leo stories put it his way: "Even more, as his infirmities increased he began to recite the Praises of the Lord himself, and afterward he got his companions to sing, that in thinking of God's praise, he might forget the anguish of his suffering and illness. Thus he did until the day of his death."[6]

Francis' "Canticle of the Sun" is the first Italian poem whose author we know, and in that sense it is the expression of a new kind of self-consciousness. (Recall our discussion in Chapter III of the first Greek lyric poet.) Brotherliness is a central theme in the "Canticle," as we have already stressed. The kindly Lord God, whom Francis addresses, that amiable feudal King of Heaven who made all creatures out of the goodness of his heart, has since been dethroned along with the earthly Kings in the age of bourgeois revolutions. The bourgeoisie has, in the classical terms of the *Communist Manifesto* (1848), "drowned the most heavenly ecstasies of religious fervor in the icy water of egotistical calculation. It has stripped of its halo every occupation hitherto honored and looked up to with reverent awe. It has accomplished wonders far surpassing . . . Gothic cathedrals; it has conducted expeditions that put to shame all former Exoduses of nations and crusades."[7]

There is no way back to Francis' God.

On the other hand, Francis' principle of brotherly love,[8] which is a bourgeois ideal just as much as capitalism is a bourgeois reality, is still not in operation, no more than his ethic of poverty.

From this angle the "Canticle of the Sun" strikes us as a youthful dream, and we have to ask ourselves repeatedly and with a certain sorrow why it didn't come true.

Brother Pacifico, whom Francis had asked for, did turn up in Rieti (whence they had brought Francis) after all. This is the story they tell: One time, when Francis was staying in Rieti because of his eye disease, in the house of the doctor Theodore the Saracen, he spoke to the companion who knew how to play the guitar: "Once before, in days long past, holy men used to play on guitars and ten-stringed harps to the glory of God. Nowadays these instruments serve only for dissipation and vanity. And so I would like you to get a guitar, discreetly, from decent people, so that we can sing religious songs together and I can forget my pain."

The brother answered: "Ah Francis, the whole town knows what sort of person I was when I still had my lute. The people would surely think I was my frivolous old self."

Francis decided to give up the whole thing.

But the following night, as he lay awake in his bed, around midnight Francis heard wondrous music played by guitars, more beautiful than he had ever listened to before. At first it sounded as if it came from a nearby room, then it moved farther away and grew fainter, came back again, and in this way gladdened the ear of the sick man for a full hour.

The next morning Francis said to his companion: "You see now, I got it after all, that solace you wouldn't give me!"

But the brothers considered this a great miracle, because in Rieti at that time there was a general curfew during the night.[9]

We cannot help conjecturing whether the good Pacifico was the secret source of the heavenly music. A half year later, in any case, as Francis lay bedridden during the last five months of his life, in the bishop's palace in Assisi, they sang to him day and night to comfort him in his sickness. We are not told whether Pacifico was there, nor do we learn whether he managed in the meantime to get hold of a lute. At all events the merriment in Francis' sickroom seems to have grown so loud that people complained about it.

This is the story they tell: One day Brother Elias noticed how Francis was consoling himself in his illness, and said to him:

"Dearest brother, the cheerfulness of you and your companions amid all your affliction and pain edifies me beyond measure. But the townspeople, though they revere you as a saint, might still be a little surprised and wonder how someone as desperately ill as yourself can be so merry. Should you not think more often of your death?"

Francis answered: "I have always thought of my end, especially during the last two years. Brother, don't bother me with your admonitions, which will only cloud over my joy!"

During this time Francis was also visited by a doctor from the town of Arezzo. Francis asked him how much longer he had to live. At first the doctor would not come out with the truth, but Francis said to him: "Don't think that I'm afraid of dying."

Then the doctor told him that it would be all over with him by the end of September or the beginning of October.

When Francis heard this, he spread out his arms and cried:

"Welcome, brother death!"

Then he said:

"Call Angelo and Leo here. They are to sing me the song of death."

When both of them had finished singing, with tears in their eyes, the song that Francis composed during his illness, Francis himself continued the song, with a new strophe:

> *Laudato sie, mio Segnore, per sora nostra morte corporale!*
> (Praised be you, my Lord, for our brother bodily death!)[10]

In the text of the divine praises that Francis sketched out on the parchment intended for Brother Leo, we find a barely translatable word used to describe one of God's attributes. It is *allegrezza*.[11]

Beyond its meaning of gaiety, it must be thought of as connoting a sense of lightness (alleviation), as the cause and manifest evidence of this good cheer. In this *allegrezza*, then, one has some access to Francis' dominant frame of mind during the last weeks of his life.

This was also the time when Francis dictated his *Testament*.

We have already seen (pp. 148–50) what melancholy traces were left behind in it by the political realities of life in his brotherhood (now become an "Order"). So it would be false to imagine Francis' thoughts in 1226 as an absolutely cloudless sky.

Nevertheless, the *Testament* (the better part of which we have already met with, bit by bit, in the earlier chapters of the book) made no compromises. Francis gives his name in the first sentence. He speaks in the first person singular; he knows he is not just anyone. In crisp, clear sentences he recounts his career and specifically formulates his wishes.

The memories he chooses to recall from the early days of the Friars Minor have a point to them. They are aimed at the new managers in his brotherhood:

"And we were content with one tunic, patched inside and out . . . with a girdle and breeches. And we did not wish to have any more."[12]

Further: "Let the brothers take care that churches, humble lodgings, and all other things that will be built for them are never accepted unless they are in harmony with holy poverty. . . ."[13]

And: "I firmly order all the brothers on obedience that, wherever they are, they are not to dare to ask for any letter from the Roman Curia, either themselves or through an intermediary, not for a church or for any convent, not on the pretext of preaching or on account of physical persecution."[14]

Finally: "And the brothers are not to say: 'This is another Rule': because this is a record (*ricordo*), admonition, and exhortation, and my testament, that I, Brother Francis, small as I am, make for you, my blessed brothers."[15]

And last of all: "And the minister general and all the other ministers and custodians shall be bound by obedience not to add or subtract from these words. And they shall always have this document with them, next to the Rule. And in the chapter meetings they hold, when they read the Rule they shall read this too. And I absolutely order all my brothers, clerics, and laymen, on obedience, that they shall not put glosses on the Rule or on these words, saying: 'They want to be understood in this way': but, just as the Lord granted me to speak and write simply and purely both the Rule and these words, so simply and purely they shall be understood and put into practice."[16]

Of the forty-two sentences in Francis' *Testament*, thirty-four begin with "and," which is a sure index of its genuineness.[17] (The manuscript tradition of the *Testament* likewise shows no later revisions.) In fact, in dictating his last will Francis discovered a mode of expression unprecedented for his age. It is in this, and not in the style of his sentences, that Francis' originality lies.

Some days before his death Francis had himself carried from the episcopal palace down to the Portiuncula.[18] This decision surely caused a great stir in Assisi, for the good burghers of the town had done everything to secure possession of what would be a precious corpse.

Celano puts it rather brutally: When Francis entered Assisi, the whole town rejoiced, the mouths of all men praised God; for the people hoped that the saint would die soon, and that was the reason for the great jubilation.[19]

After darkness fell the town militia patrolled the area around the bishop's palace, where Francis was lodged, for fear he might die suddenly and his body be taken somewhere else under cover of night.[20]

We can also be sure that the little procession following the stretcher on which Francis lay had a military escort for the short trip down into the valley. Francis had them stop once on the way and asked to be turned in the direction of the city, to bid it farewell. What he said on that occasion was remarkably unsentimental: "This town has the worst reputation in the whole region, as the home of every kind of rogue and scoundrel. So I beg you, dear Lord Jesus Christ, that it may become the home of all those who sincerely honor your name. Amen."[21]

Evidently Francis had no illusions about the prevailing attitudes in his native city.

When Francis finally lay in his hut, near the little chapel he had restored as a young man, he surprised his companions with an unexpected exertion.

This is the story they tell: As the companions stood around his bed, Francis struggled to his feet and sat down on the floor. Then he took off his clothes, and remained sitting there, naked on the ground. He laid his left hand over the scar in his right side, so that no one could see it. Then he said:

"Forgive me, but it must be. I hope God inspires you now to do what is right."

The companions began to cry. One of them, who was responsible for Francis at the time, realized that Francis wanted to strip off even the clothing that the Rule allowed him. So he took the tunic and the drawers and said:

"Francis, I'm now lending you this tunic and the underwear. Don't you dare give them away, because they don't belong to you."

Francis folded his hands and agreed. Then he said:

"You know now how I wish to die. As soon as death occurs, you must undress me just as I did before, lay me on the ground, and let me lie there for as much time as it takes to walk a mile."

Naturally, as soon as the time arrived, the companions did just as Francis had desired of them, just before his death.[22]

Later Francis dictated a few lines of farewell to Clare.[23] He also called for Brother Bernard, his first companion, and blessed him.[24]

Francis spent the night before he died sleepless and in severe pain. In the morning he had all the brothers who were staying at Portiuncula called in.[25] He laid his right hand on the head of each one of them, beginning with his representative, Brother Elias, and blessed them. Then he asked for bread, blessed it, and since he was too weak to break it, had someone else do this and distribute it to his companions.

Francis undoubtedly thought of Jesus' Last Supper with his disciples. (He also had the relevant passage from St. John's Gospel read out to him.)

The rest of the day (it was a Saturday, the third of October) would have been spent reciting the Psalms, and the brothers would have chanted the "Canticle of the Sun" for him. The last psalm that Francis himself was able to intone begins with the words, "I cry with my voice to the Lord."[26]

In the evening his death agony began.

As Francis died, an exaltation of larks is said to have flown over his hut, singing.[27]

XVI

AFTERWARD

THE "melancholy cathedral,"[1] as Goethe called the basilica of St. Francis in Assisi, is a burial church. Its walls and altars, frescoes and chapels, marble and bright stained-glass windows, the unexampled ensemble of two churches built on top of one another with a crypt beneath—all this derives its meaning from the veneration for the little corpse which it overarches.

The design for this splendid mausoleum came from Brother Elias,[2] "a sinner," as he described himself, for once telling the truth. He had Francis' body deposited provisionally in the little church of San Giorgio in Assisi.

On March 29, 1228, a man named Simon Puzarelli donated a piece of land outside Assisi to the Pope for the purpose of erecting a church to house Francis' bones. A month later the Pope issued a bull to the faithful announcing the construction of a mighty church and asking for contributions for the vast undertaking.

The Pope's name was Gregory IX, and he had been sitting on the chair of St. Peter since March of 1227. (We have already met him as the cardinal-bishop of Ostia, Count Ugolino of Segni, born around the year 1170, nephew of Innocent III and uncle of Alexander IV.)

Elias got the excavation work briskly under way, and as early as July 1228 the Pope could appear in Assisi, first to canonize Francis, and second to lay the cornerstone for the basilica.

The building project was, in modern terms, a model of advanced technology.[3] Elias planned the erection of the three elements that would combine to form a single unit: a monastery for the brothers, a church for their services, and another church for the use of ordinary believers—i.e., the laity. But the construction site proved to be too small to accommodate this scheme, so Elias decided to build the two churches, not alongside, but on top of, each other. This astonishing man, as a matter of fact, not only took care of the financial and organizational side of the project, he also stepped in as an architect, drew up designs, and contacted artists to work for him.

By the summer of 1230, after only two years, construction of the lower basilica had proceeded far enough to permit the solemn transferral of Francis' bones to their final resting place. Two thousand Friars Minor from all over Europe appeared for this great festival, and many bishops and prelates walked in the long procession that set out for the new basilica from the church of San Giorgio.

To everyone's great disappointment Elias did not allow the crowd to view the contents of the coffin. According to one story he had Francis' remains brought quietly to their new location (which was a closely guarded secret) a few days before the festival. Another tradition has it that Francis' coffin was indeed carried along in the procession, but when they came to the new church, it was quickly brought inside. Then the doors were closed, and the precious relics buried with the public excluded.

One thing is certain: Francis' grave was so well hidden that it took till 1818 to find it.

We can skip the further history of the building of the basilica.[4] It is more important to note an idea that occurred to that old fox, Ugolino. Hardly had Francis' remains been hidden away after a scene of gorgeous pomp when the papal chancellery favored the dearly beloved Friars Minor with a bull that made the *Testament* worthless.

Under the date of September 28, 1230, Pope Ugolino decreed that Francis' *Testament* had no binding power over the brothers of the Order, because Francis had drafted it without the consent of the Order's ministers.[5]

A later colleague of Ugolino's, the learned Jesuit and Cardinal Franz Ehrle (1845–1934),[6] after seven hundred years of Church history, still could find nothing wrong with all the tricks played on the dead man from Assisi. In an article he wrote on the subject he claimed that the Pope really had no other choice, given the situation. Evidently they have a great deal in common, the cardinals, bonzes, and mandarins of every age, and one wonders why we still have to listen to their monotonous pronouncements.

A further bit of deceit by Ugolino consisted in his making emphatic mention of the "friends of the Order" (briefly referred to in the Rule of 1223) and notably smoothing the way to doing business with them. From now on persons who did not belong to the Order (and hence were not subject to the "holy Rule") could be closely related to the brothers through friendly commercial connections. The Franciscans sent them all those pious souls who insisted on getting rid of their money and giving it to the Order. Then the friars could draw on their account—by check, as it were—without ever having to come into physical contact with filthy mammon.

Thus four years after Francis' death and two years after his canonization, the wishes of the little poor man from Assisi had been decisively, definitively sabotaged. The brittle official Latin of the papal bull spelled out with unmistakable clarity what the gesture of hiding Francis' bones beneath the splendid new church really meant: Francis was pushed aside, and the Order of the Friars Minor could now enter upon its glorious march into the future.

The hundred years that followed Francis' death, to which we now turn, belong to his biography because they elucidate the conflict that overshadowed the last six years of his life. We shall see how this conflict attracted the attention of the European public, and how the Pope ended it by force, with a momentous decree.

After the Pope rendered this verdict, Francis stood condemned as a heretic for having chosen to model his life on Jesus the poor man, and his whole operation had to go underground.

The Franciscans, with the thorn of a bad conscience stuck in their side, vacillated between accommodation and reform for another two hundred years after that, until the real Reformation exploded and tore half of Europe away from the Pope.

Today, after another four hundred years of progress, we live with the past experience of a plunge into barbarism and the future threat of nuclear war. Under the circumstances it could be that Francis has more to say to us than all the "architects of modernity," the Cromwells, the Napoleons, the Lincolns, the Lenins.

The basis for such an affinity, of course, is that Francis is a part of us all; we sense his presence in us as one of the repressed longings of our bourgeois existence, and as the memory of a debt that has never been paid.

THE ETERNAL GOSPEL

One day in the year 1241 a strange monk slipped through the gates of the Franciscan monastery in Pisa. (The leaning tower was under construction just around this time.) The monk had a request: He wanted to save some books from seizure by Emperor Frederick II. The pious brother had a feeling that his own monastery, located between Lucca and Pisa, was no longer safe enough. He was the abbot of this monastery, and a member of the party opposing the Emperor. The order he belonged to had been founded by a man named Joachim of Floris, and the books that he entrusted to the Franciscans were Joachim's writings.[7]

A number of Franciscans began to read these folios. We know their names, because one of them, a certain Salimbene of Parma, wrote a chronicle of current events.[8] They were four academics, and as they studied Joachim's treatises their excitement grew. What agitated them so much, and at once inspired them to become propagandists for the new ideas, was a previously unheard-of philosophy of history. It taught, in a nutshell, that a new age was dawning, and its herald was Francis of Assisi.

The originator of such revolutionary notions had died in the year 1202 in the monastery of San Giovanni in Fiore (Calabria), which he himself had founded.[9] When Joachim died, Francis was a prisoner in Perugia, only twenty years old, and Joachim would have had to be clairvoyant to recognize Francis' importance. As a matter of fact, Francis' name never occurs in the blessed abbot's books, but Joachim has a great deal to say about a "new leader" (*novus dux*) who was soon to appear. The four companions from Pisa were clear right from the start that this could be none other than Francis. They became the first cell of an intellectual party that soon had people talking. In 1257 Brother Gerard of Borgo San Donnino, the boldest of the group, was sentenced to life imprisonment for having published Joachim's writings, along with an introduction, in Paris. The title of the Foreword was *Liber introductorius in Evangelium Aeternum* (The Book of Introduction to the Eternal Gospel).

That meant the writings of Joachim, which were to light the way to the new age as the sole authoritative teaching.

Since Joachim's collected works are much too extensive to be described here, let us content ourselves with an extract in the form of a free montage.

> The Eternal Gospel of the blessed Abbot Joachim:[10]
>
> I, Joachim, was in my cell at the hour of matins, before the day had dawned, in front of me the book of Revelation by John. And suddenly the brightness of knowledge flashed upon the eyes of my spirit. There was disclosed to me the fulfillment of this book, the harmony of both Testaments, of the old and new covenant. This happened to me on the holy day of Pentecost.
>
> The secrets of Scripture point the way to three ages.
>
> In the first age we were under the law. In the second we are in the economy of grace. In the third, already near, love will rule, for ever and ever.
>
> The three ages are divided into seven periods.
>
> The first age embraces five periods, it runs from Adam to Christ. The

second age is the sixth period, it lasts for forty-two generations and is now approaching its end. The third age is the seventh period, the last one before the end of the world.

The first age is called the Old Testament, when we were slaves. The second is called the New Testament, when we were dependent sons. In the third we shall be free. The first stage was ruled by the Father, the second by the Son. In the third the Holy Spirit will blow where it wills.

At first the stars shone in the night. Then came the red light of dawn. Soon it will be day.

The first age corresponds to the simplicity of children, the second to the knowledge of a man, the third to the wisdom of old age.

First the primroses bloomed, then the roses. Soon the age of the lilies will dawn.

The holy Church is now lying, like the woman in Revelation, wailing in the pangs of childbirth. What issues forth from her shall be called a spiritual people.

When we are on the point of reaching the kingdom of love, the signs and mysteries by which we were wont to be spoken to will be exchanged for full vision. Baptism and the Eucharist will be superfluous then, and the ministers of the sacraments as well, the ordered hierarchy of priesthood, will have nothing more to do, because the Spirit will speak to the hearts of men without the intervention of authority. It will lend them wings for a life of peace. And what of the hallowed order of priests—will it grieve because it must cease when the Church of the Spirit appears?

No, the followers of Peter are never, never to grow pale with envy because they must yield to the new order of the Spirit.

For every transformation brings with it the death of what went before, as the Apostle said: When the state of completion arrives, all the partial preparations will be destroyed.

Is not the Church of today like the dead Lazarus, before Christ awakened the stinking corpse to new life? In the last days when the proud have been brought low, the Lord will favor the humble, and the plain and simple people will stand above the arrogant professors.

And a man will arise, whoever he may be, a new leader and preacher of truth, surrounded by twelve men, like an angel of heaven, and he will bring religious life to perfection.

All this I, Joachim, write, at the beginning of the last two generations before the arrival of the kingdom of freedom.

The chiaroscuro style of this enthusiastic prose, together with its subversive hints, was very much to the taste of the Franciscan malcontents. As of yet they did not make up a regular party. But their bitterness over the new developments in the Order since Francis' death went deep. The building of the grandiose church in Assisi, which required the nonstop collection of money all over Europe, was for these men a scandal that cried to heaven, a betrayal of Lady Poverty.

Around 1240 in the Marches of Ancona these zealous brothers—the *zelanti*,[11] as they were first called—already formed a tightly knit group, defied the official superiors of the Order, and wore a sort of uniform—very short tunics that barely reached the knee.

This radical branch of the Order found in Joachim's writings something it had been missing all along—an ideology. And this in turn involved an early bourgeois declaration of independence, a break with the feudal powers of the day, the barons and clergy, and a firm belief that the papal Church and the divine right of princes which it had blessed were historically obsolete and on their way out.

This ideology—and here was a novelty—set a deadline for the end of the old society and the dawn of the new, and not in the other world, as usual, but right here in this one: the year 1260.

The humble people (*minores*), who are specifically addressed in Joachim's writings as the privileged class of the new aeon, practiced the poverty ethic as it was feasible then under the quasicommunistic[12] conditions of monastic life. It goes without saying that the radical Franciscans, who were against both private and collective property to begin with, saw these *minores* as symbolic of themselves.

Invoking Joachim's harmony of the Old and New Testament—i.e., a divinely inspired logic—they claimed the third person of the Trinity for their protector. They saw the Holy Spirit as the principle of the new age, and so they were soon called the Spirituals.[13]

THE SPIRITUALS

One of them, John of Parma, had led the Friars Minor from 1247 till 1257.[14] (This remarkable man began his term of office with a three-year tour of inspection that took him on a visit to the companions in England, France, and Spain—and he walked the whole way.) Another, a respected theologian named Hugo of Digne,[15] intrepidly lectured the Pope and cardinals "as if he were speaking to children at play." Hugo died around 1257 and left behind a strong following, especially in Provence. Tuscany too saw pockets of resistance forming against the official Franciscan party line, and in the Marches of Ancona the wild mystics in short tunics continued to agitate in their lively fashion, even though many of them were severely punished by being denied the sacraments, or exiled to foreign countries or remote hermitages.

The supreme theologian of the Spirituals was Peter John Olivi.[16] Born around 1248 in southern France, he entered the Order at the age of twelve, studied in Paris, and thereafter began to teach in southern France.

For Olivi, Francis becomes the Christ of the new age. The feudal Roman Church, with all its corruption, is called the Whore of Babylon, beast from the abyss, Antichrist, and community of Satan in the writings of this passionate thinker.

Paper, as they say, will put up with anything, and one might simply write off this polemic by the Spirituals faction among the Franciscans as just another medieval theological squabble—if it were not for the fact that it made the common people, the artisans and journeymen, prick up their ears, at first in southern France and in northern Italy, but soon in other economically busy regions of Europe, especially in the Netherlands, in Flanders, and in Brabant.

From 1300 on, it became obvious that the Spirituals had found a real power base among the masses, in that comprehensive underground movement of the European lower classes which was persecuted by the Inquisition in Francis' day, under various heretical labels.

THE THIRD ORDER

Thus far we have not yet spoken of the "Third Order," which still survives in the Catholic world as a pious lay fellowship, looked after by Franciscan priests. But as late as the nineteenth century, these "tertiaries," as they are also known, were by no means only occupied with saying the rosary. As already mentioned, they tried to come up with political alternatives to the social problems of the day.

Francis surely never intended the autocratic-bureaucratic splitting of his fellowship into three Orders[17]: one for single men, one for single women, and one for (in most cases, married) "penitents" of both sexes who wished to remain with their families. Nor was it Francis' idea to have the first two Orders lead a cloistered life—that came from the managerial mentality of Church officialdom. In the ten years from 1209 till 1219 (we called them the happy years), the Franciscans went about their business quite freely, without any regimentation to speak of from higher-ups. There were itinerant men, most of them without Holy Orders or theological training, with their shelters (loci) off the beaten track, in the forest. There were the sisterhoods, women like Clare and her companions, who lived together in houses, unpropertied and unselfish. And there were (as, for example, in Greccio) extensions of the Franciscan lifestyle among people who wanted to continue earning a living and to stay with their families, but who also desired, like Francis, to "enter religion."

The precise meaning of all this can only be understood in the broad context of the rudimentary organizational efforts—which had only a very limited success and were bitterly fought by the feudal powers—of the medieval lower classes.

Modern historians talk about the "poverty movement," those collective endeavors that they neatly divide into "heretical" and "orthodox" varieties, with Cathars and Waldensians on one side, and ecclesiastically recognized groups like the Franciscans on the other. But in reality this movement was a rebellion, breaking out now in the city, now in the countryside, by the common people against the status quo.[18] There was no unity to it; it was all variegated and highly individualistic. Different groups fought among themselves. There were localized revolts here and secret conventicles there, with all different sorts of traveling agitators, and stay-at-home sympathizers.

The most restless elements in this social ferment were the weavers, clothmakers, and fullers—men and women who worked in the textile industry and were dependent on their wages.[19] In the "century of wool" (p. 31) these people were vulnerable to the ups and downs of a nascent market economy (with extensive foreign trade). Because of the sharp competition they were often thrown out of their workshops (which were also their homes) and found themselves on the highways of Europe. In the various places where the wool weavers managed to organize against the financiers and early capitalists (in Breslau, say, or Cologne or Ghent), we find them armed and tightly deployed—if they wanted to enforce their demands. To this day we talk about "weaving" a plot—and with reason.

This brief excursus into the history of the social struggles in Francis' day should demonstrate that behind the manifold groups founded in this era was an altogether simple idea that ran across the lines of class and conviction: Things can't go on the way they've been.

It is quite conceivable that among Francis' early supporters there were individuals attracted to the idea of combining several families together in an "evangelical life" without private property, and not just for reasons of piety. Another quite potent motive was the possible economic advantages of organizing production among small craftsmen or peasants along cooperative lines. And there are, in fact, indications that some such experiments were tried, possibly in the community houses of the Italian *Humiliati*,[20] where men and women lived and worked together in harmony in Francis' day.

We should note that the authorities made use of a clearly discernible strategy in dealing with such associations.[21] They demanded submission to the dogma and discipline of the Church, and they worked to limit each brotherhood and sisterhood to religious goals.

Whenever a group violated these two rules, it fell under the fatal rubric of heresy and was cruelly persecuted.

The history of the "Third Order" in the hundred years after Francis' death was, accordingly, a troubled one.

In the year 1289 the Pope issued a bull that prescribed a standardized Rule for the tertiaries.[22] All previous attempts to regiment them (scholars still dispute the dates here) had evidently not sufficed to discipline the numerous lay fellowships[23] that were living out Francis' ideas, all across Italy and beyond, without giving up their familial or economic ties.

Such groups did not always limit themselves to pious exercises and works of charity. In the Netherlands some unmarried weavers and wool workers decided to live together in community houses—certainly not just from a need to sing the Psalms in common. They knew that unity makes for strength, in this case strength to fight the economic power of the merchants' guilds in the burgeoning cities of the North. Many women as well looked for and found new forms of common life. (All by itself Cologne had over a hundred such convents for women.) When the new papal Rule for tertiaries came out, it was gladly adopted by such associations, to protect themselves from prying authorities.

The latter had long since grown to distrust the restless groups of laypeople as likely breeding grounds for heretical activities and lewd behavior. The people called them by many different names: beguines, beghards, bizocken, papelards.[24] (The derivation of these terms is unclear.) This much is certain: Beginning with the thirteenth century such groups constituted a pan-European phenomenon with considerable strength and impact. Not all these men and women remained sedentary. Many wandered across the country in little bands, spread new ideas, read translations of the Bible, and criticized the clergy.

In 1274 a (strictly orthodox) Franciscan from Tournai warned the synod in Lyon about the intrigues of the beguines, and related that in Paris they were selling French Bibles for free. Twenty years later the supporters of the heretical Olivi in southern France and northern Spain were likewise calling themselves beguines. This is the time frame within which the Eternal Gospel of the Spirituals must be viewed as a popular teaching that evoked powerful echoes in the homeland of Western heresy.

Olivi himself died peacefully in 1298. His theses had been investigated several times, and he handled himself quite adroitly: He was condemned and then rehabilitated. His friend and supporter Ubertino of Casale had spread the Spirituals' doctrine in Tuscany, where he was a teacher, and won a noticeable following.[25]

By 1299 the Franciscans had gotten nervous and for the first time the Order sharply attacked the Spirituals and recalcitrant tertiaries in southern

France.[26] At the general chapter of the Franciscans in Lyon, Olivi's books were gathered together and burned. Over three hundred followers of his teachings were punished (expulsion from the Order, imprisonment, exile to foreign provinces). In addition there was a ban on the veneration of Olivi as a saint. Around this time Olivi was extremely popular, especially among the rebellious tertiaries, the so-called beguines. In these circles his cult grew rapidly, despite the ban. Copies of treatises by the late Spiritual master went from hand to hand, along with other popular pamphlets which spoke a still cruder language.

In Italy too, things were really getting out of hand.[27]

The Spirituals there, even more radical than the ones in southern France, had already had some unpleasant experiences with the Franciscan authorities. A few of the Spirituals had gotten life imprisonment, which in those days was equivalent to a death sentence. Others had fled to Greece after the abdication of Celestine V, whom they had greeted as the "angelic Pope."[28] Celestine's successor thought them so dangerous that he sent letters to the Patriarch of Constantinople and the archbishops of Athens and Patras, demanding (in vain) their arrest and extradition.

In 1304 a large part of the group returned to Italy. Some of them (fourteen men) were immediately recognized in southern Italy and put under arrest. The inquisitor, a Dominican named Thomas of Aversa, was not one to mince words. Never before, said the inquisitor to the Spirituals, has meat fetched so high a price at the butcher's as your valuable flesh.

The inquisitor then directed a search for the other returned exiles and examined them in the prescribed manner, which included the use of torture.

Ubertino of Casale was also denounced to the papal Curia for a careless remark made during a sermon given in Perugia. (He had spoken of the "carnal," as opposed to the "spiritual," Church.) He got off lightly enough with a transfer to the hermitage on Mount La Verna. There he wrote a book with the title, *The Tree of Life of the Crucified Jesus*.[29] Externally a devotional text, it is in reality a compendium of the Spirituals' thought, with verbatim excerpts from the writings of Olivi. Ubertino was not exactly squeamish about passing judgment on the Popes. He called the then reigning Holy Father, Benedict XI, a beast from the abyss, and his predecessor, Boniface VIII, nothing less than the Antichrist of the Apocalypse.

Among the people, especially in the ranks of the small tradesmen in the new quarters between the first and second walls of towns and cities, such a message found a ready audience. Starting just around 1260 (Joachim's deadline for the dawn of the new age) a radical group based in Parma and espousing a life of poverty won many adherents.[30] It was led by a man named Gerard Segarelli, who had given away all his property and tried to enter the Franciscans, but had been rejected. Segarelli's companions liked to call one another apostles, because they wished to live as frugally as Jesus' disciples. These "Apostolics" invoked the name of Joachim and had a clear affinity with the Spirituals. They enjoyed tremendous success.

After 1290 the Inquisition began to take an interest in the Apostolics. In 1294 four of them were burned at the stake in Parma; six years later Segarelli suffered the same fate. His place was taken by Fra Dolcino, the son of a priest from Novara, who had joined the Franciscans but left before taking his vows. (The Italian Spirituals considered the Order corrupt and strongly encouraged its members to leave.) Then Dolcino met a young nun, abducted her from the convent, and together with her took the road to open revolt. He showed up in Piedmont at the head of an armed troop (5,000 men). In 1307 a crusade was organized against this rebel, and they had another slaughter for Christ. Dolcino was taken alive. Before he died at the stake, after a horrible ordeal, he was forced to watch his mistress being tortured. She too was executed, together with roughly 150 of the surviving Apostolics.

Dolcino was, in his own way, a fervent admirer of Francis.

The same is true of another Apostolic, Bentivenga of Gubbio, who joined the Franciscans and preached freedom of thought in Umbria. In 1307 he was condemned to life imprisonment, along with his followers, whose numbers had the authorities worried.

We summarize: Between 1290 and 1310 the ideology of the Spirituals made its way into the minds of the lower classes in the cities of Italy and southern France, and tied in with freethinkers from Germany and the Netherlands. The now mighty Order of the Friars Minor (around twenty thousand members all over Europe)[31] was shot through with Spirituals and Joachimites. They made up a regular opposition party. The Eternal Gospel of Abbot Joachim had become a trumpet call of liberation in a conflict where more than just the legitimacy of the old Church was on the line. The point at issue—and this lends those old stories a certain excitement—is the foundation of present-day civilization: money and private property.

The Holy See, at that time the highest authority on fundamental social and political values, had to take action.[32]

FRANCIS BECOMES A HERETIC

We get a notion of how strong (not in numbers, but in influence) the position of the Spirituals was among the Franciscans in the early fourteenth century from the fact that Pope Clement V (1305–14) at first did almost nothing in the face of an increasingly critical situation. His only move was to convene a commission of cardinals in 1309 for the purpose of thoroughly investigating the quarrel between the Spirituals and the moderate Franciscan party, the "Conventuals."[33] Both parties were represented by carefully chosen representatives: Ubertino of Casale headed the Spirituals; the minister general of the Order, Gonsalvo of Valboa, was the leader of the Conventuals.

To begin with, each delegation was given a questionnaire with four points.

The first point dealt with the controversy stirred up by the freethinkers in Umbria, many of whom were Franciscans.

The second related to the interpretation of the Rule, and the central question of poverty.

The third inquired into the evidence of the persecution undergone by the Spirituals.

The fourth examined the orthodoxy of Olivi's writings.

This questionnaire marked the beginning of a debate (conducted in writing) that lasted three years, and gave the Spirituals their only chance to co-ordinate their thinking and to make a presentation before the highest European authority on ideological questions—without arousing suspicion of heresy.

Both parties submitted memoranda in reply to the four questions, and subsequently sent in various pamphlets. As spokesman for the Spirituals, Ubertino argued so adroitly that in April 1310 the Pope dispatched a bull declaring that the complaints of the Spirituals were justified. The Pope stated further that the condition of the Order was in fact deplorable, and he called for reforms. He also put the leaders of the Spirituals under the direct control of the Holy See, thereby placing them beyond the reach of the Order's front office; and beyond that he warned Franciscan superiors in the different European provinces not to take any measures against the Spirituals.

Ubertino immediately returned to the attack, with a piece that described in detail how the Order had fallen away from Francis' original intentions, and asked the Pope to make the Franciscans go back to literal observance of the old Rule.

Ubertino's criticism was hard to refute. With all their wealth the Franciscans had become an object of public mockery, in the marketplace and in literature. A good dozen papal bulls had transformed Francis' poverty ethic into a complex system of legalistic norms. Under Bonaventure the Order had provided itself with supplementary statutes ("constitutions") to regulate the behavior of the Friars Minor down to the smallest detail, including the cut of their tunics.

But all these efforts had not managed to prevent the Franciscans from building the largest churches and the most modern houses of study anywhere. The fellowship of laymen had turned into an Order of priests that contributed bishops, cardinals, and inquisitors to the Church, and played a powerful role in politics.

Against the background of these concrete developments, Ubertino's petition to the Pope sounds rather naïve. Actually, all the Spirituals had achieved was a sort of truce. The Pope launched two further bulls, both in the year 1312.[34] The first condemned several of Olivi's theses, but without mentioning him by name. In the second the Pope censured a number of abuses among the Franciscans, piously invoked the memory of Francis, and otherwise tried to work out a compromise between the Spirituals and the Conventuals.

For a short while, up till the death of Clement V in April 1314, the Spirituals of southern France remained unmolested. They were given three friaries (in Narbonne, Beziers, and Carcassonne), where they could live as they saw fit. In Italy the Spirituals had a powerful grip on three friaries (Carmignano near Florence, Ascania near Siena, and Arezzo), and they drove out the Conventuals residing there. When the Inquisition stepped in, they fled to the protection of Frederick III in Sicily.

The Pope died in April 1314, and the cardinals took more than two years to elect a successor. Once he was finally chosen—an old but energetic and ruthless man—it became open season on the Spirituals.

There followed the final act of the struggle over the meaning and importance of property—private and collective—and its social function. Now much more was at stake than a few hundred recalcitrant Franciscans and their popular following. Instead, within a period of seven years the papacy came to a series of decisions so fundamental that they must be construed as a formal renunciation of Jesus, the poor man of the Gospels, by the leadership of the Western Church.

The Pope, named John XXII, acted swiftly and mercilessly.[35]

First he attacked the Spirituals within the Order, with the active support of the Inquisition, as we have already related. Now for the first time in the history of the Franciscans four brothers were burned to death in public.

Then it was the turn of the restless lay groups, the beguines and the bizocken, along with the other deviates like them who claimed to possess the true spirit of Francis ("Brothers of the Poor Life" [Fraticelli]). They were all excommunicated and handed over for prosecution as criminals.

A further decree was specifically directed against the Italian dissidents who had fled to Sicily, ordering the bishops there to proceed vigorously against them. (The bull directing these measures begins with the words Gloriosa Ecclesia, the "glorious Church.")

And so by 1318 the verdict had been handed down on the entire Spiritual movement. The prisons filled up, and the fires were lit. (Prominent

Spirituals like Ubertino of Casale were treated, relatively speaking, with indulgence, thus avoiding the creation of a martyr cult.)

Hard-line Franciscans in Narbonne dug up Olivi's bones, scattered them, and destroyed the grave. But Olivi's thoughts were not so easily gotten rid of. Theologians embracing them had to be engaged along a broad front, with all the intellectual weaponry available from the arsenal of orthodoxy.

This took place during the years from 1317 till 1323. The papal drumbeat at the end of all the theological cacophony marked the end of an unprecedented debate on the foundations of the future bourgeois era. Francis had been dead a hundred years.

Today we know that the two basic principles that still determine the way we act were just then emerging. They were:

Religion is a private matter.

The books have to balance.

In the year 1321 a member of the Franciscan Third Order, a convinced Spiritual and beguine, was preaching in Narbonne.[36] He was denounced to the Inquisition for making statements redolent of heresy and subjected to an interrogation by the inquisitor, John of Belna (a Dominican) in the presence of the archbishop of Narbonne. In the course of it the man defended the view that Jesus Christ and his Apostles had owned no property at all, neither individually nor in common.

As was prescribed for such trials, the inquisitor called in a council of notable jurists and theologians from the area and read them a list of all the preacher's incriminating remarks, including the thesis of Christ's absolute poverty. One of the council members was a Franciscan named Berengar Talon, a lecturer in theology at the Order's school in Narbonne. He immediately raised an objection against calling the thesis in question heretical, and invoked a papal bull from 1279. The inquisitor accused Talon of error and both appealed to the Pope in Avignon.

In Avignon they had been busy examining just this question for some time. In 1317 the Pope had appointed a Dominican cardinal to do a thorough examination of Olivi's most dangerous book, his *Commentary on the Apocalypse*. For his part the cardinal had gotten eight professors of theology to put together a comprehensive report that exhaustively refuted Olivi's Joachimite doctrine of the seven periods of history and the coming Church of the Spirit.

But the commission was not so sure of itself when it came to Olivi's theology of poverty. The crucial point here concerned the kind of poverty practiced by the Savior and his companions, which in turn would be the binding Gospel norm for Francis and *his* companions, and the whole thing caused the scholars a certain amount of embarrassment.

Olivi is right, the theologians maintained, if he asserts that Francis' rule of poverty corresponds exactly to the life led by Christ and his Apostles. Olivi errs, they continued, if he asserts that therefore the Pope has no power over the Franciscan Rule because it is identical to the Gospel, which is higher than the Pope.

This sort of hair-splitting nullified any value the report might have had, but because of it all of Olivi's theology, including his doctrine of Christ's radical poverty, was doomed.

The Pope, a little man given to anger, was at this point seventy-seven years old. He did not feel like waiting forever for clarification on the question of poverty. When on top of everything else the appeal from Narbonne came in, raising the very same point that the commission had failed to elucidate, he had the basic question phrased as crisply as possible and submitted it to the theologians, requesting a decision.

The question read: *Utrum asserere quod Christus et apostoli non habuerunt aliquid sive in proprio sive in communi sit haereticum.* (Whether it is heretical to assert that Christ and the Apostles possessed nothing, either as individuals or as a group.)

There were two possible answers.

Affirmativē.

Negativē.

We cannot appreciate the importance of the decision with which the Pope confronted the educated European world, without taking into account the unique role played by the Bible in those days in all issues of political legitimacy.

Should the answer to the Pope's jackpot question be "no," that would mean that Holy Mother Church must be accounted guilty of betraying Christ. All her possessions, which were practically immeasurable, would have been illegitimate, in the strict sense of the word.

On March 26, 1322, the Pope underlined the urgency of his question yet again, in a bull that immediately lifted the ban on all discussion of the foundations of Franciscan poverty, pronounced by his predecessor of happy memory, Nicholas III, in the year of Our Lord 1279, in a brief on holy poverty. Thus everyone was now free to voice his opinion on the subject without fear of excommunication.

In addition the Curia urged the leaders of the Franciscans to define their position on poverty as quickly as possible.

At Pentecost Franciscan officials from all over Europe met in Perugia for a general chapter.

The chapter knew that the very essence of Franciscan life was now at stake, and, putting aside all their earlier quarrels, they pulled themselves together and took an extraordinary step. They decided to write a circular letter to all Christians on the question of poverty. The letter was drawn up in two versions, one shorter, one longer, and until the end of 1322 more than a hundred copies of the Order's reply to the Pope's question circulated through Europe, from Sicily to England.

In the erudite Latin of the longer version, the letter said that Christ and the Apostles had simply used (*simplex usus facti*) the things they needed to live, totally renouncing any rights of ownership, and, naturally, excluding any provision for the future (*sollicitudo*), which is undeniably necessary for the management of both private and corporate property.

So the Pope had his answer: The radical poverty of Christ and his Apostles is a truth of faith.

The Pope was no great light in theological matters. He had gotten his degree in law, and thus he replied, first of all, by reaffirming his right to abrogate his predecessors' decisions. In their arguments the Francisans had leaned heavily on Nicholas III's brief of 1279, which resolved the issue of poverty in their favor. But now the ground of canon law they were standing on had been pulled out from under them. John XXII also expatiated on the legal questions of ownership and use, emphasizing that even the simplest use of a thing implied a form of ownership. Could his clever predecessor (John continued), the blessed Nicholas III, have been so stupid as to dispute the Franciscans' right to own every piece of cheese they had for supper?

The brutal truth that the Pope expressed was this: "My dear Friars Minor, you are without any doubt the owners of all the things you have at your disposal—and that's not the half of it. I have no intention of giving any more support to your hypocritical contrivance of considering everything Franciscans own as papal property. Earlier Popes may have played along with this game, but it's over now."

The gruff tone of the papal text reveals the total banality of the development initiated by Ugolino almost exactly one hundred years before. Now the Franciscans were dismayed to see the surplus they had piled up —which proved that their appeal to Jesus' poverty was nothing more than rhetoric.[37]

Now that the business side of the affair had been settled, the Pope could address the question of faith that he himself had posed with such precision.

On November 12, 1323, a papal bull was nailed, as was the custom, to the door of the cathedral of Avignon. It was short and to the point, as befits a dogmatic decision.

It was heresy, the Pope declared for all time, to assert that Christ and the Apostles had no personal or collective property (*Redemptorem nostrum ac Dominum Iesum Christum eiusque Apostolos in speciali non habuisse aliqua nec in communi*). It was also heresy to maintain that the

Redeemer and his Apostles did not enjoy the right of selling or giving away their belongings, which are explicitly mentioned in Holy Writ (*Iis quae ipsos habuisse Scriptura sacra testatur, nequaquam ius ipsis utendi competerit, nec illa vendendi seu donandi ius habuerint aut ex ipsis alia acquirendi*).[38]

Here, in clear contrast to the Franciscan open letter, the Redeemer and Savior of Christendom was irrevocably chained to the commodity-money-commodity cycle. And the ideal pattern of Christ traveling about with his Apostles, owning nothing, not even knowing where he would sleep the following night, was once and for all declared illicit by Christ's vicar on earth.

Let us recall that early Mass celebrated at the Portiuncula on February 24, 1208, when Francis listened to the Gospel and discovered, with incontestable certainty, that he must imitate Jesus the poor man by following those clear maxims:

No gold, no silver, no money.

No bag of provisions.

Only one tunic.

No shoes, no staff.

Let us recall Francis' conflict with the officials over the sentence from the Gospel, "Take nothing with you for your journey."

Let us recall Francis' *Testament,* in which he sums up what he considered the essence of the imitation of Christ: "And we were content with one tunic, patched inside and out . . . with a belt and breeches. And we did not wish to have any more."

The Roman Church, Inc., on the advice of farsighted members of its supervisory board, had annexed the Franciscans because it badly needed a hard-working managerial elite. Francis' obstinate insistence on living like the barefoot Jesus was something it would have to put up with for the time being.

A hundred years later the time had come to eliminate this cumbersome reminder of the past from the company's code. Francis was retroactively declared a heretic—this was the unspoken conclusion of the papal verdict of November 1323. One hundred years, almost to the day, after the promulgation of the papal Rule for the Friars Minor, Francis' deviance, his refusal to conform, was out in the open. The years after Francis' death revealed something we don't always see so clearly in his life, something that led him into many hard struggles in his time, despite his tenderness for the eucharistic body of God's Son and for the anointed hands that held it: Francis could not be a man of the Church. In more general terms, he couldn't fit into the institutional mold.

Francis' biography ends on November 12, 1323.

Some remarks that Ernst Bloch made in 1970 are worth remembering in this context: "The Sermon on the Mount turned into the Donation of Constantine. Marxism-Leninism turned into Stalinism, the *citoyen* turned into the *bourgeois*. There's a worm in every apple. We still don't really know what it is, other than the manipulations of the ruling class, that so often leads to the corruption of the best. What ever became of the Luther of 1517, or the Utopias of the American Revolution? And when the dream comes true, it's just not what we were dreaming of, and maybe its fulfillment has even perverted it into its exact opposite. What's going on here?"[39]

The question will have to go unanswered, for all its relevance to the evolution of the Franciscans. We shall have to be careful not to relish the story of their corruption in that peculiar way for which Flaubert found an unsurpassable formula: "Whenever they tell me about some low trick, it pleases me as much as if they had given me money."[40]

But rather than dwelling on such dubious sentiments, we may conclude with a question which should prove more useful: What is the reason for the gentle sense of melancholy that Francis awakens in us?

"WITHOUT ANY DOUBT HE WAS THE HAPPIER"

This is how things stand with our historical legacy (that infinite cemetery): Many figures from the imaginary museum of the human past give us the feeling of being quite close to us, though they have been dead for thousands of years. Others again seem far away, though they were alive and well only fifty years ago—Hitler, for example. This odd fact teaches us two things.

First, the number of years elapsed doesn't always have to play a vital role in the confrontation with our collective past.

Second, the reason for our interest in figures from the distant past lies in the fact that their unsolved problems are still, in an exemplary manner, the same as ours.

This goes for Francis of Assisi as well as for Socrates and Jesus.

Francis' portrait belongs in that long gallery of bourgeois individuals who felt uncomfortable with themselves and so betrayed their own class.

Karl Marx (d. 1883) fits in there too, along with Aurelius Augustinus (d. 430), even if these two "Church Fathers" don't have much else in common.

The force that drove both men so far off the track laid out for them in childhood was the rebellion against their own bourgeois makeup.

As we shall see in a moment, this rebellion is as much a part of the (masculine) bourgeois ego as acquisitiveness. For two thousand years of Western history its motto has been, "Let the dead bury their dead."[41]

It is astonishing how clearly the rage in this cry of the carpenter's son from Nazareth still echoes in our ears.

Here, in a classic example, is the moment of truth in the life of a bourgeois (aged thirty-one, at the height of a remarkable career):

"It was on a day when I was preparing a speech to be delivered in praise of the Emperor; there would be a lot of lies in the speech, and they would be applauded by those who knew they were lies. My heart was all wrought up with the worry of it all and was boiling in a kind of fever of melting thoughts. I was going along one of the streets of Milan when I noticed a poor beggar; he was fairly drunk, I suppose, and was laughing and enjoying himself. It was a sight that depressed me, and I spoke to the friends who were with me about all the sorrows that come to us because of our own madness . . . and it seemed to me that the goal of this and all such endeavors was simply to reach a state of happiness that was free from care; the beggar had reached this state before us, and we, perhaps, might never reach it at all. With the few pennies that he had managed to beg he had actually obtained what I, by so many painful turns and such devious ways, was struggling to reach—namely, the joy of a temporary happiness.

". . . And undoubtedly he was happy while I was worried; he was carefree while I was full of fears. . . . The beggar would sleep off his drunkenness that very night; but I had gone to bed with mine and woken up with it day after day after day and I should go on doing so. . . . Yes, and so . . . without any doubt he was the happier.

". . . I said much along these lines to my intimate friends at the time, and I often noticed that it was the same with them as it was with me, and I found that things were not at all well with me. . . ."[42]

We sense a kind of moral hangover in this text of Augustine, written more than fifteen hundred years ago. It articulates feelings at once classic and modern. The revolt they give rise to is always directed against bourgeois parents, and the scandal it causes may be heard reverberating through contemporary literature, as well as in certain old stories.

Let us recall the man named Valdes. This legendary precursor of Francis hears the song of Alexios[43] while out for a walk, and because of it leaves his wife and children, gives his wealth away, and lives henceforth as a penniless beggar.

The ballad that had such a powerful effect on him has been preserved. It is one of the earliest documents of Old French literature. Its story, as we now know, goes back still farther in time, to fifth-century Christian Syria,[44] in the days when the Roman Empire was pinning its last hope on baptism. The tale which people thought retelling even then concerns a rich young burgher who leaves his bride on their wedding night and goes abroad to live as a beggar.

An unknown eleventh-century French poet produced a new version of the ballad, 125 lines long, in the vernacular. Whoever he was, he had a sharp eye for the telltale signs of a certain repressed bourgeois longing, composed of guilt feelings and escapist fantasies.

The song of Alexios was as we would say nowadays, a long-running hit, and in Valdes' day every street singer had it in his repertoire.

We know nothing of what Valdes actually felt, or of his state of mind before he revolted against his own world. Nevertheless, his gesture of renunciation seems oddly familiar to us; we could imagine the man in any modern city.

We could likewise picture Augustine, with all his frustrations, dressed like a young executive or assistant professor. We could take the passage from the *Confessions* just cited, make a few cuts, and use it as the basis for a film script on the first crisis in the life of a gifted young man.

Or we might make a collage of the three figures: the blessed Alexios with his dark resentment of his father, on whom he managed to take a subtle vengeance by returning to his house as a beggar and stranger and dying there without identifying himself; Augustine, the professor of rhetoric and favorite of Milanese society, envying a drunken beggar; Valdes reaching for a beggar's staff and becoming a lay preacher.

What one of them can't tell us, the other one can, and whatever may still be missing we learn from the actions of the third. The point of all this is to recognize an amazing structural similarity in the behavior of the three men. Let us examine it a bit more closely, because it leads us directly to Francis, or rather to the Francis in us.

The most striking thing about our discontented sons of the bourgeoisie is that they no longer aspire to go upward, to the apex of the social pyramid, where you eat out of golden dishes. Instead, the attraction comes from far below, from the beggar, the social outcast pure and simple.

(In our society beggars have practically disappeared, and their role as a model for frustrated young bourgeois men has been taken over by the [idealized] proletarian, or the ghetto black or the Indian or, in a few cases, even the noble criminal.)

Why this flight to the bottom?

A preliminary answer might be because of the idea that down on the bottom you can find a way of life free from repression and from all the sublimations and defense mechanisms that constitute the bourgeois character. (It is no accident that Augustine's beggar was drunk.) Down on the bottom you can live—at least the wistful fantasy of upwardly mobile types, trained to achieve and succeed, says you can—from hand to mouth, with uninhibited women who aren't out to get married. Planning and making provisions for the future (*sollicitudo*) are no longer necessary; instead you live frugally, always on the move, in jeans and sandals. Let tomorrow take care of itself.

As we've known for at least ten years, numbers of young people from the industrialized nations have been taking flight from the homes of their bourgeois parents, most of them only for a while. According to the available information, this is a bourgeois and not a proletarian phenomenon. The children of Marx and Coca-Cola have really arrived, and they are rebelling in their fashion against their own makeup.

We have already met their ancestors.

What distinguishes these youthful fugitives from civilization from their precursors in antiquity and the Middle Ages is the fact that they lack a deep and abiding aversion to the Mammon of their fathers. But wait and see. We can't exclude the possibility that even people over forty may be led to abandon bourgeois existence—there are already some signs of this.

We can say provisionally that, as we reflect on this aspect of Francis' legacy, conceiving it in terms of the class struggle won't get us anywhere. The theory and practice of the *Easy Rider* myth are the expression of a purely bourgeois protest. The workers, even the young ones, have other things to worry about.

Here is a greeting to Stafford Beer. His last letter to me, dated February 9, 1978, came from a little house in Wales, where he has been living since 1975 as a hermit.

> Hello, Stafford!
> Have you finally given up smoking?

On the dust jacket of the book that Stafford Beer gave me, when he was in Vienna on business, is a sort of "Wanted" poster, informing the reader who Stafford is (or was): International consultant for management sciences; visiting professor of cybernetics, Manchester University; professor of statistics and operations research, the University of Pennsylvania; president of the Society for Operations Research in America and England; winner of the McCulloch Prize of the American Society of Cybernetics, and of the silver medal of the Royal Swedish Academy for engineering sciences; for thirteen years led the largest operations-research group in England; after that built up a management-consulting service and led this firm as its director; for four years leader of research and development for the largest publishing operation in the world.[45]

Stafford occasionally advised the Allende government on economic policy. His last interview with Allende took place on July 26, 1973. On September 11 of that year, as we know, Allende was to die. Stafford writes in his book:

> I have written and broadcast much
> since then
> about the assassination
> of a poor country
> by the rich world.[46]

When Stafford Beer was in Vienna around the beginning of 1975, he told me of his intention to change his way of life.

In December 1976 he wrote me in a letter, "I did the whole thing. There is a little stone cottage (no water supply!) miles from anywhere. My only possession now is a spinning wheel. My Rolls-Royce is in California. There are no books or records here with which to masturbate."

Pier Paolo Pasolini (d. 1975), writer and film director, belongs in this book as much as Stafford Beer. One of the last things Pasolini wrote before he was murdered was: "Let's make a fresh start, clench our fists, and start all over again. Then we won't be facing bourgeois forces, as we do now, forces that seem to have been in the saddle from all eternity. Then it won't be a question anymore of saving what's still to be saved. No compromise. Let's make a fresh start. Long live poverty."[47]

These two outsiders whom we have just seen are to be understood as bourgeois individuals, like the rest of us; not as objects of study, but as our kind of people. (It would be false to give an account of a trial in which we ourselves were involved, as if we had nothing to do with it, in the absurd posture of the detached scientist.) Their revolt is unromantic and persevering, their flight to the bottom unpatronizing. And they aren't the only such fools who refuse to compromise.

Let's make a fresh start.

Long live poverty.

Pasolini speaks to our bourgeois ego with Francis' voice—scarcely audible in all the noise of advertising, mass entertainment, and political hoopla that surrounds us.

But the song of Alexios won't let itself be drowned out. It's as much a part of our lives as its exact counterpoint, the conjugal bed. The old melody reminds us of the violence we have done to ourselves in the name of reason, and as the price of our liberation from a life of indigence, at nature's mercy.

That is why we can't forget Francis.

And so, like the citizens of Gubbio, we follow after his frail figure with our eyes, hoping that the wolf who threatens to devour us all may yet be tamed.

NOTES

For the reader's convenience I have listed the books and articles consulted in a separate bibliography. Hence the references are given here in abbreviated form.

CHAPTER I: *"I, Your Little Brother Francis"*

1. Cipolla, p. 87.
2. Ibid.
3. Allusion to the book of the same name by Ludwig Feuerbach, *The Essence of Christianity*, ed. E. Graham and F. W. Strothmann (New York: Ungar, 1957).
4. Francis' *Testament* (Karrer, p. 572).
5. *Fioretti*, Ch. 2 (Karrer, p. 344 ff.; Binding, p. 12 f.).
6. Jean-Paul Sartre, *L'Idiot de la Famille: Gustave Flaubert de 1821 à 1857* (Paris: Gallimard, 1971), I, 515.
7. Ibid., I, 544.
8. Samuel Beckett, *Waiting for Godot* (New York: Grove Press, 1954), p. 60.
9. Celano, I, 36 (Grau, p. 100).
10. *Divina Commedia, Paradiso,* XI, 150.
11. See Ch. XVI, n. 34.
12. Grundmann, pp. 15–20; Moore, pp. 23–136.
13. *Divina Commedia*, ibid.
14. Brooke, *Scripta*, p. 286.

CHAPTER II: *Dangerous Stories*

1. Brooke, *Scripta*, p. 7 f.
2. Ibid., p. 9.
3. Ibid., p. 5 f.
4. Ibid., pp. 26–40. For the current state of opinion on the old sources for Francis' biography, cf. Mockler, pp. 17–25; see also Grau, pp. 38–44.
5. Grau, p. 217. For Thomas of Celano, cf. Grau, pp. 28–56.
6. Mockler, p. 151; Grau, p. 53 f.
7. Quoted in Karrer, p. 295 f.
8. Brooke, *EFG*, p. 223; Mockler, p. 15; Moorman, pp. 307, 350 f.
9. Karrer, pp. 197–99. Cf. Celano, II, 28 (Grau, p. 282).
10. There is an extensive bibliography of all the extant old sources on Francis' life in Moorman, pp. 595–98. The same author provides a briefer survey of the material in the new edition of his *Saint Francis of Assisi*, p. 117 f. See also Brooke, *Coming*, pp. 23–28; Mockler, pp. 24–27.
11. Brooke, *Scripta*, p. 86.
12. Ibid., p. 94.
13. Ibid., p. 290.
14. Binding, p. 7.

15. Cf. Walther Killy, *Deutscher Kitsch* (Göttingen: Vandenhoek & Ruprecht, 1962), pp. 27–29.
16. F. Prudenzano, *Francesco d'Assisi.*
17. Cf. Roggen, p. 29.
18. Cf. Kautsky, p. 180 f.
19. Sabatier, p. xvii.
20. Moorman, in his *Saint Francis,* counts sixty modern biographies.

CHAPTER III: A Good Bourgeois

1. See Elias, I, 139–45.
2. Allusion to the book by Wolfram von den Steinen, *Der Kosmos des Mittelalters.*
3. See de Mause, pp. 112–262.
4. Le Goff, pp. 19–36.
5. Cf. Zinsel, pp. 33–37.
6. Roger Bacon (1219–84) was the first to express such a desire.
7. Cf. Mumford, pp. 316–20.
8. R. W. Müller, pp. 258–73, 326–35.
9. Ibid., p. 273.
10. Quoted in Müller, p. 274.
11. Mumford, p. 309.
12. Weber, *The Protestant Ethic and the Spirit of Capitalism,* tr. Talcott Parsons (New York: Scribner's, 1958), p. 113.
13. Quoted in Weber, p. 175.
14. Ibid., p. 181.
15. Cf. Mumford, pp. 301–8.
16. Cipolla, p. 155.
17. Quoted in Mumford, p. 270. Cf. Le Goff, p. 189.
18. "The world-historical significance of the monastic way of life in the West, as opposed to Oriental monasticism . . . lies in its rational character. It was freed from aimless rejection of the world and self-torture, in principle, by the Rule of St. Benedict, still more by the Cluniacs, even more by the Cistercians, and finally, most decisively of all, by the Jesuits. It became a systematically articulated method of rational conduct." Max Weber, *Gesammelte Aufsätze zur Religionssoziologie* (Tübingen: J. C. B. Mohr, 1963), I, 116.
19. Mockler, p. 58.
20. Cf. Ernst Piper, *Der Aufstand der Ciompi* (Berlin: Wagenbach, 1978).
21. Max Weber, *Wirtschaft und Gesellschaft* (Tübingen: J. C. B. Mohr, 1976), pp. 775–79. Cf. Le Goff, pp. 75–83.
22. Ibid., p. 805.
23. Werner, p. 23 f.
24. Ibid., p. 25 f.
25. Grundmann, pp. 22–28; Moore, pp. 139–262; Emmanuel le Roy Ladurie, *Montaillou: Cathars and Catholics in a French Village* (London: Solar Press, 1978).
26. *Hérésies,* p. 185.

CHAPTER IV: A Disgrace to the Family

1. Karrer, pp. 46–49; Celano, I, 14–15 (Grau, p. 75 f.).
2. Mockler, pp. 54–56.

3. Ibid., p. 58.
4. Ibid., p. 58 f.
5. Ibid., p. 59 f.
6. Le Goff, pp. 191–93.
7. Karrer, pp. 34–36; Celano, I, 4–6; II, 5 f.
8. *The Robbers*, V, i.
9. Karrer, p. 36 f. Cf. Celano, I, 7; II, 7.
10. Horst Herrmann, *Savonarola* (Munich: Bertelsmann, 1977), p. 259.
11. Cf. Elias, II, 88–122.
12. Celano, II, 9.
13. Ibid.
14. Ibid.
15. Ibid., II, 8.
16. Brooke, *Scripta*, p. 240.
17. Karrer, p. 566 f.
18. Celano, I, 17 (Grau, p. 78). Cf. Celano, II, 9 (Grau, p. 233). NOTE: this translation and all subsequent translations of *verbatim excerpts* from Celano are taken from Thomas of Celano, *St. Francis of Assisi: First and Second Lives of St. Francis, with Selections from the Treatise on the Miracles of Blessed Francis*, tr. Placid Hermann, O.F.M. (Chicago, Ill.: Franciscan Herald Press, 1962). The notations for Celano (e.g., "II, 9,") are the same in all editions of his work (Trans.).
19. Karrer, p. 39. Cf. Celano, II, 9 (Grau, p. 233).
20. Cf. Walter C. Langer, *The Mind of Adolf Hitler* (New York: Basic Books, 1972); Erich Fromm, *The Anatomy of Human Destructiveness* (New York: Holt, Rinehart & Winston, 1973).
21. For the years from 1203 to 1209 we follow Mockler's reconstruction.
22. Celano, I, 6 (Grau, p. 67 f.) (Hermann).
23. Brooke, *Scripta*, p. 124.
24. The term *lazaretto* recalls the numerous medieval associations dedicated to the care of the poor and sick, and the welfare of pilgrims and travelers. Cf. *KG*, 231–36.
25. Karrer, p. 40; Celano, II, 10 (Grau, p. 72).
26. Mockler, pp. 43, 76, 84.
27. Celano, I, 10 (Grau, p. 72).
28. Ibid., I, 11 (Grau, p. 72).
29. Ibid., I, 12 (Grau, p. 72 f.).
30. Ibid., I, 13 (Grau, p. 74).
31. Mockler, p. 81 f.
32. Karrer, p. 50 f.

CHAPTER V: *Making Repairs*
1. For Celano's tendency to stylize Francis as an ideal saint, see Benz, pp. 49 f., 62–76.
2. Celano, I, 16 (Grau, p. 76 f.) (Hermann).
3. Duby, pp, 165–72.
4. Karrer, pp. 48–50.
5. Brooke, *Coming*, p. 117.
6. Ibid.
7. Ibid.
8. Karrer, p. 41.

9. Celano, II, 17 (Grau, p. 242).
10. Werner, pp. 8, 20; Brooke, *Coming*, pp. 40–44.
11. Grundmann, p. 10; Wendelborn, p. 14 f.
12. Cf. Werner, p. 20.
13. Grundmann, p. 14; Wendelborn, pp. 16–19.
14. *KG*, 172 ff.; Haller, pp. 220 ff.
15. From the *Chronica maiora* of Matthew of Paris. Cf. Mockler, p. 132; Selge, p. 144 f.
16. Selge, pp. 139–51; Mockler, pp. 131–33; 141–44; 147 f. Cf. Celano, I, 32 f. (Grau, pp. 94–96); Karrer, pp. 68–73.
17. The quotation is found in the *Legenda Maior* of Bonaventure (*Analecta Franciscana*, X, 570).
18. It was customary in the Middle Ages to cut off the hair on the top of the head. The remaining circle of hair was called the *corona* (crown).
19. Quoted from Brooke, *Coming*, p. 203 f. Cf. Mockler, p. 270 f.
20. Mockler, p. 211.
21. Brooke, *Scripta*, p. 118.

CHAPTER VI: *"That's What I Want"*
1. *Time* (Mar. 20, 1978).
2. Celano, I, 83 (Grau, p. 149 f.).
3. Celano, II, 17 (Grau, p. 242) (Hermann).
4. Celano, II, 24 (Grau, p. 248).
5. Brooke, *Scripta*, p. 270.
6. Quoted from Brooke, *Coming*, 136.
7. The best-known portrait is the fresco, attributed to Cimabue (1302), in the lower church of the basilica of San Francesco in Assisi.
8. Mockler, pp. 55 ff., 62, 97–99, 161 f.
9. Karrer, p. 568.
10. Cf. Eric J. Hobshawm, *Primitive Rebels: Studies in Archaic Forms of Social Movement in the 19th and 20th Centuries* (New York: Praeger, 1959).
11. Cf. Grau, p. 83; Mockler, p. 100; Englebert, p. 53.
12. Mt. 10:5–10.
13. Celano, I, 22 (Grau, p. 83 f.).
14. Karrer, p. 569.
15. Brooke, *Scripta*, p. 202.
16. Cf. Karrer, p. 586; Englebert, p. 55.
17. Celano, I, 83 (Grau, p. 149).
18. Quoted in Brooke, *Coming*, p. 136.
19. Karrer, p. 74.
20. Cf. Englebert, who cites (p. 64) a typical sermon: "Fear and honor, praise and glorify the almighty Lord! Thank him and pray to him, the Creator of all things, Father, Son, and Holy Ghost. Don't delay in confessing your sins, for death will soon be here! Give, and it will be given to you! Blessed are those who die repentant, they will enter the kingdom of heaven! Woe to those who do not convert, for they will go into the everlasting fire! Be on your guard, avoid evil, and persevere in goodness until the end!"
21. *Fioretti*, Ch. 16 (Karrer, pp. 385–87; Binding, pp. 53–55). Celano, I, 58

(Grau, 124 f.) gives a shorter text. Its presentation of this charming incident has a certain credibility.

22. *Fioretti*, Ch. 30 (Karrer, pp. 423–26; Binding, pp. 97–99).
23. Canetti, p. 539.
24. I quote here from the manuscript of an article that appeared in 1936 in a book by Arthur Schmid, *Spanien: Das Land zwischen Afrika und Europa* (Verlag der Druckereigenossenschaft). The passage I cite was deleted before the book went to press. I should like to express my thanks here to the author of the piece, Herr Hans Keller of Geneva, who kindly made his original text available to me.
25. Cf. Le Goff, *Civilisation*, pp. 200–5.
26. R. Traub and H. Wieser, eds., *Gespräche mit Ernst Bloch* (Frankfurt am Main: Suhrkamp, 1975), p. 216.
27. Quoted in Lambert, p. 214.
28. Lambert, pp. 211–15; Moorman, p. 310 f.
29. Grigulevič, I, 195.
30. Roggen, pp. 67, 88, 92 f.
31. Foreword to Grigulevič (I, 295 f.).
32. Dirks, p. 175.
33. Karrer, p. 51; cf. Celano, II, 51 (Grau, p. 238 f.).
34. Brooke, *Scripta*, p. 140; Celano, II, 51 (Grau, p. 276 f.).
35. Ibid., p. 268.
36. Le Goff, *Civilisation*, p. 439; Cipolla, pp. 114–16.
37. Brooke, *Scripta*, p. 192.
38. Brooke, *Coming*, p. 122; Mockler, p. 252.
39. Englebert, p. 221; Hardick, p. 195.
40. Celano, II, 65 (Grau, p. 288 f.).
41. Ibid., II, 67 (Grau, p. 290 f.).
42. Ibid., II, 69 (Grau, p. 291 f.).
43. Cf. Ernest Bornemann, ed., *Psychoanalyse des Geldes* (Frankfurt am Main: Suhrkamp, 1973), pp. 93–95.
44. Müller, pp. 25, 121–34.
45. Duby, pp. 9–76.
46. *Decretum Gratiani*, Pars I, dist. 88, cap. 11. Cf. Coulton, pp. 140–50.
47. "The mystery of the gold fetish is therefore only the dazzling mystery of the commodity fetish made visible." Karl Marx, *Das Kapital*, 1 vol. (East Berlin: Dietz, 1974), p. 108.
48. Ibid., p. 92.

CHAPTER VII: *The Life of the Friars Minor Begins*

1. Gonnet-Molnar, pp. 42–83; Grundmann, pp. 28–34.
2. Quoted from Brooke, *Coming*, p. 151 f.
3. Today they belong to the Reformed confession. Apart from Italy, where they have a theological faculty in Rome, there are around twenty thousand Waldensians living in Uruguay, the descendants of Italian immigrants.
4. This is the generic term for the three main Catholic Orders that go back to Francis, the "Friars Minor," the "Conventuals," and the "Capuchins." It also applies to a group of other Catholic Orders and Societies of more recent origin, which are modeled on Francis and his tradition. The colloquial names for the various Franciscan men's Orders differ consid-

erably from the official designations. (In Austria, for example, the Conventuals are called "Minorites," while the Friars Minor are "Franciscans.") Nowadays the differences among the various branches of the Franciscans are only superficial (large or small hoods, brown or black habits, etc.). In England the Franciscans are known as the "Greyfriars," after the original color of their habit.

Because of this somewhat confusing terminology I make no distinction in this book between the terms "Franciscans" and "Friars Minor." Likewise, as a rule I use the term "Francis' brotherhood" (or "Francis' fellowship") to designate his followers (single men, single women, and families) in the early years, i.e., between 1208 and 1223.

5. *Fioretti*, Ch. 2 [Karrer, pp. 344–47; Binding, pp. 12–15; Celano, I, 24 (Grau, p. 85 f.); II, 15 (Grau, p. 239 f.)].

6. Mt. 19:21 and 16:24; Lk. 9:3.

7. Brooke, *Coming*, p. 71.

8. Karrer, p. 569.

9. *Fioretti*, Ch. 2 (Binding, p. 16).

10. Cf. Brooke, *Scripta*, pp. 110, 112, 220.

11. Mockler, p. 125.

12. Brooke, *Scripta*, pp. 318–20.

13. Cf. Mockler, p. 209 f. The formalization of the entrance procedure did not take effect until 1220.

14. Brooke, *Scripta*, p. 122.

15. *Volo entrare religionem tuam.* The meaning of *religio* in this context is "brotherhood" or "association" with a religious objective.

16. Brooke, *Scripta*, p. 122.

17. Grau, p. 93; Englebert, p. 55 f.; Mockler, p. 125. The scholarly dispute over the names of the first companions, their social origins, and the occasion of their entrance into the brotherhood has not been settled, owing to the contradictory data provided by the old sources. We know for certain that the first three were named Bernard, Peter, and Egidio, and that Bernard was a rich man, while Egidio came from the lower class.

18. Brooke, *Scripta*, p. 88; Celano, II, 22 (Grau, p. 246 f.).

19. Cf. *Fioretti*, Ch. 18 (Binding, p. 60 f.), where Francis learned during a general chapter that many companions were wearing "iron rings" and "spikes" beneath their tunics. He ordered the removal of these instruments of penance and had them thrown on a pile. More than five hundred "wire shirts" were collected in this way. The incident took place in the years between 1218 and 1220 (Brooke, *EFG*, pp. 287–89).

20. Brooke, *Scripta*, p. 300; Celano, II, 111 (Grau, p. 333 f.).

21. Elias, I, 266–83.

22. Celano, I, 79 (Grau, p. 145).

23. Karrer, p. 571.

24. Mockler, p. 163; Englebert, p. 102.

25. Celano, II, 37 (Grau, pp. 261–63; Brooke, *Scripta*, p. 150).

26. Cf. A. Holl and H. Knienieder, "Der politische Jesus: Zur Sanftlebigkeit der kritisch abwägenden Wissenschaft," in H. Rolfes, ed., *Marxismus Christentum* (Mainz: Matthias Grünewald, 1974), pp. 232–44.

27. Karrer, p. 61.

28. *Fioretti,* "The Life of Brother Juniper," Ch. 1 (Karrer, p. 449; Binding, p. 216).
29. Ibid. (Karrer, pp. 444–49; Binding, pp. 213–16).
30. Englebert, p. 111.
31. *Fioretti,* "The Life of Brother Juniper," Ch. 5 (Binding, pp. 223–26).
32. Ibid., Ch. 9 (Binding, p. 229).

CHAPTER VIII: *In Winter When the Roses Bloom*
1. A. Holl, *Mystik für Anfänger* (Stuttgart: Deutsche Verlags-Anstalt, 1977), p. 120.
2. Mockler, p. 169 f.; Englebert, p. 128 f.
3. Karrer, p. 132. Cf. Grau, p. 81 (note), on Celano's Clare legend.
4. De Mause, pp. 153–58.
5. Ibid., pp. 162, 176, 181–83.
6. Mockler, p. 171 f.
7. From the first century A.D. Christian widows and virgins provided accommodations in their houses for monks and clerics, a practice that was repeatedly condemned (cf. "Syneisakten," *Lexikon für Theologie und Kirche* [Freiburg: Herder, 1964], Vol. IX, cols. 1,229–31). There was also the institution of the so-called double monasteries, in which monks and nuns lived in common. Particularly interesting are the Irish customs: Around A.D. 500 there were monastic settlements in which married couples were admitted (see Leslie Hardinge, *The Celtic Church in Britain* [London: SPCK, 1972], pp. 172–99).
8. Brooke, *Coming,* p. 210 f.; Mockler, p. 142.
9. Karrer, p. 138 f.
10. Cf. Celano, I, 18 (Grau, p. 79 f.); II, 13 (Grau, p. 273 f.); Karrer, pp. 134–36; Mockler, pp. 172–75; Englebert, pp. 130–32.
11. Quoted from Englebert, p. 132 f.
12. *Fioretti,* Ch. 15 (Karrer, pp. 379–81; Binding, pp. 49–51).
13. Celano, I, 18 f. (Grau, pp. 79–81).
14. Ibid., II, 112 (Grau, p. 334 f.).
15. Ibid., II, 205 (Grau, p. 335).
16. Ibid., II, 207 (Grau, p. 419 f.).
17. Ibid., II, 112 (Grau, p. 335).
18. Brooke, *Coming,* p. 125.
19. Celano, I, 3 (Grau, p. 64).
20. Benz, p. 51.
21. Celano, II, 116 f. (Grau, p. 338 f.). Cf. Celano, I, 42 (Grau, p. 106 f.): "For if, as happens, a temptation of the flesh at times assailed him, he would hurl himself into a ditch full of ice, when it was winter, and remained in it until every vestige of anything carnal had remained. And indeed the others most fervently followed his example of such great mortification." (Hermann).
22. Karrer, p. 139 f. The "great adversity" is an allusion to Cardinal Ugolino's efforts to force a Benedictine Rule on the Poor Clares. Cf. Moorman, p. 38 f.
23. *Fioretti,* Ch. 33 (Karrer, pp. 429–31; Binding, p. 102 f.).
24. Karrer, p. 137 f. (note).
25. The right to dispense with all regular income—i.e., collective property-

lessness—was called *privilegium paupertatis* (the privilege of poverty). Cf. Moorman, pp. 35, 205 f.

26. Quoted from Englebert, p. 142. The bull held good only for the house of the Poor Clares in San Damiano, not for the other convents of the Order. Cf. Moorman, p. 205 f.

27. Between Gregory IX and Innocent IV (1243–54), there was Celestine IV, who died after a pontificate of barely one month.

28. Moorman, p. 211 f.

29. Quoted from Englebert, p. 143.

30. Englebert, p. 144.

31. Ibid.; Moorman, p. 212 f. The original text of the bull was discovered in 1893, when Clare's tomb was opened. The parchment was found beneath remnants of her clothing.

32. Englebert, p. 145.

CHAPTER IX: *Ten Happy Years*

1. *Der Spiegel,* No. 21 (1978).
2. Wendelborn, p. 160.
3. *Fioretti,* Ch. 10 (Karrer, p. 368 f.; Binding, p. 37 f.).
4. Josef Quint, ed., *Meister Eckhart: Deutsche Predigten und Traktate* (Munich: Carl Hanser, 1969), p. 54.
5. Celano, I, 35 (Grau, p. 98 f.).
6. *Fioretti,* Ch. 16 (Karrer, pp. 382–84; Binding, pp. 51–53). For the nature of eremitic life in the Middle Ages, see Brooke, *Coming,* pp. 44–58.
7. Following Mockler.
8. Sabatier, p. 309.
9. Grau, p. 89 (note); Karrer, p. 589 f.
10. Celano, I, 26 (Grau, p. 88 f.).
11. Erik H. Erikson, *Young Man Luther: A Study in Psychoanalysis and History* (New York: Norton, 1962), p. 118.
12. Nb. 6:24–26.
13. Karrer, p. 550.
14. William James, *The Varieties of Religious Experience* (New York: The New American Library, 1970), p. 130.
15. Ibid., p. 172.
16. 1 Jn. 4:8.
17. *Fioretti,* Ch. 9 (Karrer, pp. 364–67; Binding, pp. 35–37).
18. Lk. 6:20 (my translation).
19. Celano, I, 37 (Grau, p. 100 f.). Cf. Celano, I, 89 (Grau, p. 156): ". . . and a shoot of the ancient religion suddenly brought a great renewal to those who had grown calloused and to the very old." (Hermann).
20. Augustin Souchy, *Vorsicht: Anarchist* (Darmstadt: Luchterhand, 1977), pp. 109 f., 112.
21. Ibid., p. 120.
22. *Playboy* (Aug. 1978), p. 216.
23. *Fioretti,* Ch. 21 (Karrer, pp. 395–99; Binding, pp. 67–70).
24. Quoted from F. Heiler, *Erscheinungen und Wesen der Religion* (Stuttgart: Kohlhammer, 1961), p. 90.
25. Jörgensen, p. 286. Cf. Karrer, p. 629.
26. Mt. 5:43.

27. Brooke, *Scripta,* p. 242. *Fioretti,* Ch. 26 (Karrer, pp. 410–13); Binding, pp. 80–83). Borgo San Sepolcro lies twenty-three kilometers northwest of Arezzo.
28. Brooke, *Scripta,* p. 166.
29. Celano, I, 73 (Grau, p. 138 f.); Karrer, pp. 190–92, 605 f. Cf. Mockler, pp. 221, 226; Sabatier, pp. 198–201. Pope Honorius III (1216–27) was in Rome from May 12, 1217, until July 4, 1218 (Karrer, p. 605). The psalm that Francis quotes is Ps. 44:16. The fact that Francis had a prayer book (probably a psalter) with him is explained by the clerical obligation to recite the canonical hours.
30. G. W. F. Hegel, *The Phenomenology of Mind,* tr. J. B. Baillie (Atlantic Highlands, N.J.: Humanities Press, 1977), p. 233.
31. Ibid., p. 237.
32. Lk. 1:52.
33. Montage using Celano, II, 152 (Grau, p. 369 f.); II, 148 (Grau, p. 365 f.); Brooke, *Scripta,* pp. 202, 282, 166.
34. Selge, pp. 137, 152; Karrer, p. 606; Englebert, p. 189; Sabatier, p. 207 f.
35. Upper class = *maiores;* middle class = *mediocres;* lower class = *minores;* cf. Roggen, p. 19.
36. Brooke, *Scripta,* p. 140; cf. Celano, II, 31 (Grau, p. 256).
37. Mockler, p. 209 f.; Englebert, p. 198.
38. Roggen, pp. 66, 87.
39. Cf. Celano, II, 68 (Grau, p. 291); II, 78 (Grau, p. 301 f.).
40. Cf. Roggen, p. 87.
41. Celano, II, 147 (Grau, p. 364).
42. *KG,* 206 ff.; Brooke, *Coming,* p. 160 f.; Mockler, p. 205.
43. Mockler, p. 224. Cf. Brooke, *Coming,* p. 95.
44. Brooke, *Coming,* pp. 98 f., 189.
45. Ibid., p. 96.
46. *Fioretti,* Ch. 18 (Karrer, pp. 388–91; Binding, pp. 57–61). Mockler, p. 222 f., assigns this story to the year 1218. Karrer, p. 628, shifts it to 1219.
47. Quoted from Brooke, *Coming,* p. 208.
48. See the detailed presentation in Roggen, pp. 64–76.
49. Quoted from Brooke, *Coming,* p. 207. Cf. Karrer, p. 194 f.
50. "Otherwise, they were all so happy in their poverty that they sometimes had to interrupt the Divine Office to let the fits of infectious laughter subside." From the chronicle of the Englishman Thomas of Ecclestone, quoted in Englebert, p. 196.
51. Celano, II, 127 (Grau, p. 348 f.); cf. Karrer, p. 176.

CHAPTER X: *"Soldan! Soldan!"*

1. Following Englebert, pp. 208–10; cf. Mockler, p. 237.
2. Cf. Mockler, pp. 186, 237.
3. Celano, I, 55 (Grau, p. 119).
4. My interpretation differs on this point from Mockler's. He organizes his biography around the ideal of the Crusader, which he views as central to Francis' life.
5. Mayer, *Idee und Wirklichkeit der Kreuzzüge* (Gemmering bei München: Stahlmann, 1965), p. 52.
6. Ibid., p. 32.

7. Ibid.
8. Ibid., p. 41.
9. Ibid., p. 44 f.
10. Le Goff, p. 142. There is a survey of the scholarly literature on the Crusades in Mayer, *Idee und Wirklichkeit*, p. 73 f.
11. Celano, I, 55 (Grau, p. 119 f.).
12. The chronology of the years 1212–15 is difficult to reconstruct. Cf. Englebert, p. 146. I follow Mockler here (p. 192).
13. Celano, I, 56 (Grau, p. 120 f.).
14. *Fioretti*, Ch. 4 (Binding, p. 19 f.).
15. Mockler, p. 192 f.
16. Ibid., p. 185 f.
17. The first Franciscan Pope was Nicholas IV (1288–92).
18. Mockler, p. 214 f.
19. Ibid., p. 215 f.
20. Karrer, p. 183. (The date here cannot be conclusively determined—Karrer opts for 1216.) The story notes that Francis sang the Gospel during the Mass, one of the few indications that Francis had received the diaconate (cf. Celano, I, 86; Grau, p. 152). It is quite possible that Francis simply took it upon himself to sing the Gospel on solemn occasions, or that he was asked to do so.
21. Karrer, p. 185 f. Cf. Mockler, p. 211 f.
22. Karrer, p. 187.
23. Ibid., p. 187. Cf. Mockler, pp. 212–18. The collection of stories that reports Francis' wish to go to France is the *Scripta Leonis*. Cf. Brooke, *Scripta*, pp. 226–28, 230–32.
24. Mockler, pp. 232–34.
25. Quoted from Mockler, p. 236.
26. Celano, II, 30 (Grau, pp. 254–56).
27. Mockler, p. 234 f.
28. Brooke, *Coming*, p. 204; Mockler, p. 205 f.
29. Quoted from Englebert, p. 205 f.
30. Cf. Mockler, pp. 252, 238. Celano, I, 57 (Grau, p. 122 f.) gives a brief presentation.
31. *Fioretti*, Ch. 24 (Karrer, pp. 403–5; Binding, pp. 73–76).
32. Quoted from Mockler, p. 239.
33. I follow Mockler here, pp. 241–47.
34. Ibid., p. 243.
35. G. E. Lessing, *Nathan the Wise*, III, vii. The plot of *Nathan the Wise* (1779) derives from the second tale of the first day of Boccaccio's *Decameron*. In it Saladin, "Sultan of Babylon," asks the Jew Melchizedek which of the three "laws"—Hebrew, Muslim, or Christian—is the true one. Melchizedek replies by telling the story of a man with three sons. The man has a precious gold ring that all three sons—paradigms of virtue and greatly beloved by their father—wish to inherit. He promises the ring to all three, then has two identical copies made of it. When he dies, each of the sons gets a gold ring, and no one can tell which one is the right one. This, says Melchizedek, is like the situation of the three contending faiths professed by God's children. (Trans.)
36. Cf. Hebret Nette, *Friedrich II von Hohenstaufen* (Reinbek bei Hamburg: Rowohlt, 1975), p. 47.

37. From the Greek *katholou*.
38. Southern, pp. 136–43.
39. Englebert, p. 179.
40. Brooke, *Scripta*, p. 102.
41. Following Englebert, p. 175 f.
42. "We grant a plenary indulgence for your sins." Cf. Mayer, *Idee und Wirklichkeit*, p. 32 f., which is my source for the formula.
43. Englebert, p. 177.
44. Englebert, who agrees with Sabatier that the Portiuncula indulgence dates from Francis' lifetime, places these events in 1216. As a matter of fact, the Pope in question (Honorius III) was staying in Perugia—which is where tradition claims the indulgence was granted (cf. Brooke, *EFG*, p. 291)—from May 20 till August 12, 1216. It is also conceivable that the Portiuncula legend conflates a series of separate episodes into a single event, as so often happens in the old Franciscan sources. In that case Francis would have obtained his indulgence after several attempts, which is plausible enough.

CHAPTER XI: *As a Man in Chains*
1. I quote from Brooke, *Coming*, p. 118; cf. Selge, p. 138.
2. "What is God without man? The absolute form of absolute boredom. What is man without God? Pure madness in the form of the innocent." Martin Heidegger, *Schellings Abhandlung über das Wesen der menschlichen Freiheit* (Tübingen: Niemeyer, 1971), p. 143.
3. Elias Canetti, *Masse und Macht* (Hamburg: Claassen, 1960), p. 232 f.
4. Cf. Ch. IX, fn. 29. Brooke, *EFG*, pp. 286–91, transfers this encounter with Ugolino to 1222.
5. St. Cierge.
6. Sabatier, pp. 275–76.
7. Quoted from Selge, p. 158.
8. Goetz, p. 161 f.
9. Michel Foucault, *Madness and Civilization: A History of Insanity in the Age of Reason*, tr. Richard Howard (New York: Random House, 1965).
10. Brooke, *EFG*, p. 64; Mockler, p. 247 f.
11. Karrer, pp. 193–95.
12. Moorman, pp. 46–48.
13. Modern treatments of Francis like to represent him as losing control of his brotherhood. Lambert, for instance, writes (p. 36): "Francis was a supreme spiritual master of small groups; but he was unable to provide the impersonal organization required to maintain a worldwide order." The ideological character of such opinions is only too clear. They implicitly presuppose that Francis would have had to play the role of totalitarian commander-in-chief in order to curb his growing brotherhood. In point of fact, Francis had excellent leadership qualities, including a keen sense of the real world.
14. Selge, p. 151.
15. Thus Selge, p. 152, among others. Cf. Sabatier, p. 222.
16. Cf. Karrer, p. 196.
17. For the chronology of Francis' stay in Rome see Selge, p. 155; Brooke, *EFG*, pp. 64–67.

18. Selge, p. 155 f.
19. Ibid., p. 156.
20. Karrer, p. 196. Cf. Brooke, EFG, p. 65 f.
21. Selge, p. 152 f.
22. Celano, II, 24 (Grau, p. 248); Karrer, p. 189; cf. Brooke, EFG, p. 66.
23. Brooke, Scripta, pp. 248–52.
24. Brooke, EFG, p. 112. For the role of the first "vicars," cf. Brooke, EFG, pp. 79–81, 111–13.
25. Ibid., p. 112.
26. Karrer, p. 220 f.
27. Ibid., p. 201; cf. Celano, II, 143 (Grau, p. 360 f.). Scholars disagree on the date of Francis' resignation. Lambert (p. 34) assigns it to 1222, while Brooke (EFG, p. 106) prefers an earlier date (1217 or 1218). Grau (p. 360) argues for 1220, as does Karrer (p. 201).
28. Brooke, Scripta, pp. 218–20.
29. Quoted from Brooke, Coming, p. 204; cf. Selge, p. 157.
30. Gonnet-Molnar, pp. 123–210.
31. Ibid., p. 24; Grigulevič, I, 120–22.
32. Quoted from H. Nette, Friedrich II (Reinbek bei Hamburg: Rowohlt, 1975), pp. 61–63.
33. Quoted from Brooke, Coming, p. 209. The original continues, "nor turned by the ferocity of the Germans."
34. Gonnet-Molnar, p. 83; cf. Grundmann, p. 32.
35. Moorman, pp. 51–58; Brooke, EFG, pp. 57, 75, 89—Mockler (p. 127) suggests that we simply speak of a First, Second, and Third Rule. This would surely simplify the terminology, but at the same time it would blur the fundamental difference between the life program of 1209 and the constitution of the Order authorized by the Pope (Papal Rule) of 1223.
36. Cf. Englebert, pp. 77–79; also Moorman, Sources for the Life of Saint Francis (Gregg International, 1967). My montage uses the beginning of the Papal Rule (Brooke, Coming, p. 120), then the Gospel citations from the story of Bernard's conversion (cf. Ch. VII, fn. 6), the so-called Intentio Regulae from the Leo stories (Brooke, Scripta, pp. 202–4), the Testament (concerning the saying of the canonical hours), and the Papal Rule of 1223—which undoubtedly contains old material —in regard to preaching, alms, manual work, money, and obedience to the Pope.
37. Brooke, Scripta, pp. 206–8. Cf. Jn. 12:6 (Judas "had the money box.").
38. Englebert, pp. 220–27; Sabatier, pp. 235–52; Lambert, pp. 28–42; Brooke, EFG, p. 107; Selge, p. 137.
39. Brooke, Scripta, p. 222. For the conferences cf. Brooke, EFG, pp. 86–89.
40. Celano, II, 209 (Grau, p. 421 f.). Cf. Celano, II, 188 (Grau, p. 400 f.): "When he was afflicted with grave infirmity, he raised himself upon his couch and said in vehemence of spirit: 'Who are these who have snatched my Order and that of my brothers out of my hands? If I go to the general chapter, I will show them what my will is.' " (Hermann).
41. Brooke, Scripta, pp. 284–86.
42. I quote from Brooke's version of the Papal Rule, Coming, pp. 120–25.
43. Lambert, pp. 41, 84.

44. Brooke, *Coming*, p. 123.
45. Ibid., p. 125.

CHAPTER XII: *"They Will Throw Their Books out the Window"*
1. Steenberghen, p. 105; *KG*, 319 f.
2. Moorman, pp. 64, 66, 137.
3. *KG*, 318 ff.
4. Le Goff, p. 282 f.
5. Steenberghen, pp. 353 f., 452–57.
6. Grundmann, p. 42; Steenberghen, p. 92; Cohn, pp. 141–46; Ley, p. 104.
7. Cohn, p. 142.
8. The presentation that follows makes use of Steenberghen's research (pp. 75–183, 335–62, 481–512).
9. Ibid., pp. 185–253.
10. Ibid., p. 394.
11. Cipolla, p. 161.
12. Zilsel, pp. 14–29.
13. *Testament* (Karrer, p. 568).
14. Celano, I, 82 (Grau, p. 147 f.). Cf. Karrer, p. 569.
15. Quoted from Grau, p. 148, n. 322.
16. "And we ought to honor and revere all theologians and ministers of the divine word, as those who minister to us spirit and life." Brooke, *Coming*, p. 117.
17. Brooke, *Scripta*, p. 186; cf. Celano, II, 91 (Grau, p. 312).
18. Cipolla, p. 162.
19. Brooke, *Scripta*, pp. 51–53. Text: ibid., pp. 202–22.
20. Cf. Celano, II, 189 (Grau, p. 401 f.): "Not the bark, but the pith, not the shell, but the kernel, not the many things, but the much." The "wordy circumlocutions, ornaments, and embellishments, vain displays and curiosities" are consigned, in this passage, to "those who are marked for a fall." (Hermann).
21. Cf. D. Schiller, *Wallenstein's Camp*, First Act.
22. Brooke, *Scripta*, pp. 208–16 (greatly abridged).
23. Karrer, p. 209; Celano, II, 195 (Grau, p. 407 f.); Brooke, *Scripta*, pp. 208–12 (montage).
24. Quoted from Alain Peyrefitte, *The Chinese: Portrait of a People*, tr. Graham Webb (Indianapolis, Ind.: Bobbs-Merrill, 1977), p. 177.
25. Ibid., p. 171.
26. Brooke, *Coming*, p. 122.
27. Celano, II, 161 (Grau, p. 377).
28. Karrer, p. 71.
29. Cf. J. D. Bernal, *The Social Function of Science* (London: Routledge, 1967).
30. *Fioretti*, Ch. 8 (Karrer, pp. 360–64; Binding, pp. 32–34). *The Little Flowers of St. Francis* (Boston, Mass.: Daughters of St. Paul, 1976), pp. 76–79 (no translator given).
31. Brooke, *Scripta*, pp. 144–46.

CHAPTER XIII: *The Flame Was God*
1. Erika Bourguignon provides a good introduction to the latest research in this area in F. D. Goodman, J. J. Henney, and E. Pressel, *Trance,*

Healing, and Hallucination (New York: John Wiley, 1974), pp. v–xvi.

2. Cf. Grau, p. 114, n. 197.
3. Celano, II, 96 (Grau, p. 318).
4. Ibid., II, 201 (Grau, p. 413).
5. Ibid., II, 95 (Grau, p. 317).
6. From Ash Wednesday to Holy Saturday, and from the Assumption (Aug. 15) to the feast of St. Michael (Sept. 29).
7. The *Fioretti*, Ch. 14 (Karrer, p. 377 f.; Binding, p. 48), gives an interesting account of the goings-on during a group trance, with Francis playing the part of charismatic leader. At the end of the session a vision appears, and everyone is "as if dead." Anyone who has studied the material in the Goodman, Henney, Pressel book will rate this story as thoroughly believable.
8. Felicitas D. Goodman, *Speaking in Tongues* (Chicago, Ill.: University of Chicago Press, 1974), p. 72.
9. Mt. 25:40.
10. Brooke, *Scripta*, p. 148.
11. Celano, I, 84–87 (Grau, pp. 150–53).
12. Brooke, *Scripta*, p. 234 (cicada); ibid., pp. 176–78 (examples of Francis' respect for nature).
13. Celano, I, 58–61 (Grau, pp. 124–27). The "lake of Rieti" is today called Lago di Piediluco (sixteen kilometers northwest of Rieti). Alviano is seventeen kilometers south of Todi.
14. Karrer, p. 520.
15. Brooke, *Scripta*, p. 234.
16. Celano, II, 170 (Grau, p. 385 f.).
17. *Fioretti*, Ch. 57 (Karrer, pp. 503–6; Binding, pp. 174–76).
18. *Abyssus abyssum invocat* (Vulgate).
19. Celano, I, 94 f. (Grau, p. 162 f.) (Hermann, slightly altered). Wendelborn, pp. 335–37, in contrast to Celano, puts the stigmatization in the year of Francis' death.
20. *Fioretti*, Ch. 57 (Karrer, p. 507).
21. Brooke, *Scripta*, p. 254.
22. Quoted from ibid., p. 8. Italian text: Karrer, p. 550.
23. Text in Karrer, p. 552.
24. One can still find it today in the older monasteries and churches of the Order.
25. Celano, I, 90 (Grau, p. 157 f.). Cf. Benz, pp. 97–104.
26. Brooke, *Scripta*, pp. 186–88.
27. Ibid.
28. *Lexikon für Theologie und Kirche* (Frankfurt am Main: Herder & Herder, 1964), Vol. IX, col. 1,081.
29. A perusal of all the sources that describe Francis as the object of demonic wrath reveals a marked increase in such attacks during his last years.
30. *Fioretti*, Ch. 56 (Karrer, p. 202; Binding, p. 173).
31. Brooke, *Scripta*, p. 258.
32. Ibid., p. 260.
33. This term is also found in the Leo stories (*temptatus et accidiosus*). Brooke, *Scripta*, p. 260. Cf. Josef Pieper, *Über die Hoffnung* (Olten:

Summa Verlag, 1948), pp. 55–63; Benz, pp. 123–27; Grau, p. 346, n. 293.

34. Celano, II, 115 (Grau, p. 337 f.).

35. Erving Goffman, *Stigma: Notes on the Management of Spoiled Identity* (Englewood Cliffs, N.J.: Prentice-Hall, 1963).

CHAPTER XIV: Il Santo

1. Brooke, *Coming*, p. 212 (I have put the narrative in the first person).
2. Brooke, *Scripta*, p. 272; Celano, II, 133 (Grau, p. 353).
3. *Fioretti*, Ch. 58 (Binding, p. 185 f.).
4. Celano, III, 155 (Grau, p. 505).
5. Ibid., III, 121 (Grau, p. 498).
6. Ibid., III, 175 (Grau, p. 510).
7. Moorman, pp. 75–80; Sabatier, pp. 275–308; Englebert, pp. 286–99; Wendelborn, pp. 338–40.
8. Celano, I, 99–101 (Grau, pp. 168–72); II, 25 (Grau, p. 249 f.).
9. Brooke, *Scripta*, pp. 284–86 (this story is rather unflattering for Elias). See also ibid., p. 64.
10. Ibid., p. 182.
11. Ibid.
12. Ibid. Cf. Grau, p. 131, n. 256.
13. Celano, II, 196 (Grau, p. 409 f.).
14. Brooke, *Scripta*, pp. 180–82.
15. Brooke, *Coming*, p. 121.
16. Brooke, *Scripta*, p. 184.
17. Ibid., p. 274.
18. Ibid., p. 184. Cf. Celano, II, 90 (Grau, p. 312).
19. Brooke, *Scripta*, p. 118.
20. Ibid., pp. 112–16. For the testamentary character of these sayings see Brooke, *Scripta*, p. 118, n. 1; also Wendelborn, p. 329 f.
21. A condensation of the sayings in Brooke, *Scripta*, pp. 112–16.
22. Ibid., pp. 116–18.
23. Cf. Wendelborn, p. 327 f.
24. I have chosen the letters whose core, at least, is authentic.
25. Karrer, p. 554 (abr.).
26. Quoted from Sabatier, pp. 297–300 (condensed). Wendelborn, p. 328, dates this letter 1224. Cf. Brooke, *EFG*, pp. 288, 106 ("toward the end of his life").
27. Quoted from Brooke, *Coming*, p. 127 (abr.).
28. Quoted from Wolfram von den Steinen, ed., *Franz von Assisi: Die Werke* (Reinbek bei Hamburg: Rowohlt, 1958).
29. Brooke, *EFG*, p. 108. For the use of the terms "vicar" and "minister general," see ibid., pp. 106–22.
30. The *locus classicus* where Francis calls himself a fool is found in Brooke, *Scripta*, pp. 286–88. Cf. also Roggen, p. 73.
31. Brooke, *Scripta*, pp. 156–58. Cf. Celano, I, 52 (Grau, p. 116 f.). Karrer (p. 218) assigns this episode to the winter of 1220–21.
32. Brooke, *Scripta*, pp. 158–60. Cf. Celano, II, 131 (Grau, p. 352). The Martinmas fast lasted from All Saints' Day (Nov. 1) till Christmas. The story may have occurred in the winter of 1225.
33. Brooke, *Scripta*, pp. 158–60.

34. Le Goff, p. 243.
35. Celano, II, 78 f. (Grau, pp. 301–3).
36. *Fioretti*, Ch. 55 (Karrer, p. 491 f.; Binding, p. 162 f.).

CHAPTER XV: *The Song of Death*

1. Celano, II, 106 (Grau, pp. 326–28): Grau, p. 327, n. 243; Mockler, pp. 199 f., 202, n. 9; Moorman, pp. 25, 66.
2. Mockler, p. 106 f.; cf. Brooke, *Scripta*, p. 166.
3. Brooke, *Scripta*, pp. 162–66. For the text of the "Canticle of the Sun" see Karrer, pp. 520–22.
4. Brooke, *Scripta*, p. 166.
5. Ibid.
6. Ibid.
7. Karl Marx and Friedrich Engels, *The Communist Manifesto*, tr. Samuel Moore (New York: Washington Square Press, 1964), pp. 61–62.
8. For the relationship between bourgeois ideals and social realities cf. Agnes Heller, "Aufklärung und Radikalismus: Kritik der psychologischen Anthropologie Erich Fromms," in Adelbert Reif, ed., *Erich Fromm: Materialien zu seinem Werk* (Vienna: Europa-Verlag, 1978), pp. 184, 200, 211.
9. Brooke, *Scripta*, pp. 130–32.
10. Ibid., pp. 198–202, 264.
11. Karrer, p. 552.
12. Ibid., p. 568.
13. Ibid., p. 570.
14. Ibid.
15. Ibid., p. 572.
16. Ibid.
17. Wendelborn, p. 330.
18. Brooke, *Scripta*, p. 262.
19. Celano, I, 105 (Grau, p. 176).
20. Brooke, *Scripta*, p. 198.
21. Ibid., p. 262.
22. Ibid., pp. 294–96. Cf. Celano, II, 214 f. (Grau, p. 426 f.).
23. Ibid., p. 280.
24. Ibid., pp. 274–76.
25. Ibid., p. 290. Cf. Celano, I, 108 (Grau, p. 178 f.); II, 217 (Grau, p. 429 f.). *Fioretti*, Ch. 6 (Karrer, pp. 355–57; Binding, p. 27 f.). Cf. Brooke, *EFG*, pp. 17 f., 97.
26. Ps. 141.
27. Brooke, *Scripta*, p. 282.

CHAPTER XVI: *Afterward*

1. Quoted from Karrer, p. 11.
2. Immediately after Francis' death, Elias sent a letter to all the higher officials of the Order. He signed it, "Brother Elias, a sinner." Moorman, p. 83. For Elias' activities between March 1228 and the summer of 1230, see Moorman, pp. 85–88.
3. For large-scale medieval technology, see Otto Ullrich, *Technik und Herrschaft* (Frankfurt am Main: Suhrkamp, 1977), pp. 60, 314 f. Also Martin Warnke, *Bau und Überbau: Soziologie der mittelalterlichen*

Architektur nach den Schriftquellen (Frankfurt am Main: Syndikat, 1976), p. 154.

4. Moorman, p. 99 f.; Brooke, *EFG*, pp. 119, 122.
5. Moorman, p. 90; Lambert, pp. 78–88.
6. Cf. Franz Ehrle, "Die Spiritualen: Ihr Verhältnis zum Franziskanerorden," in *Archiv für Literatur und Kirchengeschichte*, III, 572.
7. Benz, p. 175.
8. Salimbene of Parma, Rudolf of Saxony, Bartholomaeus Guisculus, and Gerard of Borgo San Donnino. Cf. Benz, p. 176.
9. Cf. Gert Wendelborn, *Gott und Geschichte: Joachim von Fiore und die Hoffnung der Christenheit* (Vienna: Böhlau, 1974). For more literature on Joachim, see ibid., pp. 293–98.
10. I follow Benz's presentation here (pp. 4–58).
11. Moorman, pp. 108–11.
12. Kautsky, I, 199.
13. The term *spiritualis* meant, in general, the opposite of *mundanus* (worldly); cf. Brooke, *Scripta*, p. 138.
14. Moorman, pp. 112–14, 146; Lambert, pp. 103–15; Brooke, *EFG*, pp. 255–72.
15. Moorman, pp. 118, 189.
16. For a discussion of Olivi's teaching, see Benz, pp. 256–332.
17. Cf. Roggen, pp. 63, 71 ff. (Francis had no intention of founding an Order in the traditional sense.) For the early history of the "Third Order" see Moorman, pp. 40–45.
18. Cf. R. I. Moore, *The Origins of European Dissent* (London: Allen Lane, 1977), p. 321 f.
19. Kautsky, I, 146–60; Cohn, p. 147.
20. Cf. *Hérésies*, p. 178 f. For the parallels between the *Humiliati* and Francis' brotherhood, see Grundmann, p. 31.
21. *Hérésies*, pp. 97–100.
22. Moorman, p. 217.
23. Roggen thinks there is still no conclusive proof that the Third Order had a Franciscan origin. Goetz, p. 159, conjectures that the Third Order at first consisted merely of a loose affiliation of already existing lay groups with Francis' brotherhood. Cf. Moorman, p. 216 f.
24. Grundmann, p. 48. On the beguines and beghards, see ibid., pp. 47–58, and the bibliography in *Hérésies*, p. 445 f. (Nos. 473–509). For the Olivi beguines see Moorman, p. 197.
25. Moorman, p. 197 f.
26. Lambert, pp. 171–74, 177 f., 217 f. (the influence of Olivi).
27. Moorman, pp. 188 f., 194–96; Lambert, pp. 167–76.
28. The expression goes back to the writings of Joachim, and was applied by the Spirituals to Pope Celestine V, whom the cardinals removed from his hermitage and placed in the papal chair in the year 1294. On December 13 of that year the Pope voluntarily resigned, and was placed under house arrest until the end of his life.
29. *Arbor Vitae Crucifixae Jesus;* cf. Lambert, pp. 174–76, and Benz, p. 332.
30. *KG*, 310 f.; *Hérésies*, pp. 188–94; Grundmann, p. 49 f.
31. Moorman, pp. 307, 350 f.; Brooke, *EFG*, p. 283.
32. On the political background of this intervention, cf. Haller, V, 166.
33. Moorman, pp. 199–304; Lambert, pp. 184–201.

34. Moorman, p. 203 f.; Lambert, pp. 198–201.
35. Moorman, pp. 307–19; Lambert, pp. 208–46.
36. For the reconstruction of this affair and its consequences, see J. Koch, "Der Prozess gegen die Postille Olivis zur Apokalypse," in *Recherches de Théologie Ancienne et Médiévale*, V (1933), 302–15.
37. There are two versions of this bull; Lambert, pp. 230–35.
38. The Latin text may be found in Denzinger-Schönmetzer, *Enchiridion Symbolorum, Definitionum et Declarationum de Rebus Fidei et Morum* (Barcelona: Herder, 1973), 35th ed., No. 930 f.
39. Oskar Schatz, ed., *Hat die Religion Zukunft?* (Graz: Styria, 1971), p. 133.
40. Jean-Paul Sartre, *L'Idiot de la Famille: Gustave Flaubert de 1821 à 1857* (Paris: Gallimard, 1971), I, 444.
41. Mt. 8:22.
42. *The Confessions of St. Augustine*, tr. Rex Warner (New York: The New American Library, 1963), pp. 119–20.
43. Gerhard Rohlfs, ed., *Sankt Alexius* (Tübingen: Niemeyer, 1953).
44. Ibid., p. 3 f.
45. Stafford Beer, *Platform for Change* (New York: John Wiley, 1975).
46. Ibid., p. 453.
47. Pier Paolo Pasolini, *Freibeuterschriften* (Berlin: Wagenbach, 1978), p. 132. (As a precaution, I have omitted the last sentence of the text. It reads: "Long live the communist struggle for the necessities of life." Pasolini was expelled from the Italian Communist Party in 1949.)

BIBLIOGRAPHY

SINCE my book is not primarily intended for specialists, I cite here, for the most part, the works I consulted that might also prove helpful to the interested layman. For that reason I provide a brief commentary after each one.

The handiest collection of material from the original sources for Francis' life is the one edited by Otto Karrer, first published in 1945 by the Manesse Verlag (Zürich). The new edition (1975) dispenses with the extensive and informative notes, for which reason I quote from the 1945 edition.

For the *Fioretti* I have drawn upon the translation by Rudolf G. Binding (*Die Blümlein des heiligen Franziskus von Assisi* [Frankfurt am Main: Insel Taschenbuch, 1973]). The differences between Karrer and Binding are explained by the fact that Karrer translates from the shorter Latin version of the *Fioretti*, while Binding uses the Italian version.

For both biographies by Thomas of Celano and his so-called *Book of Miracles* I quote from the complete German edition of Englebert Grau (Werl [Westphalia]: Dietrich-Coelde-Verlag, 1964).*

In the case of the Leo stories I refer to an English edition: Rosalind B. Brooke, *Scripta Leonis, Rufini et Angeli Sociorum S. Francisci* (Oxford: Clarendon Press, 1970). Along with its scholarly introduction this critical edition offers the Latin text and an English translation.

The Dietrich-Coelde-Verlag (Werl in Westphalia) is also the publisher of *Die Schriften des heiligen Franziskus* (ed. Kajetan Esser and Lothar Hardick), *Leben und Schriften der heiligen Klara von Assisi* (Englebert Grau), *Franziskus, Engel des sechsten Siegels: Sein Leben nach den Schriften des heiligen Bonaventura* (Sophronius Clasen), as well as *Die Dreigefährtenlegende des Hl. Franziskus* (Clasen-Grau).†

For the text of the 1223 Rule and the chronicle of Jordan of Giano, as well as the letters of Jacques de Vitry, I quote from the English translation of these important sources by Rosalind B. Brooke, *The Coming of the Friars* (London: George Allen & Unwin, 1975). In the notes this is abbreviated as "Brooke, *Coming.*"

For the Church history of the period the *Handbuch der Kirchengeschichte* (Freiburg: Herder, 1968), Vol. III, Part 2, may be recommended for the background it provides. It is abbreviated as *KG* in the notes.

All other titles are listed in alphabetical order.

Armstrong, Edward. *Saint Francis: Nature Mystic.* Berkeley: University of

* All the foregoing materials may be found in English translation in Marion A. Habig, ed., *St. Francis of Assisi: English Omnibus of Sources* (Chicago: Franciscan Herald Press, 1977) (Tr.).

† All the early biographical material on Francis may also be found in Marion A. Habig, ed., *St. Francis of Assisi: Omnibus of Sources of the Life of St. Francis* (Chicago, Ill.: Franciscan Herald Press, 1975) (Tr.).

California Press, 1975. (Diligent compilation, with commentary, of all the texts on Francis' relationship to animals.)

Benz, Ernst. *Ecclesia Spiritualis: Kirchenidee und Geschichtstheologie der franziskanischen Reformation.* Stuttgart: Kohlhammer, 1964. (Scholarly study done in 1934 on the theological positions taken in the early Franciscan sources, and on the writings of the Spirituals.)

Brooke, Rosalind B. *Early Franciscan Government.* Cambridge: Cambridge University Press, 1959. Abbreviated as *EFG.* (Monograph on the development of the legal structure of the Franciscan Order up to 1274.)

Cipolla, Carlo, ed. *The Fontana Economic History of Europe: The Middle Ages.* London: Collins, 1973. (Collection of articles on the economic situation in Europe between 500 and 1500.)

Cohn, Norman. *The Pursuit of the Millennium.* New York: Oxford University Press, 1970. (Fully documented treatment of medieval heretical movements between 1200 and 1550.)

Coulton, G. G. *The Medieval Scene: An Informal Introduction to the Middle Ages.* Cambridge: Cambridge University Press, 1967. (Good popular introduction to the Middle Ages by one of the most prominent scholars in the field. Coulton also wrote an essay on Francis entitled "Two Saints" [Norwood Editions, 1977].)

De Mause, Lloyd, ed. *The History of Childhood.* New York: Harper & Row, 1975. (Collection of articles on the history of childrearing from the end of antiquity to the modern period. The articles by both Lyman and McLaughlin bring much new material to light on conditions in the Middle Ages.)

Dirks, Walter. *Die Antwort der Mönche.* Frankfurt am Main, 1953. (Popular treatment of Francis and his brotherhood, among other things.)

Duby, Georges. *The Early Growth of the European Economy: Warriors and Peasants from the Seventh to the Twelfth Centuries,* tr. Howard B. Clarke. Ithaca, N.Y.: Cornell University Press, 1974. (Excellent study by a scholar associated with the journal *Annales,* which for forty years has labored to investigate long-term economic, demographic, and social change in history, as opposed to the tendency, as dominant now as ever, to put wars and dynastic dates in the foreground of historical discussion.)

Elias, Norbert. *The Civilizing Process: The History of Manners,* tr. Edmund Jephcott. 2 vols. New York: Urizen Books, 1978. (Essential study of the emergence of Western civilization.)

Englebert, Omer. *St. Francis of Assisi: A Biography,* tr. Eve Marie Cooper. Chicago, Ill.: Franciscan Herald Press, 1965. (Substantial biography, from the point of view of a pious Franciscan.)

Galli, Mario Von. *Living Our Future: St. Francis of Assisi and the Church of Tomorrow.* Chicago, Ill.: Franciscan Herald Press, 1976. (A Catholic journalist tries to present Francis in real-life terms. Color photos by Dennis Stock.)

Gobry, Ivan. *Franz von Assisi.* Reinbek bei Hamburg: Rowohlt, 1958. (A biography, full of pious rhetoric, with special attention to the history of the Franciscan Order, along with excerpts from the most important original sources.)

Goetz, Walter. *Italien im Mittelalter.* Leipzig: Koehler & Amelang, 1942. (A collection of scholarly articles, some of which deal with Francis.)

——. *La Civilisation de l'Occident Médiéval*. Paris: Arthaud, 1964. (Illustrated cultural history of the Middle Ages.)

——, ed. *Hérésies et Sociétés dans L'Europe préindustrielle*. Paris: Mouton, 1968. Abbreviated as *Hérésies*. (Collection of scholarly articles on the history of medieval and early modern heretics.)

Gonnet, Jean, and Molnar, Amedeo. *Les Vaudois au Moyen Âge*. Turin: Claudiana, 1974. (Standard work on the history of the Waldensians in the medieval period.)

Grigulevič, J. R. *Ketzer, Hexen, Inquisitoren: Geschichte der Inquisition*. East Berlin: Akademie-Verlag, 1976. (This two-volume presentation by a Russian scholar offers a good overview, with occasional inaccuracies.)

Grundmann, Herbert. "Ketzergeschichte des Mittelalters," *Die Kirche in ihrer Geschichte*, Vol. II. Göttingen: Vandenhoek & Ruprecht, 1967. (Short scholarly treatment of the subject—indispensable.)

Haller, Johannes. *Das Papsttum: Idee und Wirklichkeit*. Reinbek bei Hamburg: Rowohlt, 1965. (This five-volume history of the papacy goes as far as 1334. It was published between 1934 and 1945 and represents the German tradition of critical scholarship in the field of historical research.)

Hardick, Lothar. "'Pecunia et denarii': Untersuchungen zum Geldverbot in den Regeln der Minderbrüder," *Franziskanische Studien*, 40 (1958), 193–217, 313–28; 41 (1959), 268–90. (This monograph has some interesting material from the economic history of Francis' period.)

Jörgensen, Johannes. *St. Francis of Assisi: A Biography*, tr. T. O'Conor Sloane. Garden City, N.Y.: Doubleday, 1955. (Sentimental biography first published in 1907.)

Kautsky, Karl. *Vorläufer des neueren Sozialismus*. 2 vols. East Berlin: J. H. W. Dietz, 1976. (Marxist analysis of the medieval and early modern history of heresy. First appeared in 1896.)

Lambert, M. D. *Franciscan Poverty: The Doctrine of the Absolute Poverty of Christ and the Apostles in the Franciscan Order, 1210–1323*. London: SPCK, 1961. (Scholarly monograph on the issue of Franciscan poverty.)

Le Goff, Jacques. *Le Moyen Âge (1060–1330)*. Paris: Bordas, 1971. Abbreviated as Le Goff. (Excellent presentation of medieval history.)

Ley, Hermann. *Geschichte der Aufklärung und des Atheismus*, Vol. II, Pt. 2. East Berlin: VEB Verlag der Wissenschaften, 1971. (Marxist philosophy of history, with a good presentation of the theology of the Spirituals.)

Mayer, Hans Eberhard. *Idee und Wirklichkeit der Kreuzzüge*. Germering bei München: Stahlmann Verlag, 1965. (A selection of Middle High German, Latin, and Old French text from the era of the Crusades. Mayer also wrote *Geschichte der Kreuzzüge*. Stuttgart: Kohlhammer, 1965.)

Mockler, Anthony. *Francis of Assisi: The Wandering Years*. Oxford: Phaidon, 1976. (Richly factual biography, dealing only cursorily with the years 1220–26. Some informative digressions on the historical background of Francis' life.)

Moorman, John R. H. *A History of the Franciscan Order*. Oxford: Clarendon Press, 1968. (Indispensable standard work.)

——. *Saint Francis of Assisi*. London: SPCK, 1976. Abbreviated as Moorman, *Saint Francis*. (Good short biography. This well-known expert on Francis was until 1975 the Anglican bishop of Ripon.)

Müller, Rudolf. *Geld und Geist: Zur Entstehungsgeschichte von Identitätsbewusstsein und Rationalität seit der Antike*. Frankfurt am Main: Campus, 1977. (Fundamental study of the connection between the use of money and bourgeois self-consciousness in the West.)

Mumford, Lewis. *The Myth of the Machine*. Vol. I, *Technics and Human Development*. New York: Harcourt Brace Jovanovich, 1967. (Comprehensive cultural history of technology, from a critical point of view. Superb handling of the relevant literature.)

Roggen, Heribert. *Die Lebensform des heiligen Franz von Assisi in ihrem Verhältnis zur feudalen und bürgerlichen Gesellschaft Italiens*. Mecheln: St. Franziskus-Uitgeverij, 1965. (Sociological study from a conservative slant.)

Sabatier, Paul. *Life of St. Francis of Assisi*, tr. Louise Seymour Houghton. New York: Scribner's, 1912. (Pioneering biography, first published in 1894. If one disregards the style, which sounds somewhat outdated today, the book is still rewarding.)

Selge, Kurt-Victor. "Franz von Assisi und die römische Kurie," *Zeitschrift für Theologie und Kirche*, 67 (1970), 139–61. (Scholarly essay with careful treatment of the original sources.)

Southern, R. W. *Western Society and the Church in the Middle Ages* (Vol. 2 of *The Pelican History of the Church*). Hammondsworth: Penguin Books, 1976. (Richly documented medieval Church history, with an informative presentation of the mendicant Orders.)

Steenberghen, Ferdnand van. *Die Philosophie im 13. Jahrhundert*. Paderborn: Schöningh, 1977. (Technical monograph, with generous use of original sources. Conservative Catholic slant.)

Wendelborn, Gert. *Franziskus von Assisi: Eine historische Darstellung*. Vienna: Böhlau, 1977. (Scholarly but readable biography. The presentation of the "religious and social movements preceding and accompanying the early Franciscan movement" is commendable. Extensive bibliography.)

Werner, Ernst. *Häresie und Gesellschaft im 11. Jahrhundert*. East Berlin: Akademie-Verlag, 1975. (Scholarly essay focusing on the often overlooked social-political variables of heresy.)

Zilsel, Edgar. *Die soziale Ursprünge der neuzeitlichen Wissenschaft*. Frankfurt am Main: Suhrkamp, 1976. (Collection of essays on the history of science, with an informative Introduction by W. Krohn.)

INDEX